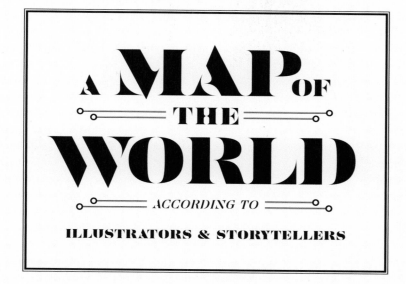

A MAP OF THE WORLD

ACCORDING TO

ILLUSTRATORS & STORYTELLERS

gestalten

PREFACE

WRITTEN BY

ANTONIS ANTONIOU

Only few graphic representation devices have been such a fountainhead of wonderment, controversy, and utility as maps have. What seems to have begun on a more intuitive level has evolved over time into a sophisticated visual instrument. Maps have proven to be a versatile medium through which to express our inquisitive nature and make sense of our physical world. Within a singular visual, we are able to impose order by appropriating reality and its complex layers. It is an endeavor that emanates an intoxicating sense of power in harnessing knowledge.

Maps have forged, through time, as many connectives as they have distinctions. Early maps were rare, intricate constructs. Their status as unique works of art spoke of social hierarchies. In the Middle Ages, the division between known and unknown worlds was used as an analogy for the relationship between good and evil. Steeped in religiosity, medieval mappae

Map by Takayo Akiyama, see page 78

mundi gave life lessons, merging human knowledge, myth, and spirituality in a surreal landscape of precautionary tales for the afterlife. During the Age of Discovery, the distinction was reworked for the Old and New Worlds. A spirit of exploration opened up the way for cultural cross-pollination and unrepentant exploitation. Discovery and conquest found expression in maps that became affirmations of power, national pride, and the enlightenment of the brutes. With the shift from religious to industrial centers, then fashion and art capitals, and major breakthroughs in printing technology, maps became more accessible and diverse, crossing over to other fields. The late twentieth century migration from analogue to digital worlds revolutionized mapping once more and brought about exciting potentials and unavoidable tensions. Throughout these changes, one commonality remained: with each connection, each discovery, other divisions were created and new frontiers appeared, ready to be discovered, tamed, and mapped.

Be it affirmations of the expanses of ruthless empires or napkin squiggles showing the way to a party, the thematics of cartography range from the trivial to survival. Think kitsch tourist guides, political propaganda maps, or a dangerous mix of the two. Patches of color that show who owns what, pinks and yellows that yell out "Mine!" The atlas, for many the greatest expression of cartography, synthesizes physical, geopolitical, socioeconomic, and other domains in a gesamtkunstwerk that operates on countless levels. Maps serve basic utilitarian purposes as administrative tools and references for mobility and navigation. Maps catalogue the pleasures and horrors of mankind. Urban crime maps show pockets of a different hell, island resort maps show hints of someone else's idea of heaven, transposing the concepts from the Middle Ages to today. Catastrophe and death are codified in maps of earthquake zones, tornado paths, or oil spills. Cartographies of hedonism depict the best shops, the top restaurants, the hottest bars. Maps make compelling promises. The promise of adventure to a child with a map of Disneyland is also formidable advertising. Treasure maps promise thrills in the quest for that coveted X. Maps operate as both records of change and glimpses into the future. They help grasp greater concepts, detect patterns, prognosticate, and reveal new layers of meaning. Weather data can be mapped to help understand the climate, population shifts visualized to aid the design of cities and the politics of urban planning. Maps are no less real when conjuring up fantastic landscapes and utopias. Cartography can be an incredible form of escapism, as maps act as proxies for experiences, real or fabricated. Whatever their purpose or subject matter, even the most rudimentary of maps have an inherent beauty, an attraction in their way of ordering things.

The map's purpose and intended audience define the map maker's design choices. These typically involve a selection of the elements to be included and their corresponding level of detail within the constraints and technicalities of the transformation from three-dimensionality to a two-dimensional projection. The selected elements go through cosmetic surgery for the sake of legibility and readability, are adjusted, simplified, or enhanced in a process referred to as generalization. The map is usually set to an appropriate scale that gives a human reference for dimensions and values. Text and icons based on semiological conventions are the most basic systems layered over the map to make information meaningful. Color and patterns are used to establish further hierarchies as more systems come into play. We are so familiar with this language of maps that we trust it and never dare question it. Maps that abide by established pictorial conventions receive almost automatic credibility.

Yet the most pervasive characteristic in cartography has been the bias of maps. "There is no 'view from nowhere' for even the most scrupulously 'detached' observer" (Martin Jay, Downcast Eyes). In this sense, to map is to lie, or at least to subject the truth to personal preconceptions and ideologies. In the history of the art of map-making, cartographic taboos and conventions have been steadfastly raised while objectivity remains a chimera. The modernist ideal of the disappearance of the hand of the creator has proven hard to reach, leaving behind an illusion of universality that is oftentimes confused with familiarity. The maps in the following pages belong to a different camp, the heretics, disregarding dogma, exploring new cartographic languages, un-

Map by Yuko Kondo, see page 79

ashamedly embracing ambiguity—a cartographic cult of personality. Maps drawn as imaginative and profound as the unique history and spatiality—the genius loci—of the places they depict, maps that acquire a musicality and sublimity even when conveying prosaic information.

Throughout history, the definition of maps has expanded to encompass everything from genes to galaxies to intangible concepts. The book refocuses on the more traditional definition that starts with geography, only to eventually transcend it. Here, mapping is a personal affair and, like in portraiture, can be caricatural, abstract, mysterious—with or sans smirk. Oscar Wilde wrote "... every portrait that is painted with feeling is a portrait of the artist, not of the sitter" (The Picture of Dorian Gray). These are maps you shouldn't trust yet cannot help but fall for—they are the femmes fatales of cartography. Some will take you where you want to go, or thereabouts. Most will certainly act as catalysts for explorations, daydreams, and critical observation. Cities are distilled to single icons or elevated to planet-

ary status, whole neighborhoods or states are omitted willy-nilly, streets disappear, choked with swarms of colorful characters, all in a potpourri of perspectives and jumbled scales as orientation becomes mere decoration. For all their idiosyncratic glory, these maps feel at least more candid.

This nonconformist attitude does not exclude the world of digital mapping. Sophisticated geo-tools opened up unimagined possibilities in cartography, befitting a fast-paced, multi-dimensional, networked world. Online maps, with GoogleMaps at the top, are now powerful brands with a consistency of language that is as familiar and even iconic as any material product. Amongst this growing field of behemoths, a small number of visual practitioners are staking their claim with playful experimentation and provocation, translating the solemnity of data into intriguing cartographies that make for wonderful quantitative storytelling. In their work lies proof that in the perceived inhumanness of automation, beauty and drama can still be found.

Geographic information systems and other geo-tools provide an unprecedented level of empowerment, and in tandem with the internet, have helped jump-start revolutions, expedite social change, and decipher complex natural systems. Real time mapping entails an eerie immediacy in the simultaneity between the real and the virtual, almost touching godhood. These transformations leave the relevance of maps in a constant state of flux. In the larger context of globalization, maps are becoming homogeneous, victims of generic uniformity. As more is being mapped, we spend less time with maps. Propagated everywhere and noticed nowhere, maps are increasingly devalued as an influential visual tool. This book documents the contrarians. Creative cartographers around the world are reacting against this culture of mundane anonymity by generating deeply personal maps, using their signature as resuscitator.

Sparse or elaborate but never boring, these maps reveal stimulating narratives that beg interaction and discovery. They act as an antidote to cartographic monotony and the modern-day obsession for accuracy. As important is the fact that they are all contemporary, part of the creative zeitgeist. By documenting these works, their ephemeral temperament is shed to reveal a lasting message with human nature at its core. Ultimately, it's about storytelling. It's about re-humanizing the process of understanding our surroundings and through this, ourselves. In all their differences, these maps allow space for dreaming.

ATLANTIC
OCEAN

GERMANY

BELGIUM

CZECH

Zaogli

Portovenere

AUSTRIA

FRANCE

Cap d'Ail

Fotre dei Marmi

LIECHT
SWITZ

Verdon Gorges

Mo
SLOVENIA

St Paul de Vence

Lleida

Rovijn

Krk

Palamos

Nice

Monte Carlo

Florence

PORTUGAL

Madrid

SPAIN

Girona

Porto Vecchio

Benicassim

Bonifacio

Nap

Valencia

La Maddalena

ITALY

Capri

Malaga

Palma

Porto Cervo

Tarifa

Ibizia

Barcelona

TUNISIA

MED

Cirkewwa

MOROCC

ALGERIA

KEY TO LOCATIONS

 BUSINESS

ARCHITECTURE

HOTEL

DIVE

A ACTIVITY

FESTIVAL

AIRPORT

GALLERY

SHOP/MARKET

RADIO STATION

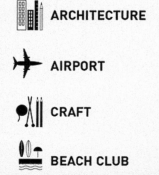 CRAFT

BEACH

BOAT STOP

RESORT

 BEACH CLUB

HIKE/CITY WALK

 CAFE/BAR

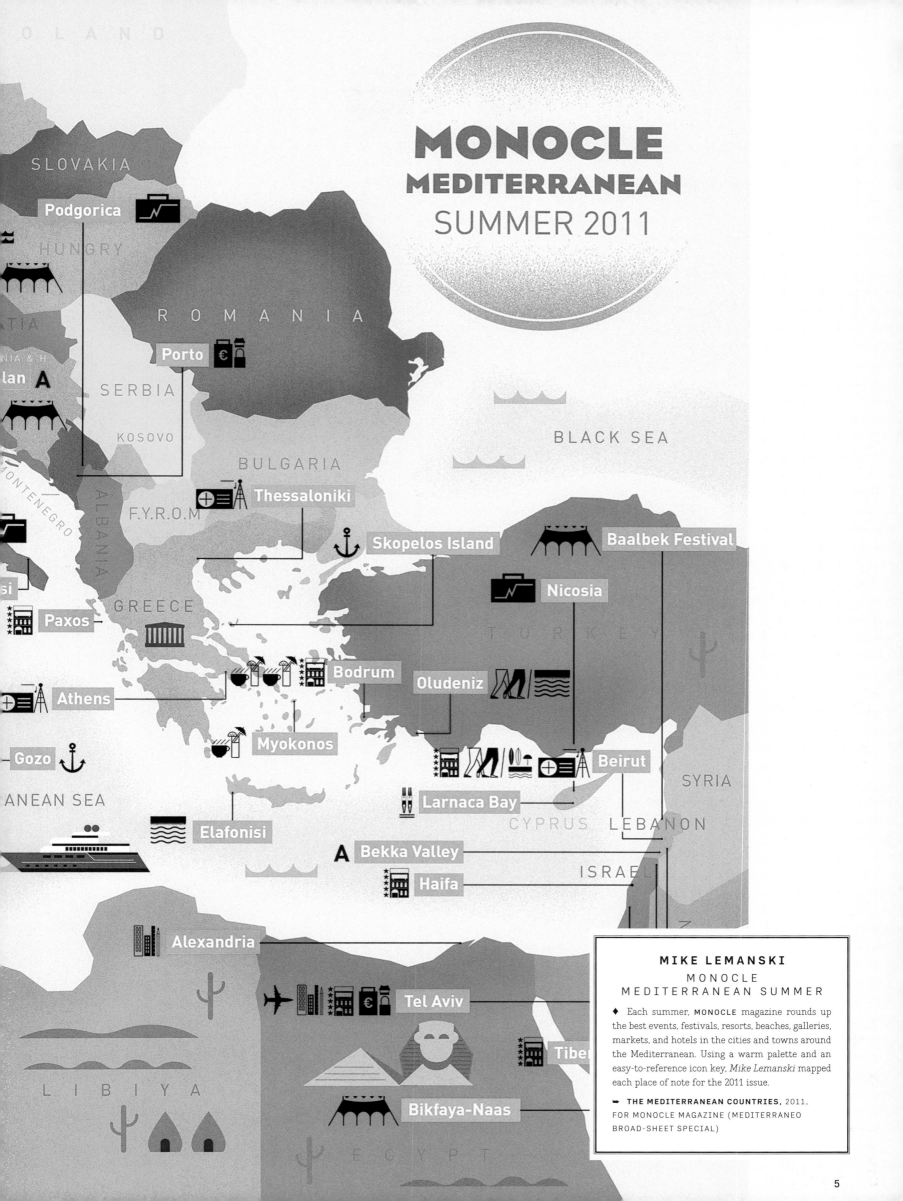

MONOCLE
MEDITERRANEAN
SUMMER 2011

MIKE LEMANSKI
MONOCLE
MEDITERRANEAN SUMMER

♦ Each summer, MONOCLE magazine rounds up the best events, festivals, resorts, beaches, galleries, markets, and hotels in the cities and towns around the Mediterranean. Using a warm palette and an easy-to-reference icon key, *Mike Lemanski* mapped each place of note for the 2011 issue.

➥ THE MEDITERRANEAN COUNTRIES, 2011. FOR MONOCLE MAGAZINE (MEDITERRANEO BROAD-SHEET SPECIAL)

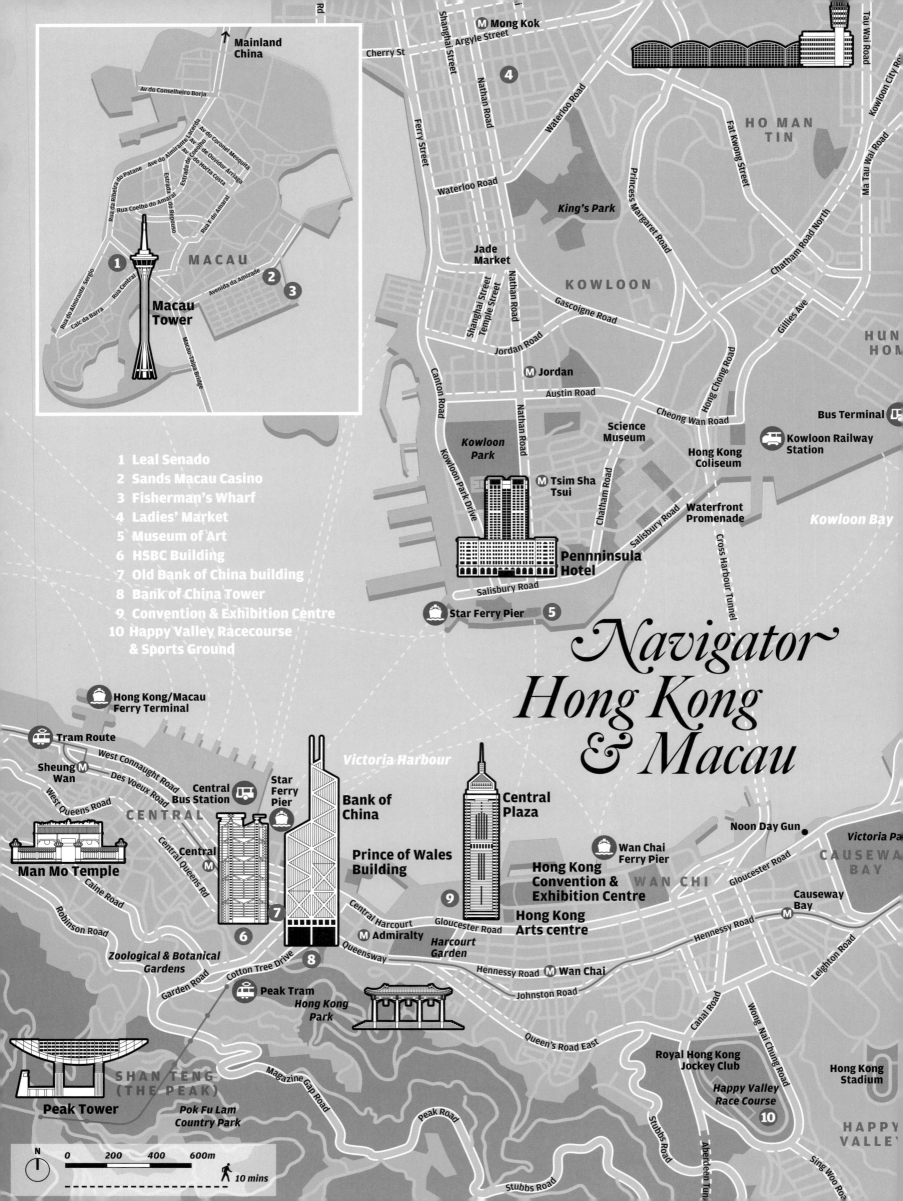

Navigator Hong Kong & Macau

1 Leal Senado
2 Sands Macau Casino
3 Fisherman's Wharf
4 Ladies' Market
5 Museum of Art
6 HSBC Building
7 Old Bank of China building
8 Bank of China Tower
9 Convention & Exhibition Centre
10 Happy Valley Racecourse & Sports Ground

Navigator Toronto

St George · 1 · 2

Spadina

Museum

Wellesley

Church & Welleseу
Gay Village

Queen's Park

3

University
of Toronto

King's College
Field

Queen's
Park

College

Allen Gardens

Gerrard Street East

GARDEN
DISTRICT

Spadina Crescent

KENSINGTON
MARKET

CHINATOWN

Ryerson
Polytechnic
University

Toronto
Bus Terminal

Dundas

Dundas Square

St Patrick

4

5

Eaton
Centre

Osgoode
Hall

Skating Rink

Queen

Moss Park

Osgoode

6

DOWNTOWN

St James's Park

King

7

ENTERTAINMENT
DISTRICT

FASHION
DISTRICT

St Andrew

8 · 9

Roy Thompson
Hall

Metro
Hall

Hockey Hall of Fame

Streetcars
Harbourfront & Spadina

Bus Station

Union Station
Toronto Central Station

Clarence Square Park

CN Tower

Victoria Memorial Park

City Core Golf
& Driving range

Skydome
Home of the Toronto Blue Jays

Roundhouse Park

Roundhouse

Shaker Cruise Lines
Niagra-on-the-Lake

Old Fort York
Historic Site

Garrison
Commons

Toronto Island
Ferry Terminal

Coronation Park

Maple Leaf
Quay

John Quay

York Quay

Skating Rink

Toronto Inner Harbour
Lake Ontario

Spadina Quay

Toronto City Centre
Airport Ferry

Toronto City
Centre Airport

HARBOURFRONT

1	Bata Shoe Museum
2	Royal Ontario Museum
3	Massey College
4	Art Gallery of Ontario
5	Sharp Centre
6	City Hall
7	Toronto Sculpture Garden
8	Design Exchange
9	Toronto Dominion Centre
10	Ydessa Hendeles Foundation

Navigator Marseille

1 Bibliothèque Alcazar
2 Musée d'Histoire
3 Musée de la Mode
4 Stade Vélodrome
5 Unité d'Habitation
6 Hôtel de Ville
7 Cathédrale de la Major
8 Fort Saint-Jean
9 Palais du Pharo
10 Notre Dame de la Garde

Mediterranean Sea

Navigator London

1 Vyner Street
2 Hygge
3 The Flea Pit
4 Start
5 Find
6 Exhibit
7 The Black Tulip
8 Wright Brothers
9 Thorsten van Elten
10 Pied à Terre
11 Cork Street
12 Paul Smith
13 Nobu Berkeley
14 Automat
15 Maze
16 Chair
17 Bill Amberg
18 The Ledbury
19 The Cowshed
20 Bamford & Sons

RUSSELL BELL

WALLPAPER* NAVIGATOR MAPS

♦ The *Navigator Maps* for WALLPAPER* ran as a monthly series of tear-out maps in the magazine. Each map highlighted ten of the best things to see and do within the featured city accompanied by a selection of simply illustrated landmark buildings.

➥ LEFT PAGE: HONG KONG AND MACAU / CHINA, RIGHT PAGE: TORONTO / CANADA; MARSEILLE / FRANCE, LONDON / UK, 2006, FOR WALLPAPER* MAGAZINE

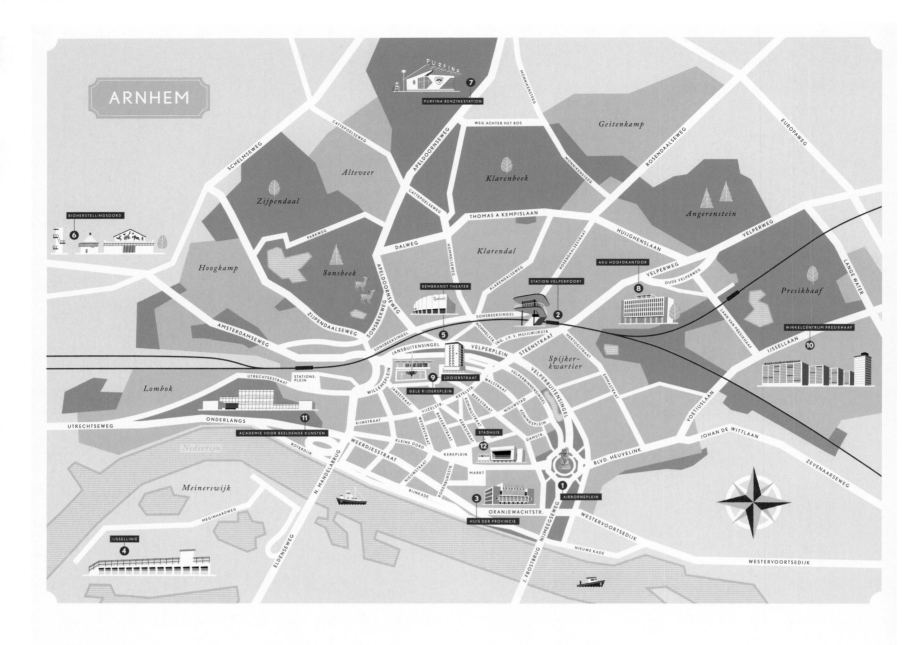

ARNHEM

PURFINA · PURFINA BENZINESTATION ⑦

BIOHERSTELLINGSOORD ⑥

Schelmseweg · Catteposelseweg · Apeldoornseweg · Weg achter het bos · Geitenkamp · Monnikhuizen · Europaweg · Rozendaalseweg

Alteveer · Klarenbeek · Angerenstein · Velperweg

Zijpendaal · Catteposelseweg · Thomas a Kempislaan · Huijghenslaan · Lange Water

Parkweg · Dalweg · Klarendal · Oude Velperweg · Presikhaaf

Hoogkamp · Sonsbeek · Rembrandt Theater ⑤ · Station Velperpoort · AKU HOOFDKANTOOR ⑧ · Velperweg · WINKELCENTRUM PRESIKHAAF ⑩

Amsterdamseweg · Zijpendaalseweg · Sonsbeeksingel · Sonsbeeksingel · Jansbuitensingel · Velperplein · Steenstraat · Spijker-kwartier · IJssellaan

Lombok · Utrechtsestraat · Stations-plein · Willemsplein · LOOIERSTRAAT ⑨ · Jansstraat · Walstraat · Velperbinnensingel · Velperbuitensingel

Utrechtseweg · ONDERLANGS · ACADEMIE VOOR BEELDENDE KUNSTEN ⑪ · Rijnstraat · Vijzelstr · Ketelstr · Bakkerstraat · Nieuwstad · Koningsplein · Johan de Wittlaan · Zevenaarseweg

Nederrijn · Boterdijk · Weerdjesstraat · Kleine Oord · Weverstraat · STADHUIS ⑫ · Damstr

Meinerswijk · N. Mandelabrug · Nieuwstraat · Kerkplein · Markt · BLVD. HEUVELINK

Meginhardweg · Eldenseweg · Rijnkade · Rosendaalstr · ③ · AIRBORNEPLEIN ① · WESTERVOORTSEDIJK

IJSSELLINIE ④ · HUIS DER PROVINCIE · ORANJEWACHTSTR. · J. FROSTBRUG NIJMEEGSEWEG · NIEUWE KADE · WESTERVOORTSEDIJK

ESTHER AARTS

ARNHEM POST WAR RECONSTRUCTION MAP

♦ Cities such as Arnhem in the Netherlands, lost many of their buildings during the Second World War. Using an illustration style that recalls Germany's post-war reconstruction era (1945-1969), *Esther Aarts* mapped 12 buildings in Arnhem that represent the typical architecture of that time.

➥ **ARNHEM / NETHERLANDS**, 2011, FOR CASA CENTRUM VOOR ARHCITECHUUR EN STEDENBOUW ARNHEM, TEXT: TON SCHULTE, LAYOUT: KARINA DIMITRIU, PICTURES: GELDERS ARCHIEF ARNHEM

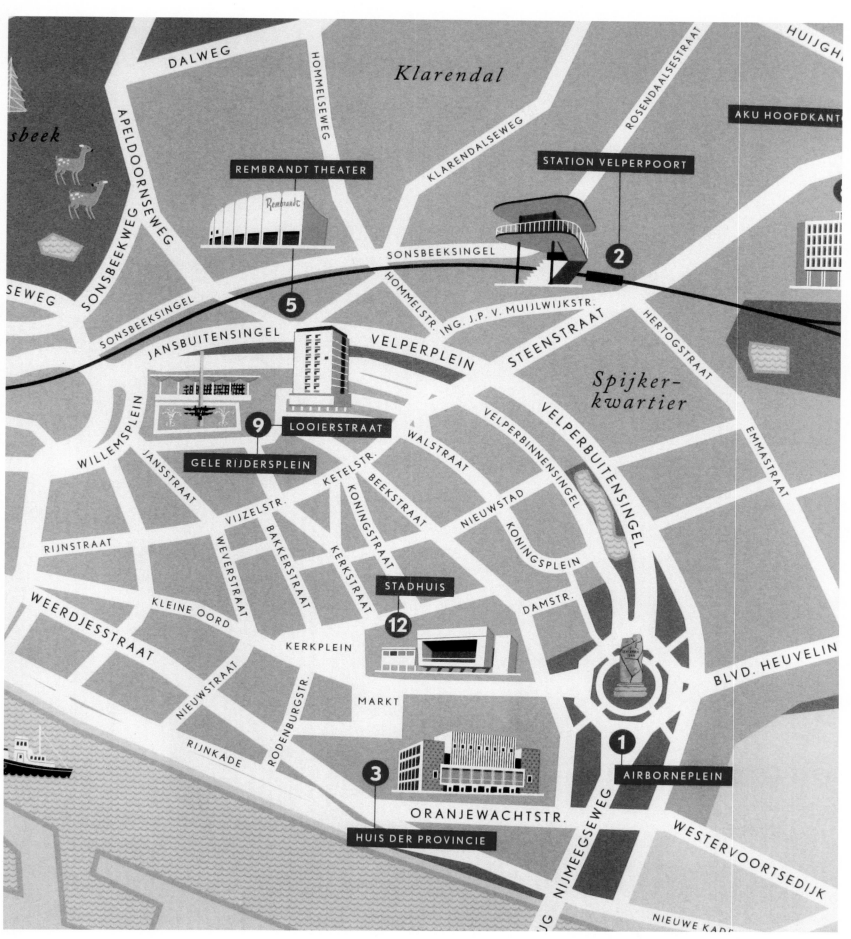
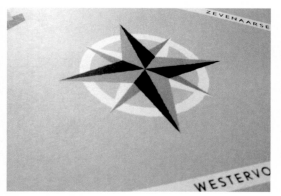

DOROTHY

FILM MAP

◆ Loosely based on vintage street maps of Los Angeles, the Film Map is made up entirely of Hollywood film titles. It features over 900 film classics such as Lost Highway, On the Waterfront, Reservoir Dogs, Jurassic Park, Nightmare on Elm Street, Valley of the Dolls, and Chinatown. An A–Z key lists each of the featured films, including their release dates and directors.

➝ LOS ANGELES / USA, 2012, PERSONAL PROJECT

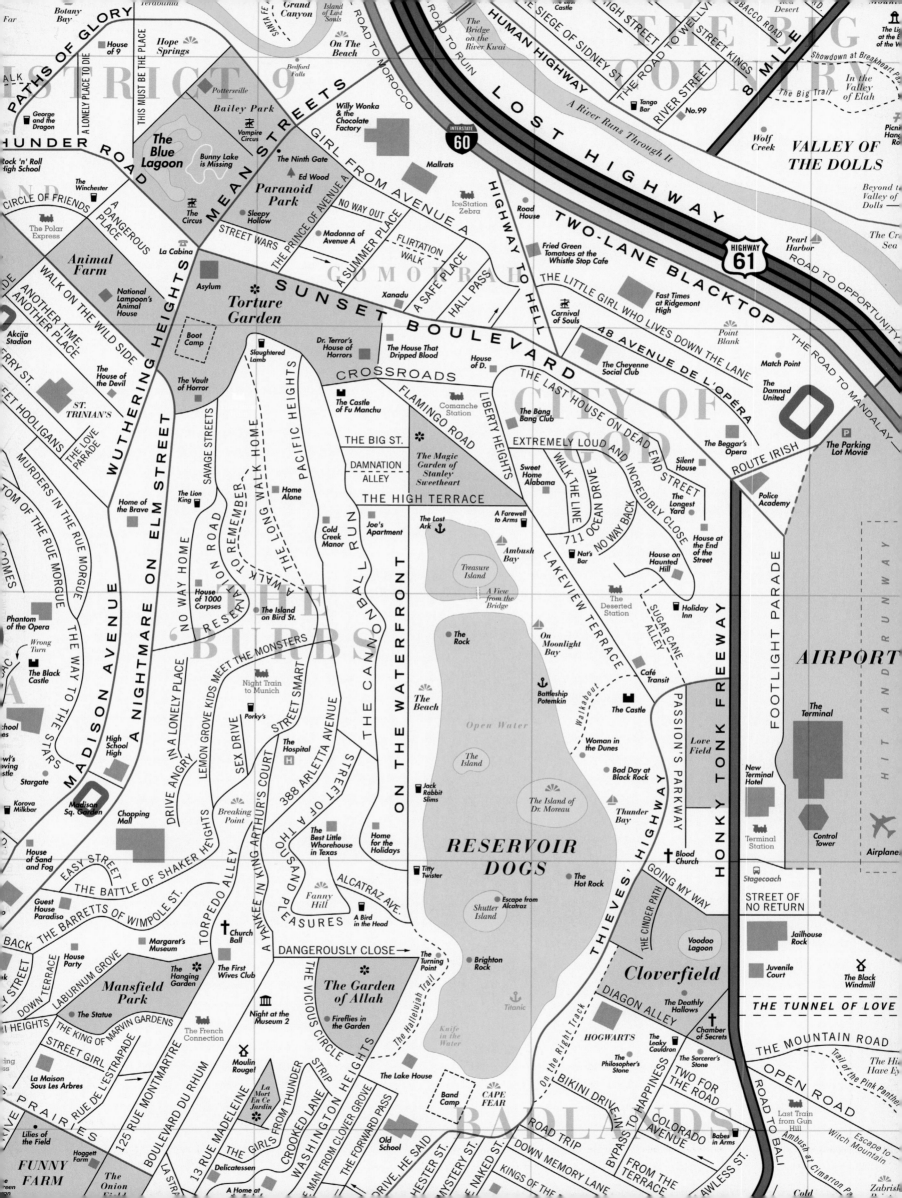

JON FRICKEY
MEINE STADT (MY CITY)

♦ Each map by *Jon Frickey* brands the city it represents with a combination of type, illustration, and color. His Meine Stadt series for NEON MAGAZINE illustrate the personal recommendations from locals for the most unique sights and venues their city has to offer.

➥ LEFT PAGE: VARIOUS, 2007–2012, RIGHT PAGE: MUNICH / GERMANY, 2012, FOR NEON MAGAZINE

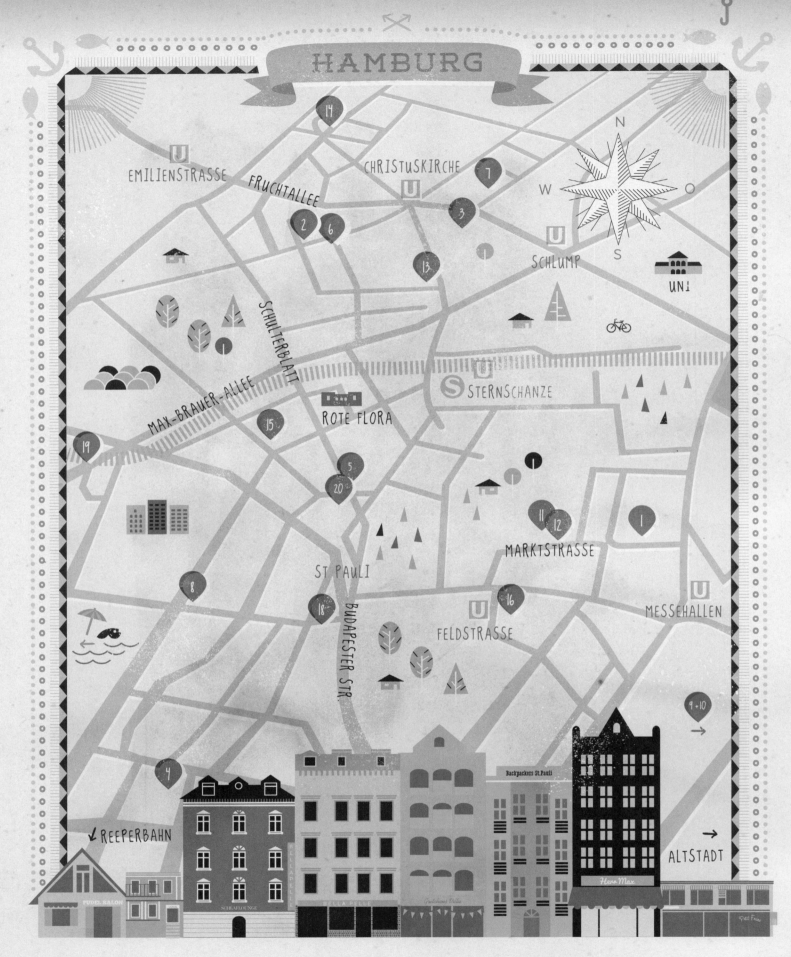

ANNA HÄRLIN
MAP OF HAMBURG CITY
➤ HAMBURG / GERMANY, 2011, FOR CUT MAGAZINE

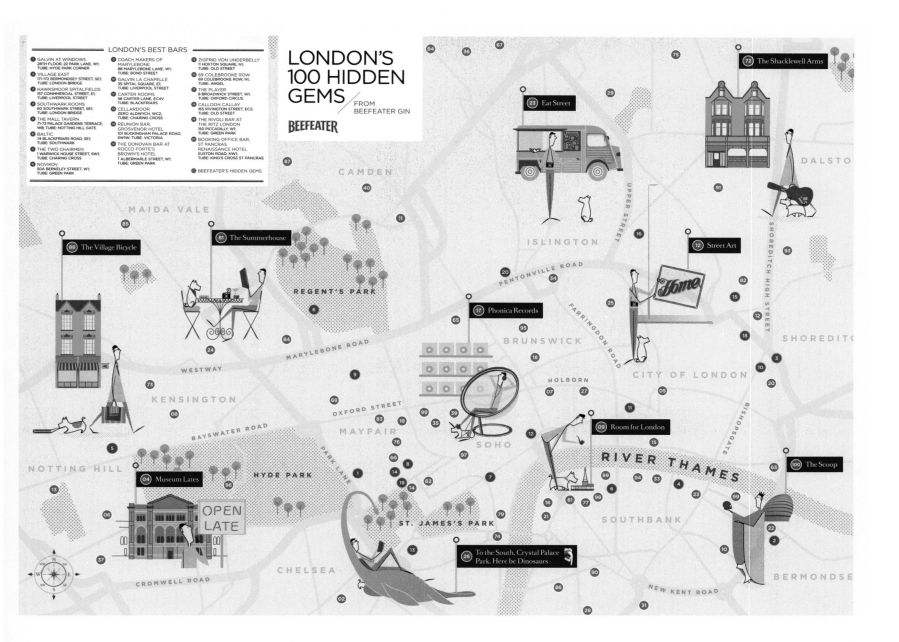

LONDON'S 100 HIDDEN GEMS
/ FROM BEEFEATER GIN

BEEFEATER

LONDON'S BEST BARS

01 GALVIN AT WINDOWS
28TH FLOOR, 22 PARK LANE, W1;
TUBE: HYDE PARK CORNER

02 VILLAGE EAST
171-172 BERMONDSEY STREET, SE1;
TUBE: LONDON BRIDGE

03 HAWKSMOOR SPITALFIELDS
157 COMMERCIAL STREET, E1;
TUBE: LIVERPOOL STREET

04 SOUTHWARK ROOMS
60 SOUTHWARK STREET, SE1;
TUBE: LONDON BRIDGE

05 THE MALL TAVERN
71-73 PALACE GARDENS TERRACE,
W8; TUBE: NOTTING HILL GATE

06 BALTIC
74 BLACKFRIARS ROAD, SE1;
TUBE: SOUTHWARK

07 THE TWO CHAIRMEN
1 WARWICK HOUSE STREET, SW1;
TUBE: CHARING CROSS

08 NOVIKOV
50A BERKELEY STREET, W1;
TUBE: GREEN PARK

09 COACH MAKERS OF MARYLEBONE
88 MARYLEBONE LANE, W1;
TUBE: BOND STREET

10 GALVIN LA CHAPELLE
35 SPITAL SQUARE, E1;
TUBE: LIVERPOOL STREET

11 CARTER ROOMS
56 CARTER LANE, EC4V
TUBE: BLACKFRIARS

12 CELLARDOOR
ZERO ALDWYCH, WC2;
TUBE: CHARING CROSS

13 REUNION BAR,
GROSVENOR HOTEL
101 BUCKINGHAM PALACE ROAD,
SW1W; TUBE: VICTORIA

14 THE DONOVAN BAR AT
ROCCO FORTE'S
BROWN'S HOTEL
1 ALBERMARLE STREET, W1;
TUBE: GREEN PARK

15 ZIGFRID VON UNDERBELLY
11 HOXTON SQUARE, N1;
TUBE: OLD STREET

16 69 COLEBROOKE ROW
69 COLEBROOKE ROW, N1;
TUBE: ANGEL

17 THE PLAYER
8 BROADWICK STREET, W1;
TUBE: OXFORD CIRCUS

18 CALLOOH CALLAY
165 RIVINGTON STREET, EC2;
TUBE: OLD STREET

19 THE RIVOLI BAR AT
THE RITZ LONDON
150 PICCADILLY, W1;
TUBE: GREEN PARK

20 BOOKING OFFICE BAR,
ST PANCRAS
RENAISSANCE HOTEL
EUSTON ROAD, NW1;
TUBE: KING'S CROSS ST PANCRAS

● BEEFEATER'S HIDDEN GEMS

72 The Shacklewell Arms
23 Eat Street
88 The Village Bicycle
81 The Summerhouse
12 Street Art
17 Phonica Records
09 Room for London
100 The Scoop
04 Museum Lates
26 To the South, Crystal Palace Park. Here be Dinosaurs

OPEN LATE
Home

MAIDA VALE
CAMDEN
ISLINGTON
DALSTON
REGENT'S PARK
PENTONVILLE ROAD
BRUNSWICK
SHOREDITCH
SHOREDITCH HIGH STREET
FARRINGDON ROAD
UPPER STREET
MARYLEBONE ROAD
WESTWAY
KENSINGTON
CITY OF LONDON
BISHOPSGATE
OXFORD STREET
HOLBORN
MAYFAIR
SOHO
RIVER THAMES
BAYSWATER ROAD
PARK LANE
NOTTING HILL
HYDE PARK
SOUTHBANK
ST. JAMES'S PARK
BERMONDSEY
CHELSEA
CROMWELL ROAD
NEW KENT ROAD

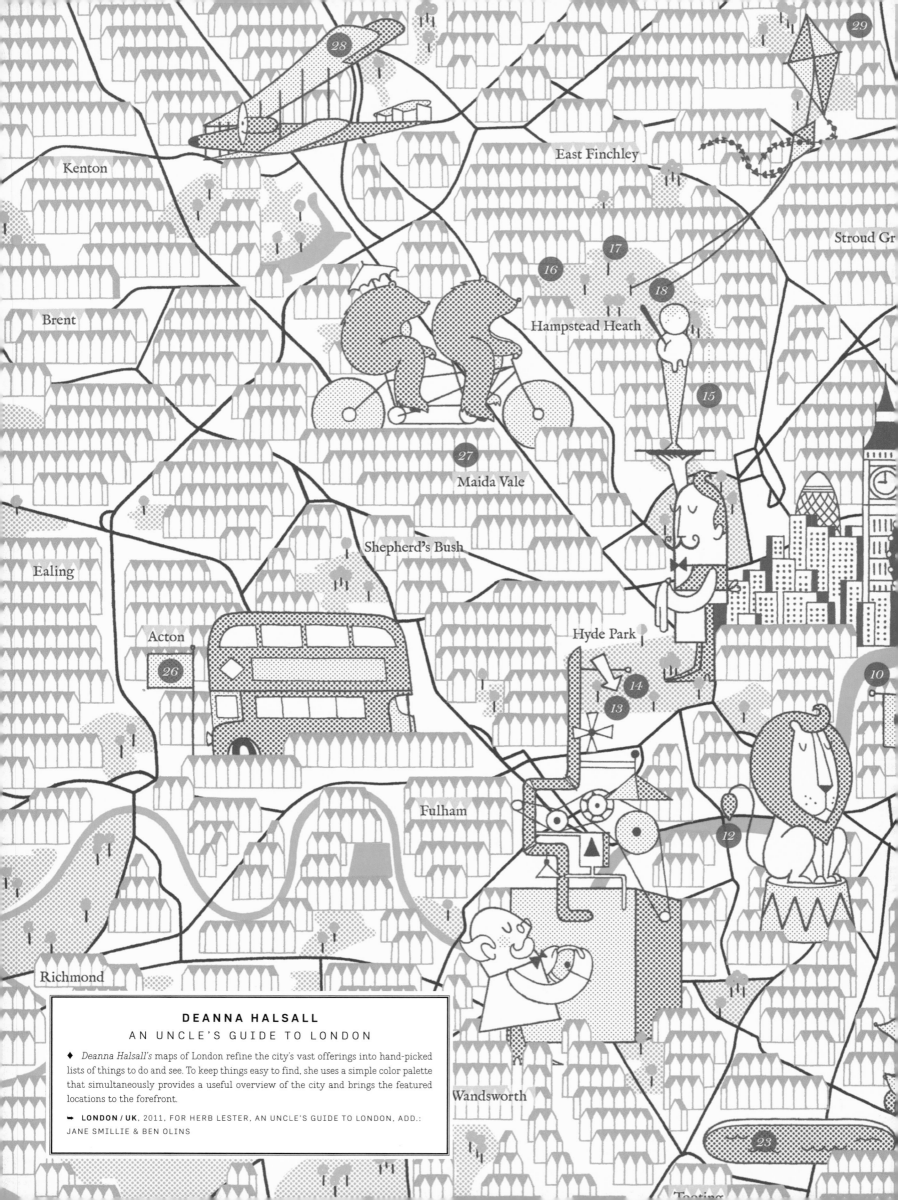

Kenton

East Finchley

Stroud Gr

Brent

Hampstead Heath

Maida Vale

Ealing

Shepherd's Bush

Acton

Hyde Park

Fulham

Richmond

DEANNA HALSALL

AN UNCLE'S GUIDE TO LONDON

♦ *Deanna Halsall's* maps of London refine the city's vast offerings into hand-picked lists of things to do and see. To keep things easy to find, she uses a simple color palette that simultaneously provides a useful overview of the city and brings the featured locations to the forefront.

➡ **LONDON / UK**, 2011, FOR HERB LESTER, AN UNCLE'S GUIDE TO LONDON, ADD.: JANE SMILLIE & BEN OLINS

Wandsworth

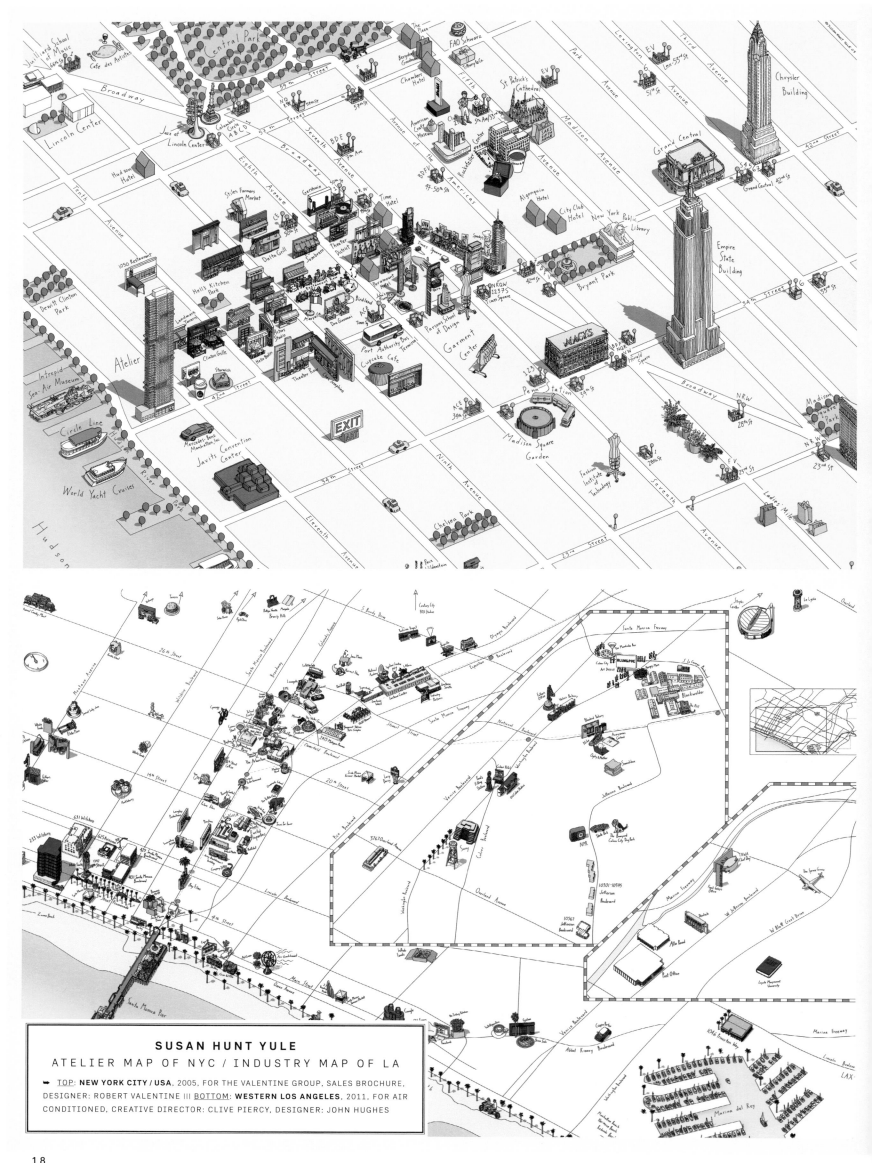

SUSAN HUNT YULE

ATELIER MAP OF NYC / INDUSTRY MAP OF LA

➤ TOP: **NEW YORK CITY / USA**, 2005, FOR THE VALENTINE GROUP, SALES BROCHURE, DESIGNER: ROBERT VALENTINE III BOTTOM: **WESTERN LOS ANGELES**, 2011, FOR AIR CONDITIONED, CREATIVE DIRECTOR: CLIVE PIERCY, DESIGNER: JOHN HUGHES

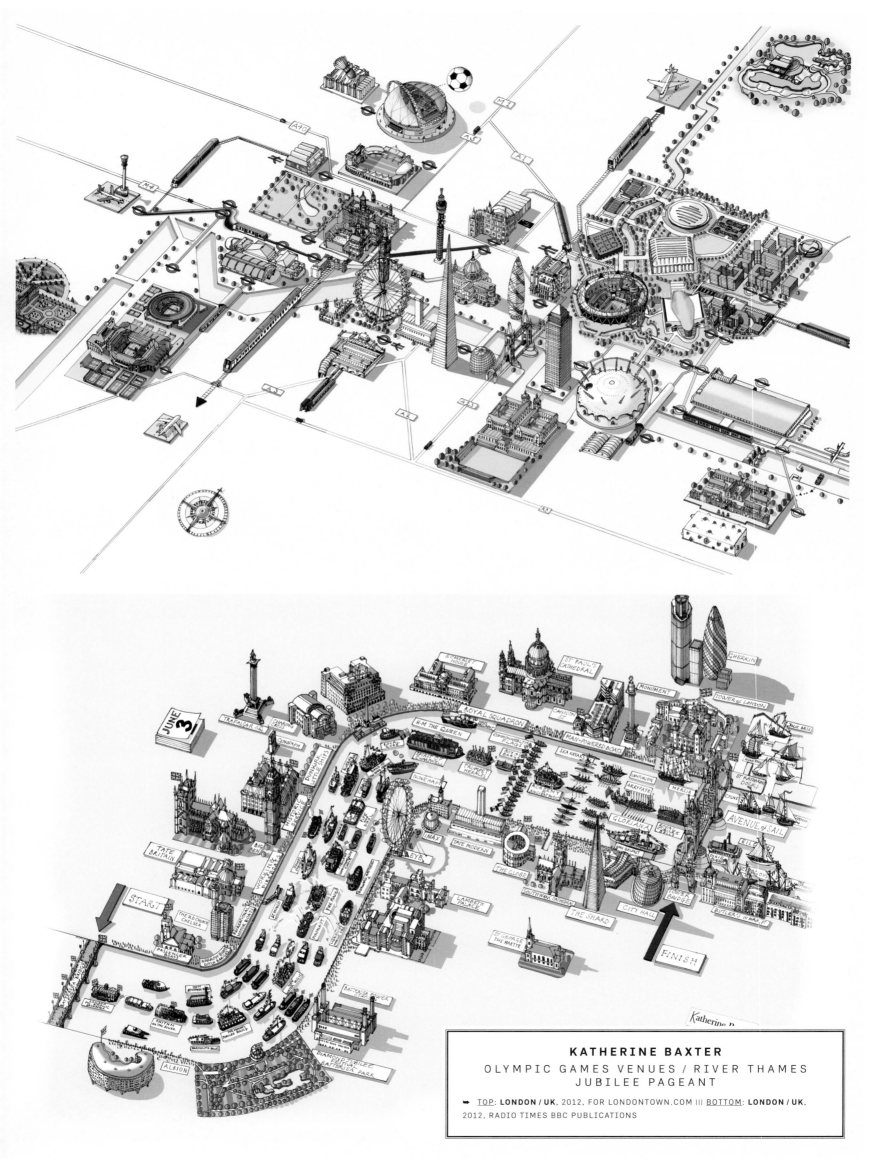

KATHERINE BAXTER

OLYMPIC GAMES VENUES / RIVER THAMES
JUBILEE PAGEANT

→ TOP: **LONDON / UK**, 2012, FOR LONDONTOWN.COM ||| BOTTOM: **LONDON / UK**,
2012, RADIO TIMES BBC PUBLICATIONS

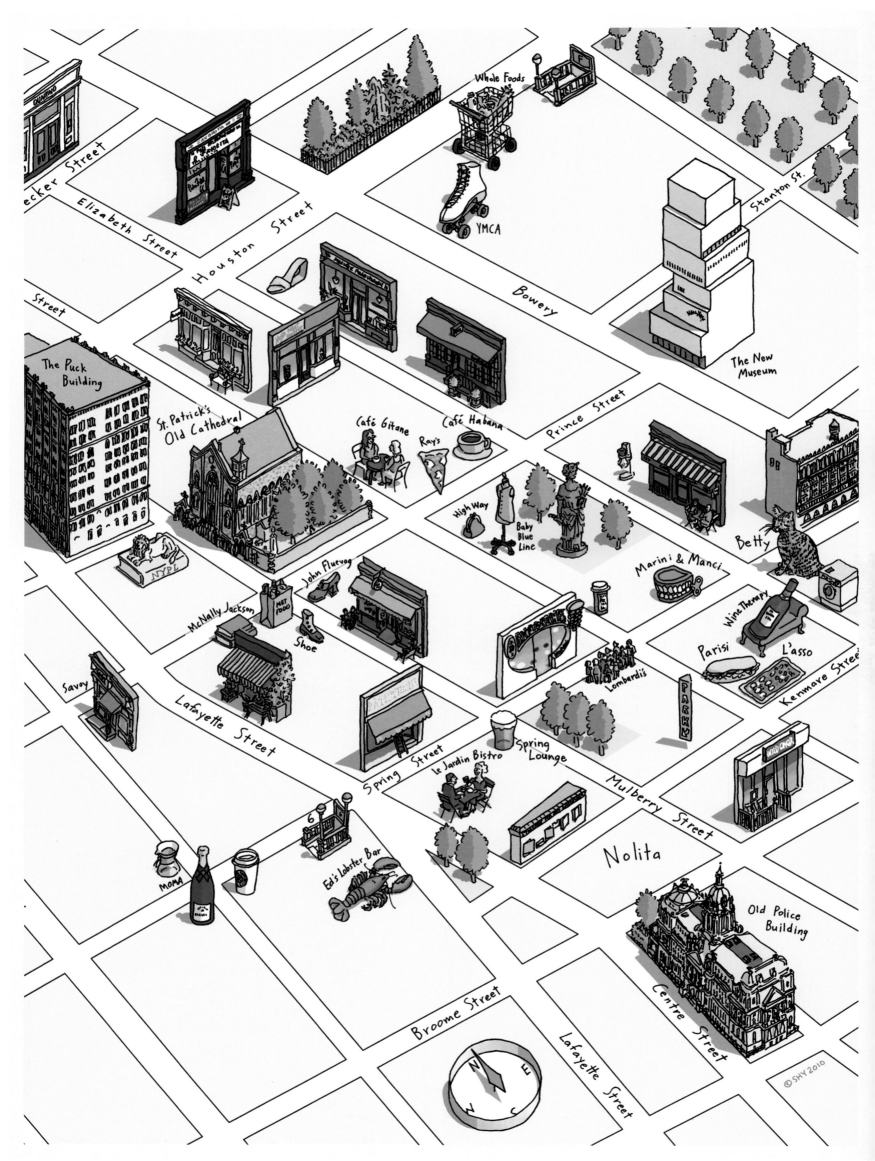

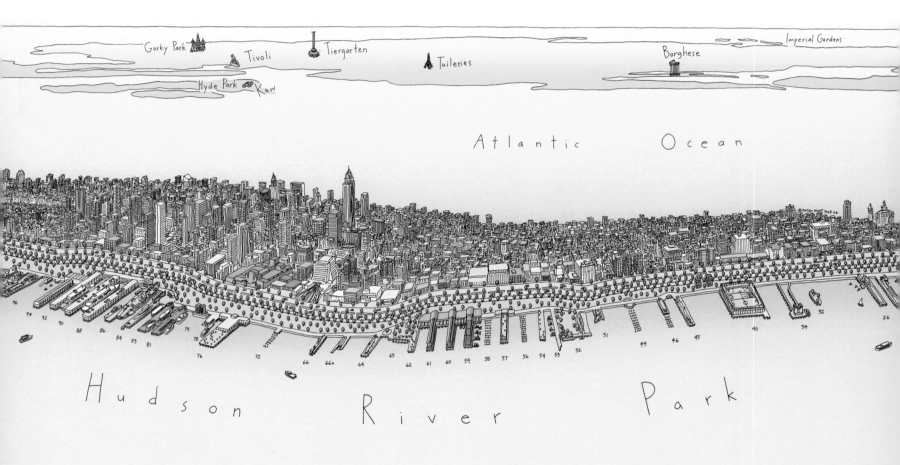

Gorky Park   Tivoli   Tiergarten   Tuileries   Borghese   Imperial Gardens

Hyde Park   Kew

Atlantic   Ocean

Hudson   River   Park

KATHERINE BAXTER
LONDON POSTER / NEW YORK POSTER

♦ Although the draftsmanship of *Katherine Baxter's* maps recalls the traditional precision of cartography, she uses a modern touch to illustrate complex urban areas. Her work manages to be both intricately detailed and clear, presenting only the most relevant information for maps of London or Manhattan.

➤ LEFT PAGE: **LONDON / UK**, 2005, FOR THE TIMES NEWSPAPER, RIGHT PAGE: **NEW YORK CITY / USA**, 2006, FOR THE TIMES NEWSPAPER

Seaton
Sidmouth

Clappentail Park

MORGAN'S GRAVE
25

Clappentail Lane

Portland Court

Ware Lane

Upper Westhill Road

Highcliff Rd.

Westhill Road

Hill Rise Rd.

UMBRELLA COTTAGE

CORAM TOWER

Sidmouth Road

Pound Road

CATHOLIC CHURCH

Coram Avenue

LIBRARY

P

HOLMBUSH CAR PARK

7

Pine Walk

UNDERCLIFF

Shire End

Cobb Road

Cobb Lane

BELMONT HOUSE

Sohe Lane

Pound Street

MINI GOLF

LANGMOOR & LISTER GARDENS

BOWLING GREEN

BOAT CLUB

PUTTING GREEN

P

Orme Terrace

JANE AUSTEN GARDEN

3

Marine Parade

Cart Road
15

13

SAILING CLUB

LIFEBOAT STATION AND HARBOUR MASTER

Front Beach

Lucy's Ledge

Cobb Gate

HARBOUR (BOAT TRIPS)

NORTH WALL

MARINE AQUARIUM

1

27

GRANNY'S TEETH

THE COBB

7

24

KEITH ROBINSON
LYME REGIS TOWN MAP

♦ *Keith Robinson* designed the map of the seaside town of Lyme Regis to appeal to visitors of all ages. The finished map, which measures 6×4 feet, is displayed at the town's seafront and features local landmarks, history, and idiosyncratic architecture. It is also sold as a fold-up tourist map and can be used as a guided walking tour of the town.

➥ **LYME REGIS, DORSET / UK**, 2011, FOR LYME REGIS TOWN COUNCIL

BORGARMYND

REYKJAVIK CENTER

♦ The birdview of Reykjavík, Iceland, highlights the city's areas of interest for visitors and tourists. Intricate details included in the map provide a better understanding of the city as a whole by showing the context of each location and views of surrounding areas.

➥ **REYKJAVIK / ICELAND**, 2010–2011, FOR REYKJAVIKCENTERMAP.COM, 50,000 FREE COPIES PUBLISHED EVERY YEAR, ADD.: SNORRI ÞÓR TRYGGVASON, PÉTUR STEFÁNSSON, SNORRI ELDJÁRN SNORRASON

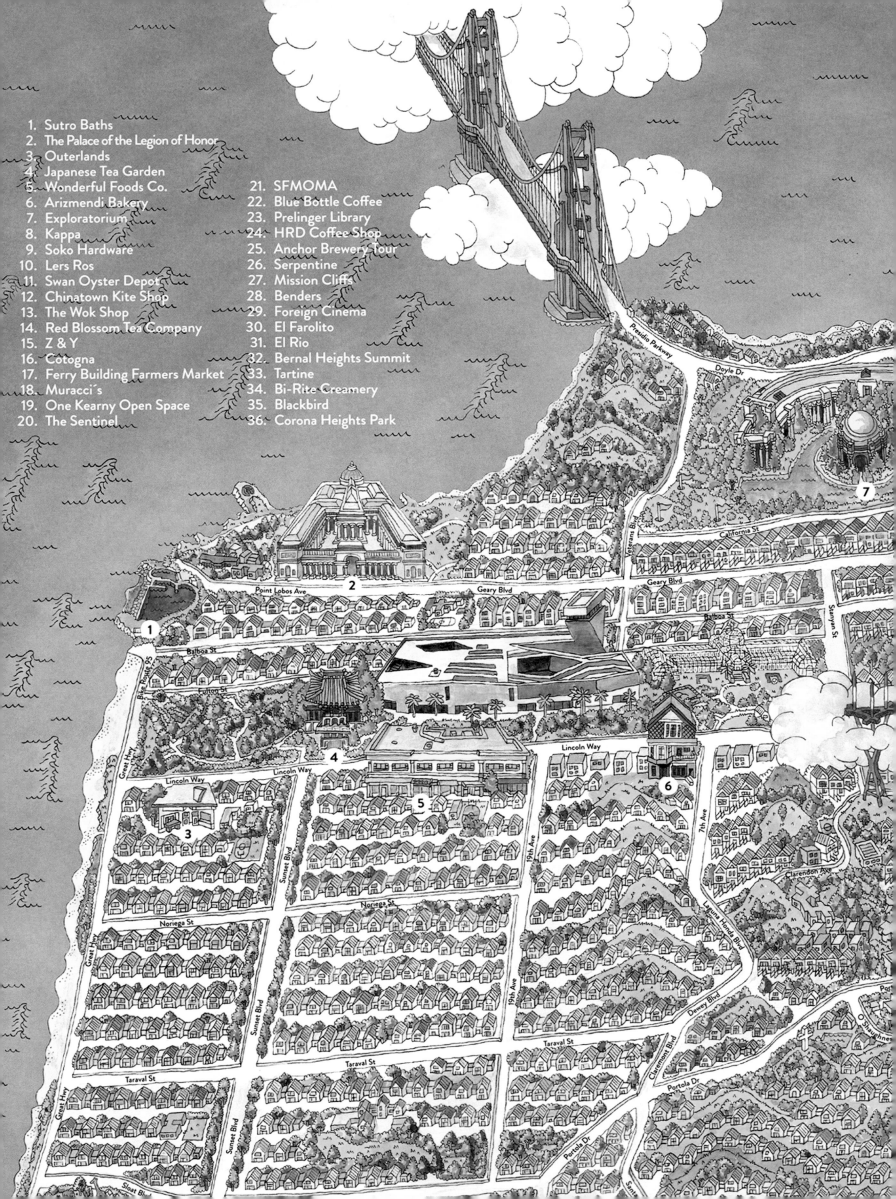

1. Sutro Baths
2. The Palace of the Legion of Honor
3. Outerlands
4. Japanese Tea Garden
5. Wonderful Foods Co.
6. Arizmendi Bakery
7. Exploratorium
8. Kappa
9. Soko Hardware
10. Lers Ros
11. Swan Oyster Depot
12. Chinatown Kite Shop
13. The Wok Shop
14. Red Blossom Tea Company
15. Z & Y
16. Cotogna
17. Ferry Building Farmers Market
18. Muracci's
19. One Kearny Open Space
20. The Sentinel
21. SFMOMA
22. Blue Bottle Coffee
23. Prelinger Library
24. HRD Coffee Shop
25. Anchor Brewery Tour
26. Serpentine
27. Mission Cliffs
28. Benders
29. Foreign Cinema
30. El Farolito
31. El Rio
32. Bernal Heights Summit
33. Tartine
34. Bi-Rite Creamery
35. Blackbird
36. Corona Heights Park

THE OPEN COMPANY MAPS **SAN FRANCISCO**

BORGARMYND

SAN FRANCISCO

➥ **SAN FRANCISCO / USA**, 2011–2012, FOR THE OPEN COMPANY, PRINTED ON WATERPROOF TEAR-RESISTANT TYVEK, FOLDED USING A SPECIAL ORIGAMI TECH-NIQUE. ADD.: SNORRI ÞÓR TRYGGVASON, PÉTUR STEFÁNSSON, SNORRI ELDJÁRN SNORRASON, TRYGGVI ÁRNASON, ERIC MELTZER, AEN TAN

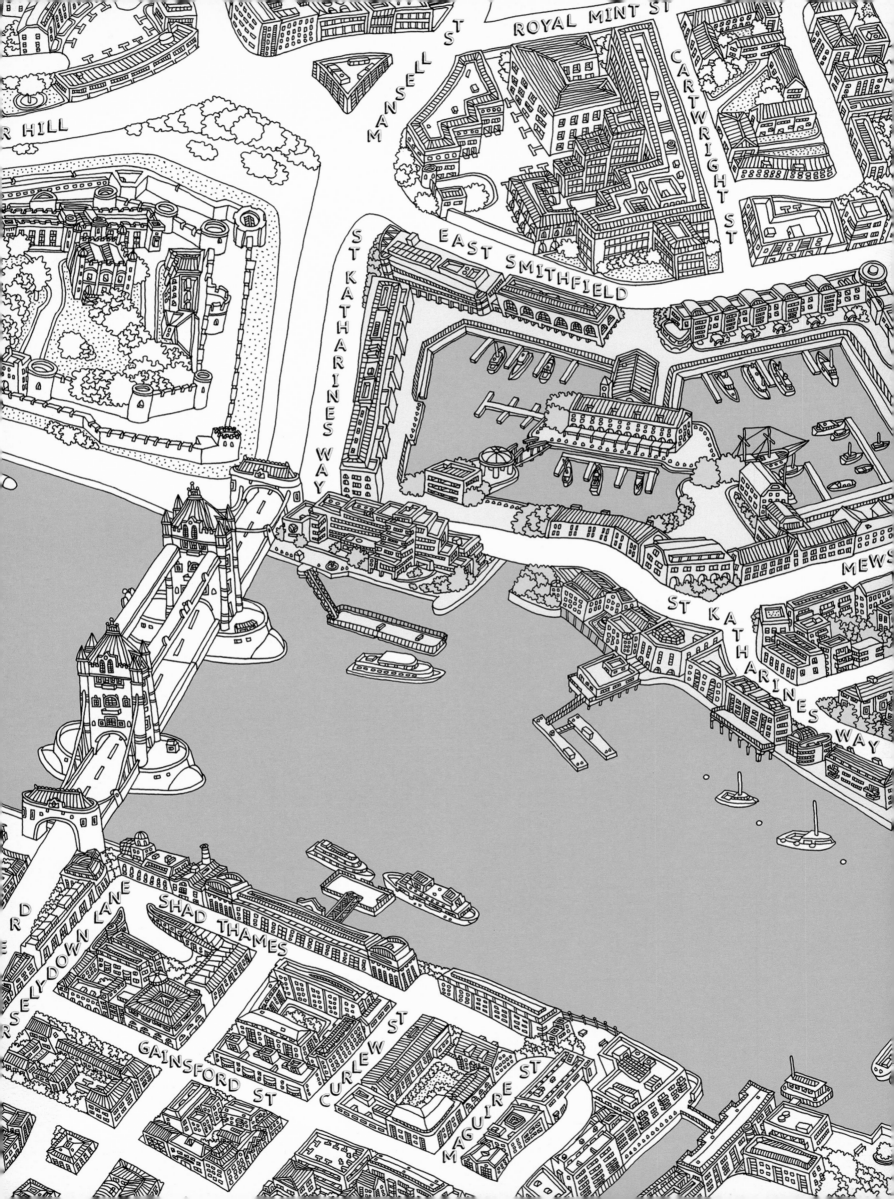

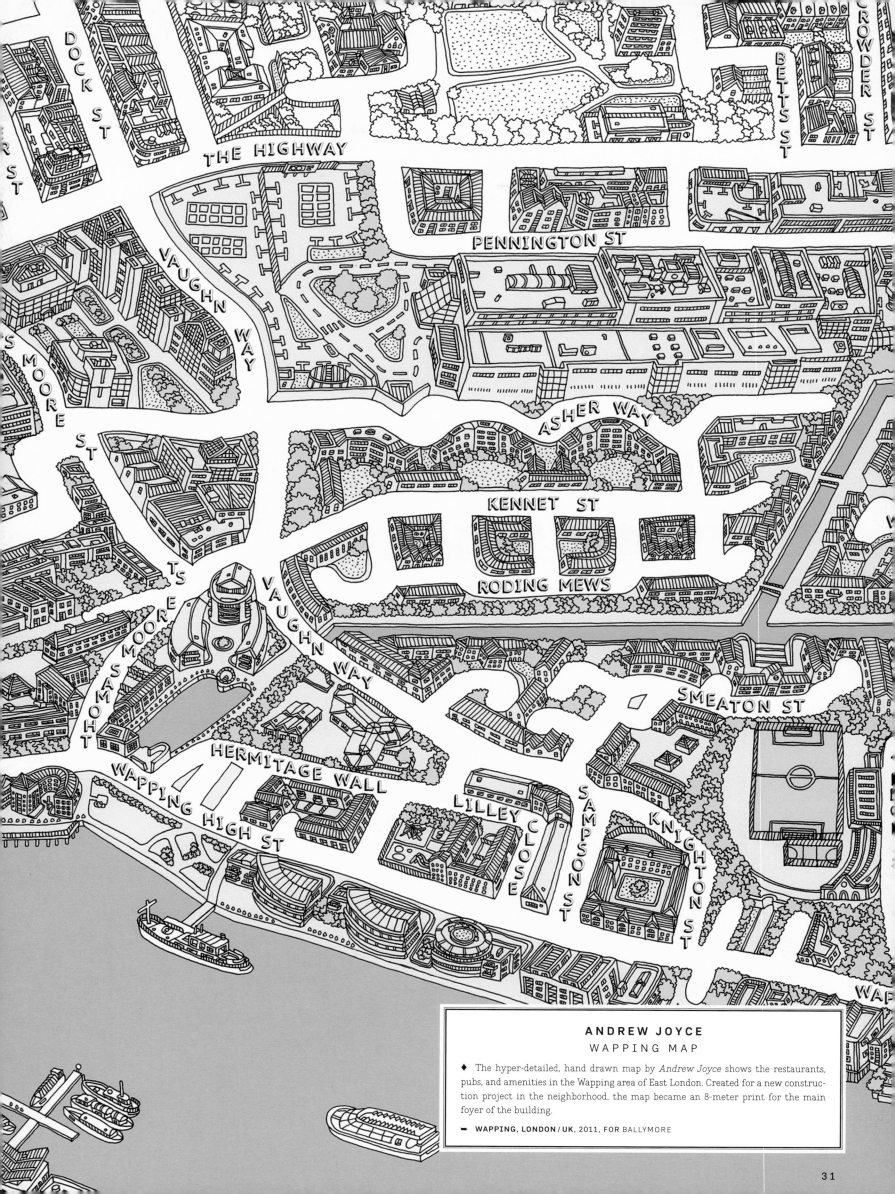

DOCK ST

CROWDER ST

THE HIGHWAY

BETTS ST

PENNINGTON ST

VAUGHN WAY

MOORE ST

ASHER WAY

KENNET ST

RODING MEWS

THOMAS MOORE ST

VAUGHN WAY

SMEATON ST

HERMITAGE WALL

WAPPING HIGH ST

LILLEY CLOSE

SAMPSON ST

KNIGHTON ST

WAP

ANDREW JOYCE

WAPPING MAP

♦ The hyper-detailed, hand drawn map by *Andrew Joyce* shows the restaurants, pubs, and amenities in the Wapping area of East London. Created for a new construction project in the neighborhood, the map became an 8-meter print for the main foyer of the building.

➡ WAPPING, LONDON / UK, 2011, FOR BALLYMORE

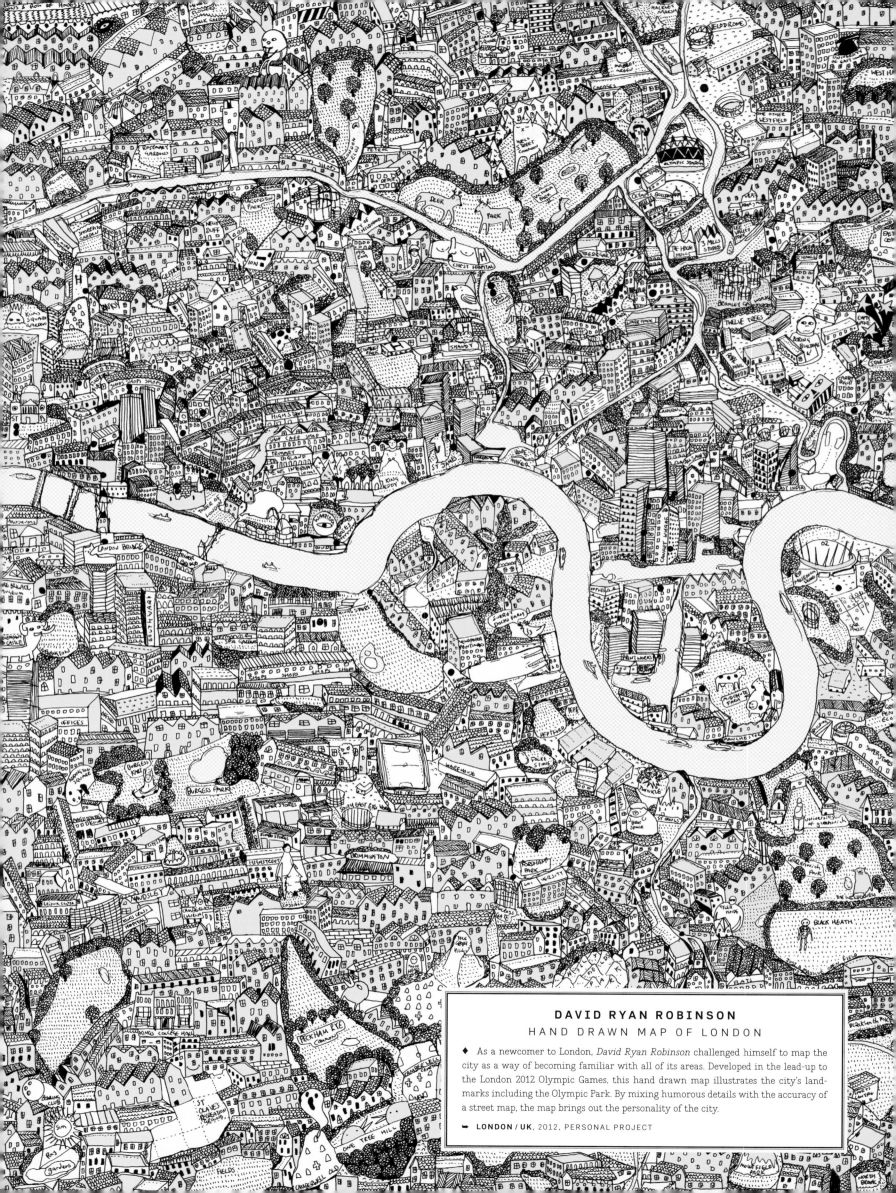

DAVID RYAN ROBINSON
HAND DRAWN MAP OF LONDON

♦ As a newcomer to London, *David Ryan Robinson* challenged himself to map the city as a way of becoming familiar with all of its areas. Developed in the lead-up to the London 2012 Olympic Games, this hand drawn map illustrates the city's landmarks including the Olympic Park. By mixing humorous details with the accuracy of a street map, the map brings out the personality of the city.

↳ **LONDON / UK**, 2012, PERSONAL PROJECT

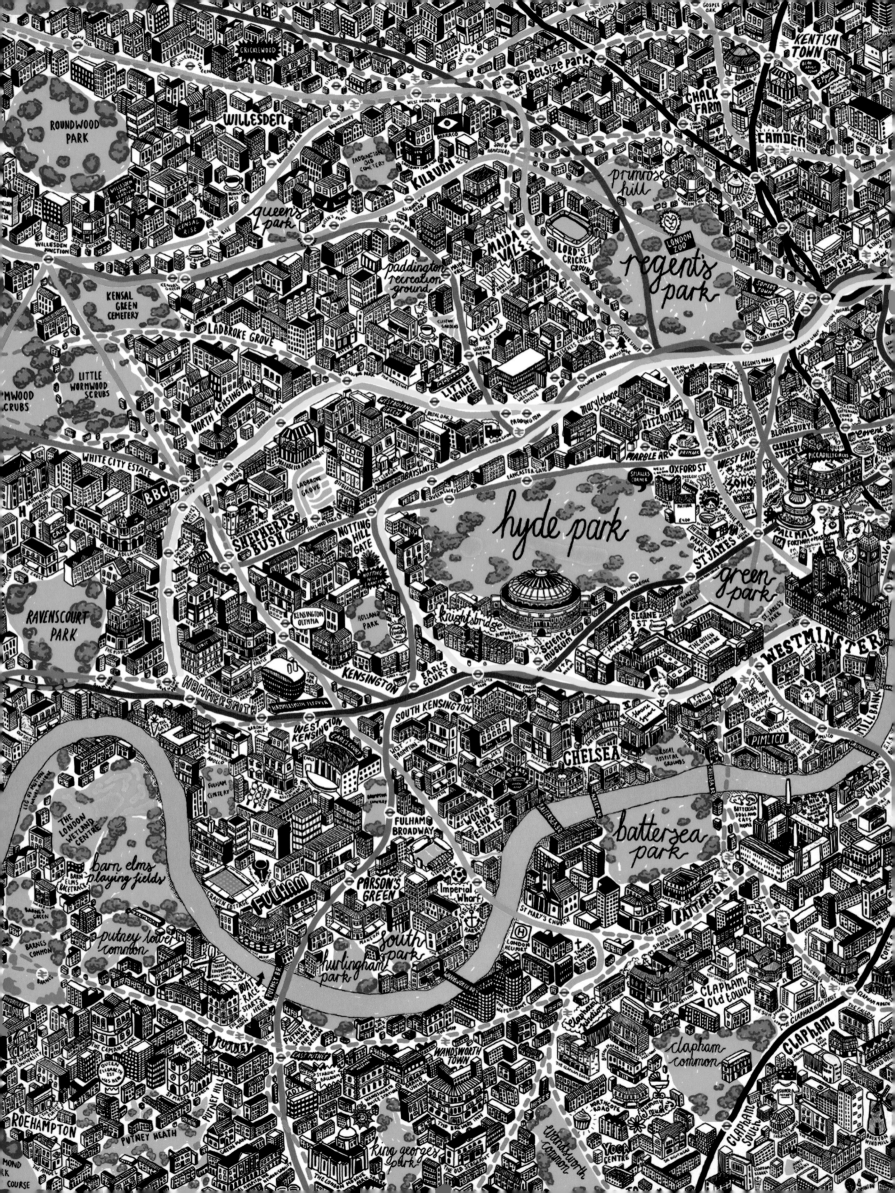

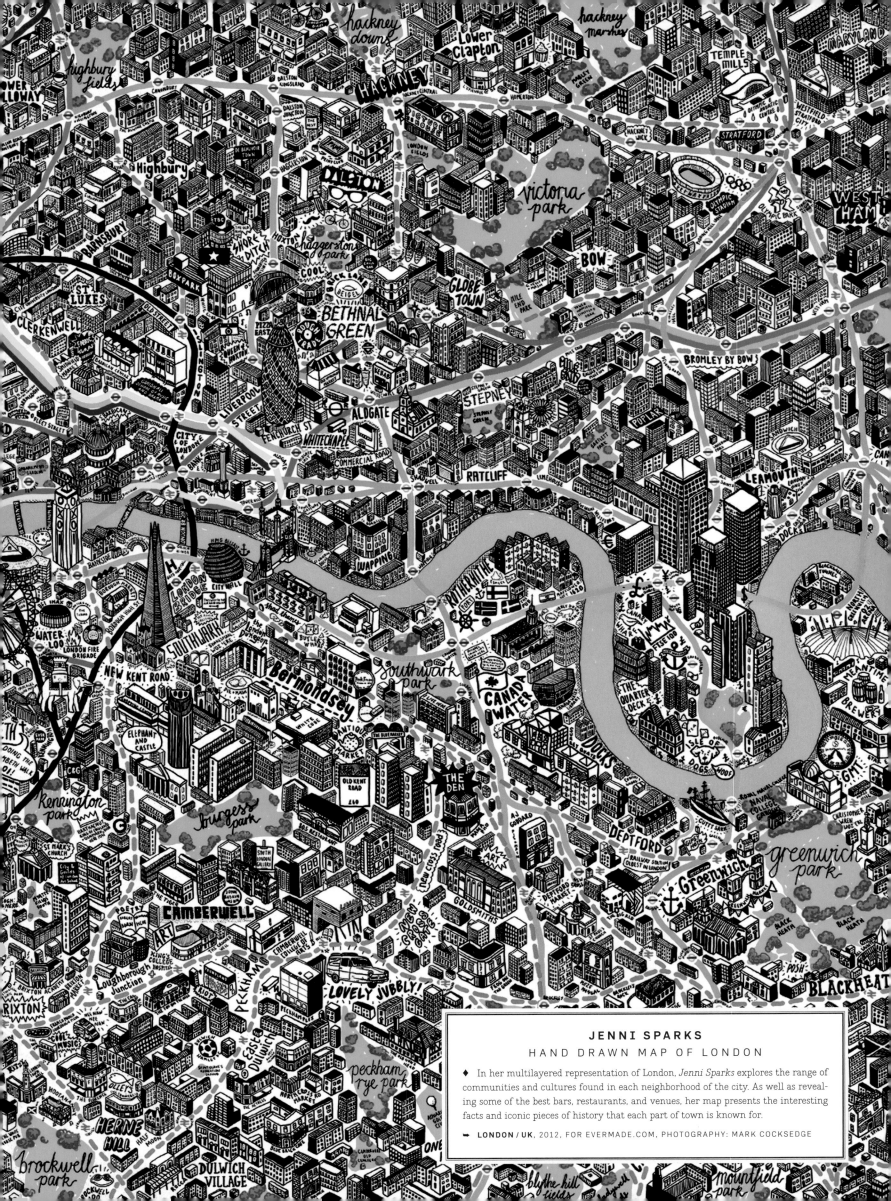

JENNI SPARKS
HAND DRAWN MAP OF LONDON

♦ In her multilayered representation of London, *Jenni Sparks* explores the range of communities and cultures found in each neighborhood of the city. As well as revealing some of the best bars, restaurants, and venues, her map presents the interesting facts and iconic pieces of history that each part of town is known for.

➥ **LONDON / UK**, 2012, FOR EVERMADE.COM, PHOTOGRAPHY: MARK COCKSEDGE

JAMES GULLIVER HANCOCK
VENEZIA

♦ Created for an Italian shopping feature in ICON MAGAZINE, the illustrated maps of Rome, Torino, and Venice by *James Gulliver Hancock* are used for detailed visual guides to the best shopping each city has to offer. Later added were the green spaces, city squares, and architectural icons that surround each of the shopping districts.

↪ **VENICE / ITALY**, 2011, FOR ICON MAGAZINE / ITALY, LEFTLOFT / MONDADORI

VENEZIA

VIA DEI CORONARI

HI NUOVI

VIA DEL GOVERNO VECCHIO

VIA GIULIA

ROMA

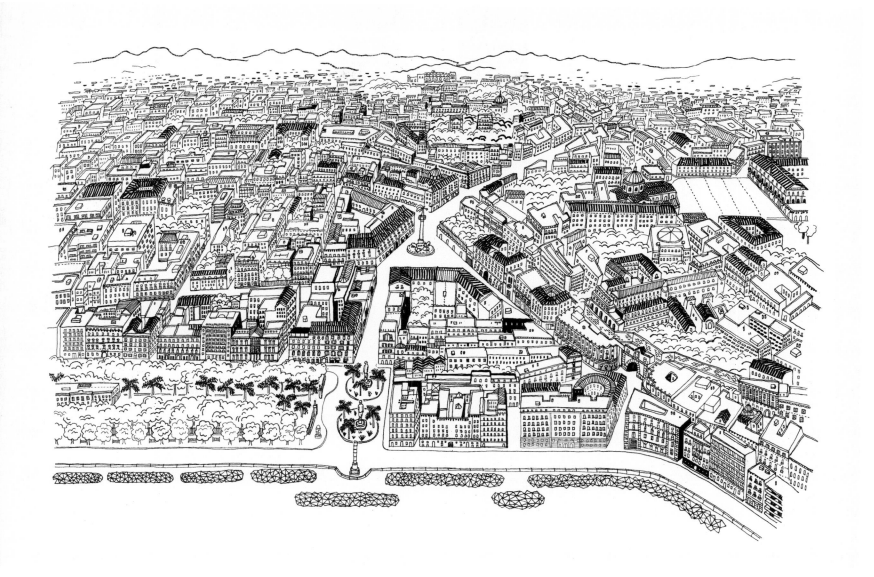

JAMES GULLIVER HANCOCK
ROMA / NAPOLI

➥ LEFT PAGE: **ROME / ITALY**, RIGHT PAGE: **NAPLES / ITALY**, 2011, FOR ICON MAGA-
ZINE / ITALY, LEFTLOFT / MONDADORI ITALY

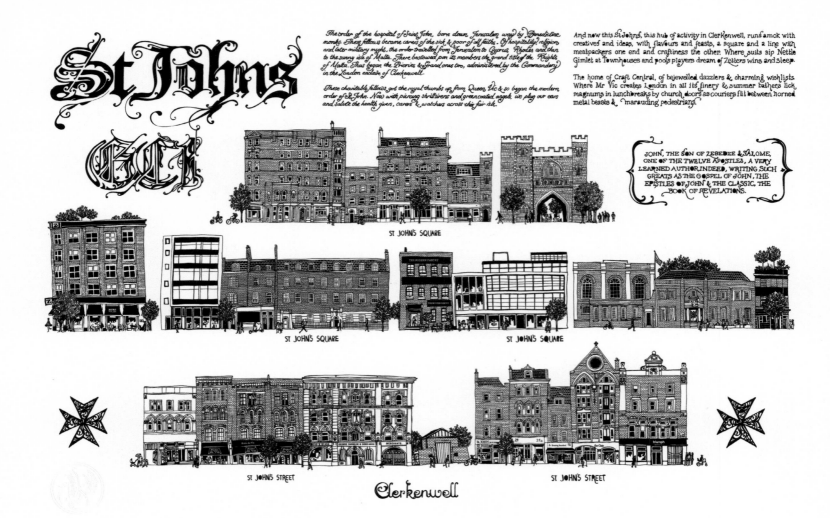

St Johns

The order of the hospital of Saint John, born down Jerusalem way by Benedictine monks. These fellows became carers of the sick & poor of all faiths. Of hospitality, religion, and later military might, the order travelled from Jerusalem to Cyprus, Rhodes and then to the sunny isle of Malta. There bestowed pon its members the grand title of the Knights of Malta. Thus began the Priories & grand ones too, administered by the Commandery in the London enclave of Clerkenwell.

These charitable fellows got the royal thumbs up from Queen Vic & so began the modern order of St John. Now with piercing shrill sirens and green coated angels, we plug our ears and salute the health givers, carers & watchers across this fair isle.

And now this St Johns, this hub of activity in Clerkenwell, runs amok with creatives and ideas, with flavours and feasts, a square and a line with meatpackers one end and craftiness the other. Where suits sip Nettle Gimlet at Townhouses and pools players dream of Zetters wine and sleep.

The home of Craft Central, of bejewelled dazzlers & charming wishlists. Where Mr Vic creates London in all its finery & summer bathers lick magnums in lunchbreaks by church doors as couriers flit between horned metal beasts & marauding pedestrians.

JOHN, THE SON OF ZEBEDEE & SALOME, ONE OF THE TWELVE APOSTLES, A VERY LEARNED AUTHOR INDEED, WRITING SUCH GREATS AS THE GOSPEL OF JOHN, THE EPISTLES OF JOHN & THE CLASSIC, THE BOOK OF REVELATIONS.

ST JOHN'S SQUARE

ST JOHN'S SQUARE

ST JOHN'S SQUARE

ST JOHN'S STREET

Clerkenwell

ST JOHN'S STREET

VIC LEE
THE LONDONEREAS

♦ In this series, Vic Lee investigates London streets that have retained their original guise as a village high street. Local shops, eateries, and businesses are shown in succession from one end of the street to the other, showcasing traditional architecture as well as subsequent additions. These street maps serve as reminders of how places grow and change over time.

➡ LEFT PAGE: ST. JOHNS, LONDON / UK ||| TOP RIGHT: CITY UNIVERSITY, LONDON / UK, 2011 / 2012, FOR CITY UNIVERSITY LONDON ||| BOTTOM RIGHT: COLUMBIA ROAD, LONDON / UK ||| NEXT SPREAD: PORTOBELLO RD., LONDON / UK, 2010–2012, PERSONAL PROJECT

CITY UNIVERSITY LONDON

Established in 1894 as the Northampton Institute, through the generosity of the Earl of Northampton and other benefactors, this centre of education in the City of London nurtured lawyers, economists, chemists, engineers and horologists to name a few of its disciplines. Renamed for its ties to the City of London in England's finest year, 1966, this University boasts the Lord Mayor of London as its Chancellor. Where Olympians once swam and boxed in London's first foray into the ringed arena in 1908, the future Olympians of business and industry now study. One of the world's top universities, City is a place of environmental awareness and sustainability, of interaction, inspiration and enjoyment: 'where the world comes together in a city made of knowledge and understanding, handshakes and deals, experimentation and industrialisation, growth and prosperity, cultures and memories.'

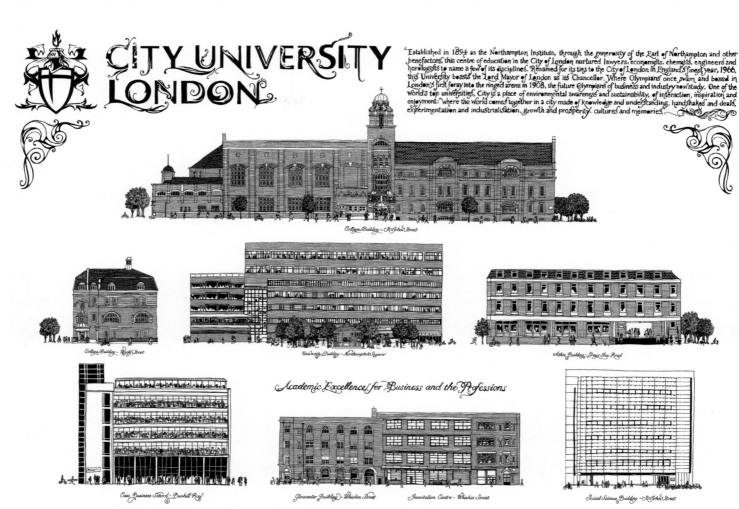

College Building ~ St John Street

College Building ~ Rosoman Street *University Building ~ Northampton Square* *Askin Building ~ Goswell Road*

Academic Excellence for Business and the Professions

Cass Business School ~ Bunhill Row *Gloucester Building ~ Whiskin Street* *Innovation Centre ~ Whiskin Street* *Social Science Building ~ St John Street*

And now to some luminaries: the famous and well heeled, the educated and inspiring, those that have carried books through the halls, scribbled notes and lunched in the parks. From Academia the likes of L. Bruce Archer, George Daniels, George Fabienden and Professor Ebrahim Moosa. From Government, Politics and Society, we have Mohandas Mahatma Gandhi, Muhammad Ali Jinnah, Jawaharlal Nehru, Clement Atlee, Liu Mingkang, Dursun Yilmaz, Margaret Thatcher, Tony Blair, Sir Stelios Haji-Ioannou and Aris Spiliotopoulos. From the world of Media and Entertainment, Steven Maguire, Dermot Murnaghan, Michael Fish, Kirsty Lang, Dr Joel Rubin and Faisal Islam, to name but a few that have passed through the City doors.

COLUMBIA ROAD Flowering Market

This former place, Nova Scotia Gardens, this Columbia Road, named in honour of the philanthropist Baroness Coutts, who built Columbia Market for the traders to ply their wares. Once the stomping ground of sheep heading to the chopping blocks of Smithfields & a notorious gang of resurrection men

This Columbia Road, where upholsterers adorned furniture & wood was buffed and polished. This now Sunday home to pansies and poppies, to stems and gems, to walking palms on crowded streets, terracotta pots and dysfunctional art. Where the call of the florist is louder than the bird in the cage and the masses flock religiously

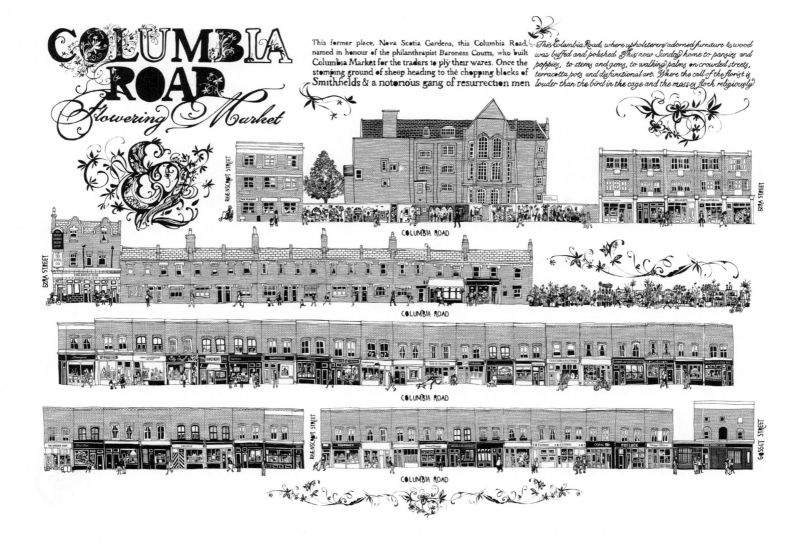

COLUMBIA ROAD

COLUMBIA ROAD

COLUMBIA ROAD

COLUMBIA ROAD

PORTOBELLO ROAD

SO NAMED AFTER A PORT IN THE GULF OF MEXICO, PUERTO BELLO, WHERE ONCE WERE SHIPPED TREASURES AND FAYRE & THE GREAT ADMIRAL VERNON LED THE BRITISH FLEET IN THE WAR OF JENKINS EAR, A PLACE ONCE OF HAYFIELDS, ORCHARDS AND GREENERY. WHERE SERVANTS, COACHMEN, MESSENGERS, AND COSTERMONGERS EARNED A DECENT CRUST AND A MR WHYTE PROPOSED A RACING EMPORIUM TO ENVY ASCOT OR EPSOM.

And now this road with famed market is a hive of buzzing snappers and shoppers, lookers & and pouters. Where rhubarb meets truffled cakes & tarnished gold rubs against glittered tops. The home of uber stars & dubious divas, paps & pets - the road to racks & runes.

43

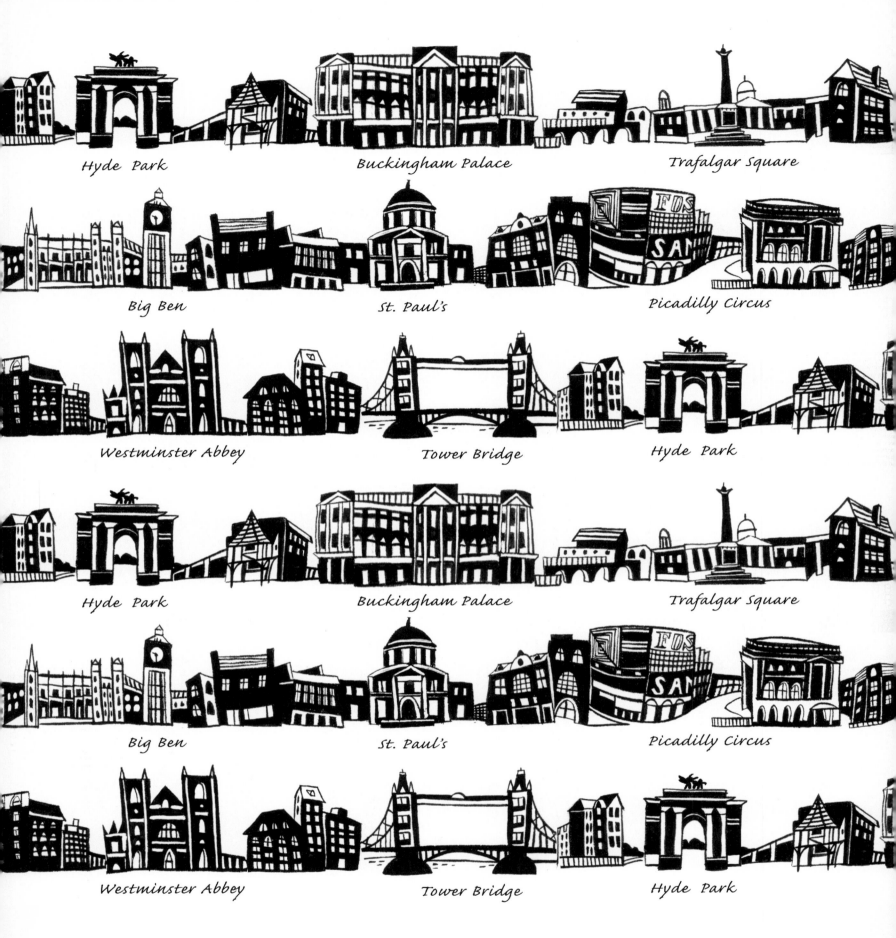

Hyde Park

Buckingham Palace

Trafalgar Square

Big Ben

St. Paul's

Picadilly Circus

Westminster Abbey

Tower Bridge

Hyde Park

Hyde Park

Buckingham Palace

Trafalgar Square

Big Ben

St. Paul's

Picadilly Circus

Westminster Abbey

Tower Bridge

Hyde Park

MARILENA PERILLI
LONDON TEXTILE

♦ *Marilena Perilli* creates a panorama of London buildings by stringing together notable landmarks such as Big Ben, Tower Bridge, and Westminster Abbey. The final drawings were printed on a line of plates, saucers, glasses, linens, and store displays. They were also printed as a limited edition city map collection.

➥ **LONDON / UK**, 2012, FOR FISHES EDDY

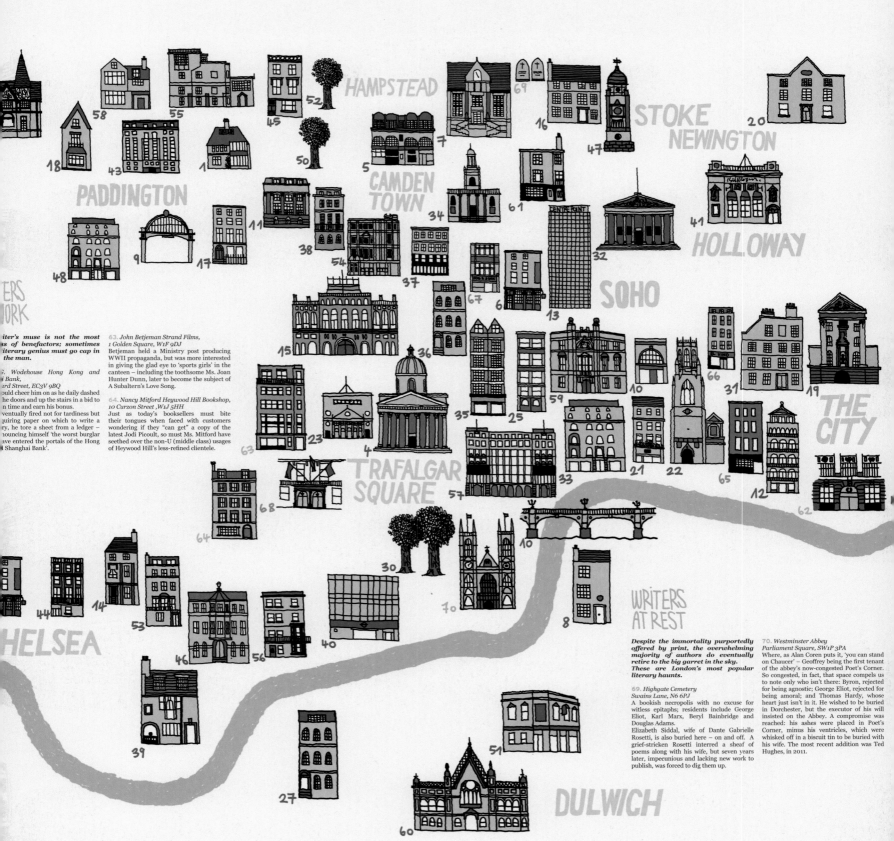

HAMPSTEAD

STOKE NEWINGTON

PADDINGTON

CAMDEN TOWN

HOLLOWAY

SOHO

THE CITY

TRAFALGAR SQUARE

CHELSEA

WRITERS AT REST

DULWICH

63. *John Betjeman Strand Films,*
1 Golden Square, W1F 9DJ
Betjeman held a Ministry post producing WWII propaganda, but was more interested in giving the glad eye to 'sports girls' in the canteen – including the toothsome Ms. Joan Hunter Dunn, later to become the subject of *A Subaltern's Love Song*.

64. *Nancy Mitford Heywood Hill Bookshop,*
10 Curzon Street ,W1J 5HH
Just as today's booksellers must bite their tongues when faced with customers wondering if they "can get" a copy of the latest Jodi Picoult, so must Ms. Mitford have seethed over the non-U (middle class) usages of Heywood Hill's less-refined clientele.

...riter's muse is not the most ...as of benefactors; sometimes ...literary genius must go cap in ...the man.

..., Wodehouse Hong Kong and ... Bank,
...rd Street, EC3V 9BQ
...ould cheer him on as he daily dashed ...he doors and up the stairs in a bid to ...n time and earn his bonus.
...eventually fired not for tardiness but ...quiring paper on which to write a ...ry, he tore a sheet from a ledger – ...nouncing himself 'the worst burglar ...ave entered the portals of the Hong ...Shanghai Bank'.

Despite the immortality purportedly offered by print, the overwhelming majority of authors do eventually retire to the big garret in the sky. These are London's most popular literary haunts.

69. *Highgate Cemetery*
Swains Lane, N6 6PJ
A bookish necropolis with no excuse for witless epitaphs; residents include George Eliot, Karl Marx, Beryl Bainbridge and Douglas Adams.
Elizabeth Siddal, wife of Dante Gabrielle Rosetti, is also buried here – on and off. A grief-stricken Rosetti interred a sheaf of poems along with his wife, but seven years later, impecunious and lacking new work to publish, was forced to dig them up.

70. *Westminster Abbey*
Parliament Square, SW1P 3PA
Where, as Alan Coren puts it, 'you can stand on Chaucer' – Geoffrey being the first tenant of the abbey's now-congested Poet's Corner. So congested, in fact, that space compels us to note only who isn't there: Byron, rejected for being agnostic; George Eliot, rejected for being amoral; and Thomas Hardy, whose heart just isn't in it. He wished to be buried in Dorchester, but the executor of his will insisted on the Abbey. A compromise was reached: his ashes were placed in Poet's Corner, minus his ventricles, which were whisked off in a biscuit tin to be buried with his wife. The most recent addition was Ted Hughes, in 2011.

THIBAUD HEREM

WRITING LONDON MAP

♦ Produced in collaboration with Herb Lester for the British Library London, the Writing London Map illustrates the locations of fictional and real stories in British literature. Detailed drawings of buildings and locations are accompanied by information about writers such as George Orwell, J.G. Ballard, and H.G. Wells.

➥ **LONDON / UK**, 2012, FOR HERB LESTER ASSOCIATES

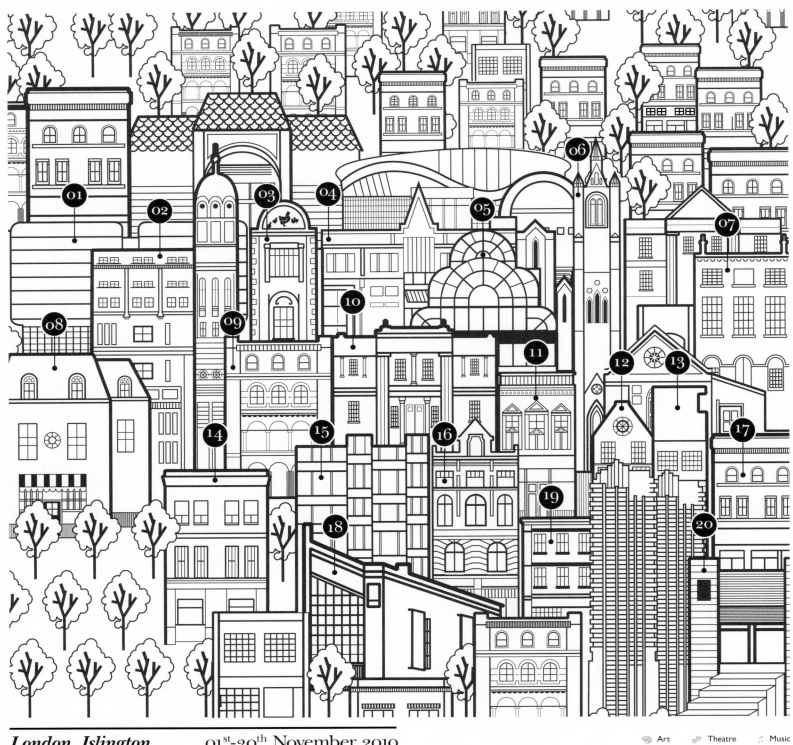

London, Islington   01st–30th November 2010   Art   Theatre   Music

MARTA PUCHALA

REFORMAP

♦ London resident *Marta Puchala* was always overwhelmed by event posters that didn't effectively communicate where the event would take place. She developed the Reformap to challenge the conventions of both the map and the event poster. Instead of using the traditional top-down view provided by maps, her solution allows the viewer to associate the events with familiar places and to navigate using actual landmarks.

➥ ISLINGTON, LONDON / UK, 2010,
PERSONAL PROJECT

01 — Pangolin London, N1
www.pangolinlondon.com
27.10–04.12
Ann Christopher:
Marks on the age of Space
Sculpture
09.09–24.12
William Pye
Sculpture
Opening Times: 10:00–18:00

02 — Scala, N1
www.scala-london.co.uk
13.11
Riot Cabaret:
A Wotever Extravaganza
Comedy
Time: 19:30
14.11
Die Antwoord
Rap-Rave
Time: 19:30
15.11
16.11
Boyce Avenue
Rock
Time: 20:15
17.11
Jazzanova
Nu-jazz, Electronica, Chill out
Time: 22:00
18.11
Adam Ant, I. Rae & the Thistles

03 — Hen & Chicken Theatre, N1
www.unrestrictedview.co.uk
13.11
Totally Tom
Comedy
Time: 13:00
The Fold Up Sketch Show
Comedy
Time: 17:30
14.11
Mr Fairbrother and Friends
Comedy
Time: 18:30

04 — The Garage, N5
13.11
Ladyfest:
N. Click, Battant, Vile Vile
Dance
Time: 15:30
14.11
Severin
Electro
Time: 20:00
17.11
J. Matranga, Lost On Campus
Rock
Time: 22:00

05 — Business Design, N1
www.businessdesigncentre.co.uk
07.11–14.11
Country Living Magazine
Fairs & sales
19.11
Vision10
Fairs & sales
Opening Times: 9:00–19:30

06 — Union Chapel N1
www.unionchapel.org.uk
15.11
Tom Jones, Lauren Pritchard
Pop, Soul
Times: 18:00
16.11
Poalo Nutini, Rumer
Pop rock, Folk, Blues
Times: 18:00
17.11
Hurst
Pop rock, Folk, Blues
Times: 18:00

07 — Estorick Collection, N1
www.estorickcollection.com
21.09–19.12
Against Mussolini: Art and
the Fall of a Dictator
Modern Italian Art
Opening Times: 10:00–18:00

10 — King's Head Theatre, N1
www.kingsheadtheatre.org
16.11
Big Girls Blues Band
Funk, Blues, Soul
Time: 21:00
18.11
Hairy Pretty Things
Musical, Comedy
Time: 18:11
19.11–21.11
Cubs in Their Eyes
Musical, Comedy, Sketch
Time: 19:30

11 — Little Angle Theatre, N1
www.littleangeltheatre.com
2.10–31.12
Handa's Surprise
Puppetry
Time: 10:30, 12:00, 13:30, 15:30
10.11–31.12
Fantastic Mr Fox
Puppetry
Time: 11:30, 13:30, 16:00
20.11–30.01.2011
Alice In Wonderland
Puppetry
Time: 14:15, 17:00

12 — Victoria Miro1, N1
www.victoria-miro.com
06.10–13.11
Hernan Bas, Isaac Julien,
Yayoi Kusama
Painting, Sculpture, Film
17.11–22.01.2011
Francesca Woodman
Photography
Opening Times: 10:00–18:00

13 — The Lexington, N1
www.thelexington.co.uk
16.11
White Light
Indie, Electro, Retro, Pop
Time: 23:00
13.11
Underground Railroad: Laura J Martin
Rock, Pop, Dance
Time: 20:00
14.11
Cash For Cars & Mr Tom
Rock, Pop, Dance
Time: 15:00

14 — Cubitt, N1
www.cubittartists.org.uk
17.09–25.10
Design Research Unit: 1942 – 72
Graphic Design
Privet View Times:18.30–20.30
13.11
Curators' Choice
Portfolio Sales
4.11. Times: 12:00–21:00
5.11. Times: 11:00– 16:00

15

18 — The Slaughtered Lamb, EC1V
www.theslaughteredlambpub.com
16.11
The Global Breakdown:
Mickey Perez
Soul, Funk, Disco, Hip Hop & House
Time: 19:00
23.11
The Wooden Sky
Brooke Parrott, Goodnight Lenin
Indie rock, folk rock
Time: 20:00

19 — Barbican Centre, EC2Y
www.barbican.org.uk
02.11
Afro Celt Sound System:
Caoimhin Ó Raghallaigh
Dance
4.11 – 13.11
Complicite: Shun-kin
Puppetry
Time: 19:45, 14:30
13.11
Brad Mehldau-Highway Rider
Dance
Time: 19:30

20

What's going on?
www.islington.gov.uk

© Copyright 2010 Marta Puchala. All rights reserved.
All event listings were correct at time of publication but are subject to change, please check website for up-to-date information.

46

SAHAR GHANBARI

LONDON / PARIS / NEW YORK

♦ After spending time getting to know New York City, *Sahar Ghanbari* became curious about representing personal relationships to cities. To explore this idea, she created visual identities for other places she had a connection to. Her process included mapping out routes within cities, then meticulously drawing the buildings and locations that made up her understanding of each place.

➥ TOP LEFT: **LONDON / UK**, TOP RIGHT: **PARIS, FRANCE**, BOTTOM: **NEW YORK CITY / USA**, 2011

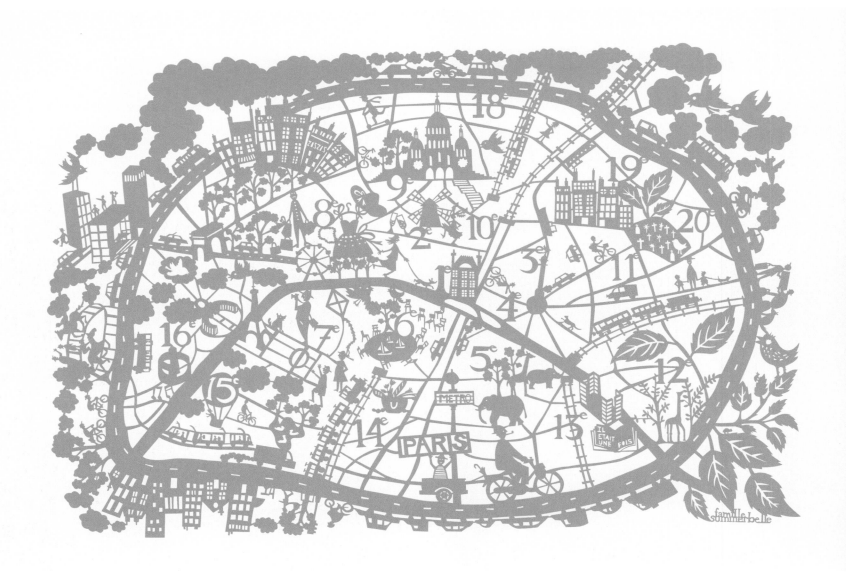

FAMILLE SUMMERBELLE
PAPER CUT MAPS

♦ The city maps by *Famille Summerbelle* are hand cut from single sheets of paper. Working with the traditional art form of paper cutting, which can be used to create lifelike portraits of people and places, these large format works become intricate guides to the landmarks and personalities of each city they represent.

➥ LEFT PAGE: **PARIS / FRANCE, SAN FRAN-CISCO / USA**, RIGHT PAGE: **NEW YORK CITY / USA**, NEXT SPREAD: **LONDON / UK**, 2009–2011, PERSONAL PROJECT

HAMPSTEAD

Primrose Hill

CAMDEN

ZOO

LORDS CRICKET GROUND

Regents Park

CAMDEN LOCK · CH

Little Venice

KINGS · X

OXFORD · ST

BLOOMSBURY
LAMBS CONDUIT ST
BRUNSWICK CENTRE

HYDE PARK

BOND STREET

SAVILE ROW

REGENT STREET

SHAFTESBURY · AV ·

NOTTING HILL

Portobello Road

THE SERPENTINE

SOHO

Marylebone High Street

MAYFAIR

KNIGHTSBRIDGE

SLOANE · ST ·

St James Park

BIRDCAGE WALK

CHARING CROSS ·

EMBANKMENT

Kensington Gardens

HARRODS

GREEN PARK

Kings Road
CHELSEA

V & A

VICTORIA

BUCKINGHAM PALACE

FULHAM

PIMLICO

TATE BRITAIN

WESTMINSTER

RIVER THAMES

BATTERSEA PARK

RICHMOND
Kew Gardens

VIC LEE

LONDON

➥ LONDON / UK, 2012, FOR ELLE DECORATION CHINA

AMSTERDAM

BLOEMGRACHT ◄ LEIDSEGRACHT

PRINSENGRACHT ◄ HERENGRACHT

SINGEL ► REGULIERSGRACHT

BROUWERSGRACHT ◄ AMSTEL

KEIZERSGRACHT ◄ TORENSLUIS

OUDE ZIJDS ACHTERBURGWAL

PLANTAGE ◄ ENTREPOTDOK

NOORDZEEKANAAL ◄ ROKIN

PRINSENGRACHT ◄ BLAUWBRUG

REGULIERSGRACHT

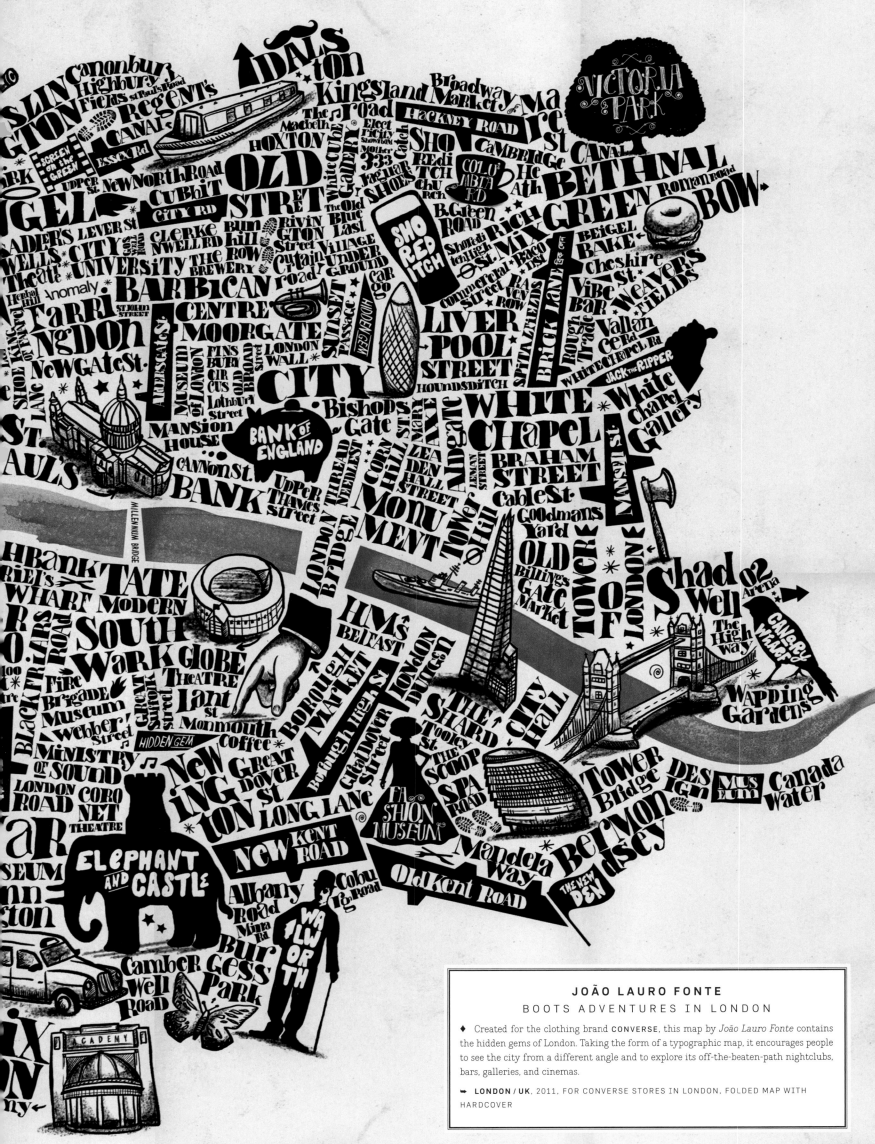

JODY BARTON
MYSTERIOUS AFRICA

♦ *Jody Barton* works with cultural stereotypes about countries and continents to create maps that are provocative comments on the political nature of mapping. With distorted hand drawn place names, he makes reference to Western ignorance of the diversity of the African continent.

➥ **AFRICA**, 2012, PERSONAL PROJECT

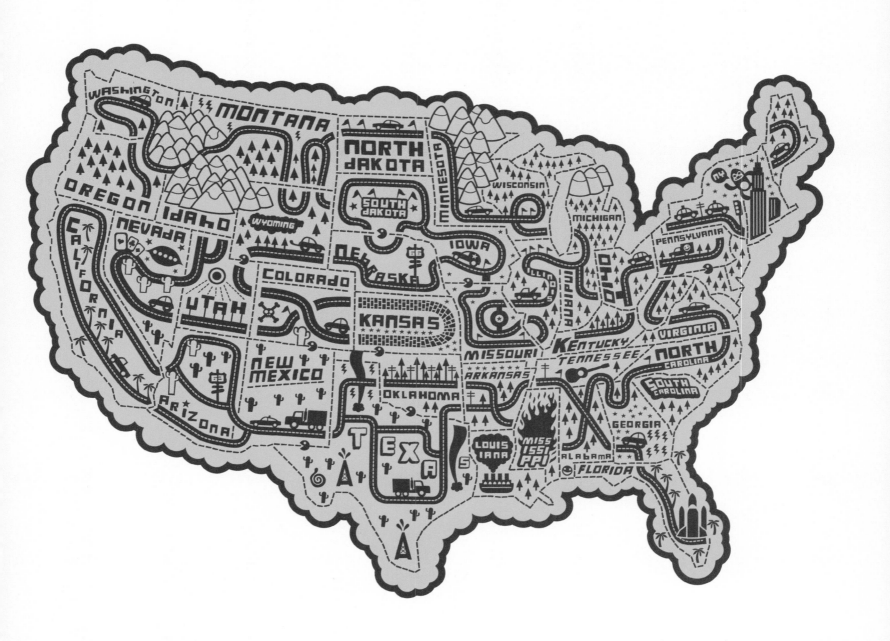

HELLO YELLOW STUDIO
HELLO MAP

♦ The continents in *Hello Yellow's* world map are composed of hand drawn typefaces. Each typeface spells out the greeting "hello" in the language of the region it corresponds to. Arranged in a dynamic order, the words emphasizes the diversity of languages and cultures all over the world.

➥ **WORLD**, 2007, PERSONAL PROJECT

ARTWORK BY
ZSUZSANNA ILIJIN

61

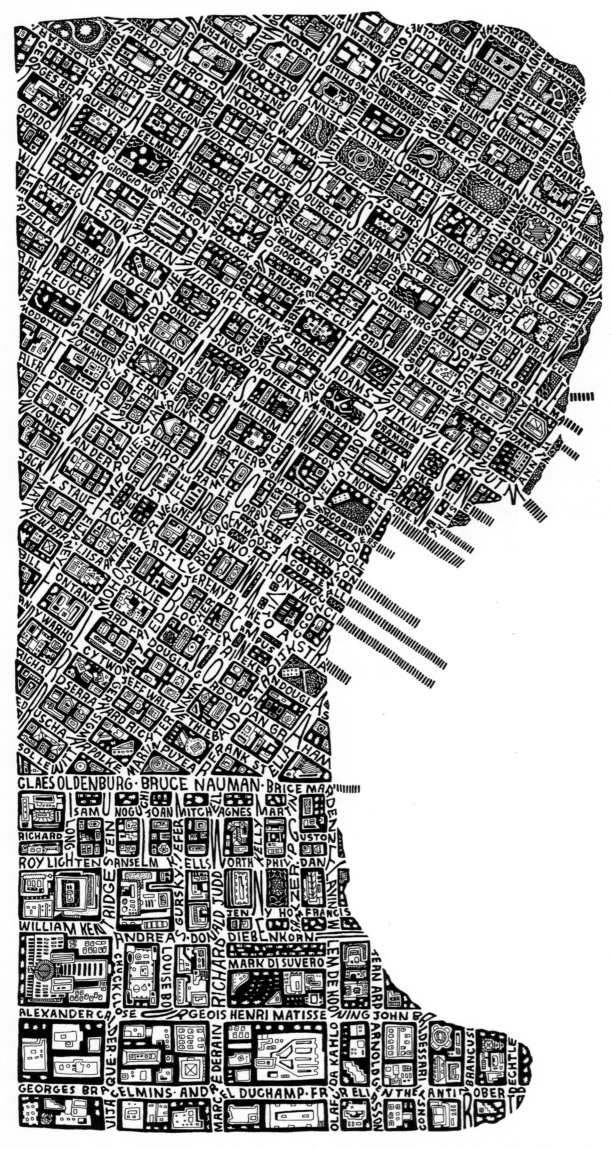

STEPHEN WALTER
SIMILANDS / THE ISLAND

♦ Central to *Stephen Walter's* work are the phenomena of place. His drawings at
first appear to be highly detailed and accurate maps of countries and cities, but a
closer look reveals intricate worlds constructed with tangled words and symbols that
form hidden meanings and contradictions.

➥ LEFT PAGE: **W**, RIGHT PAGE / NEXT SPREAD: **THE ISLAND**

THE BRITISH ISLES / IMAGINARY, 2006–2008, PUBL. BY / COURTESY OF STEPHEN
WALTER & TAG FINE ARTS

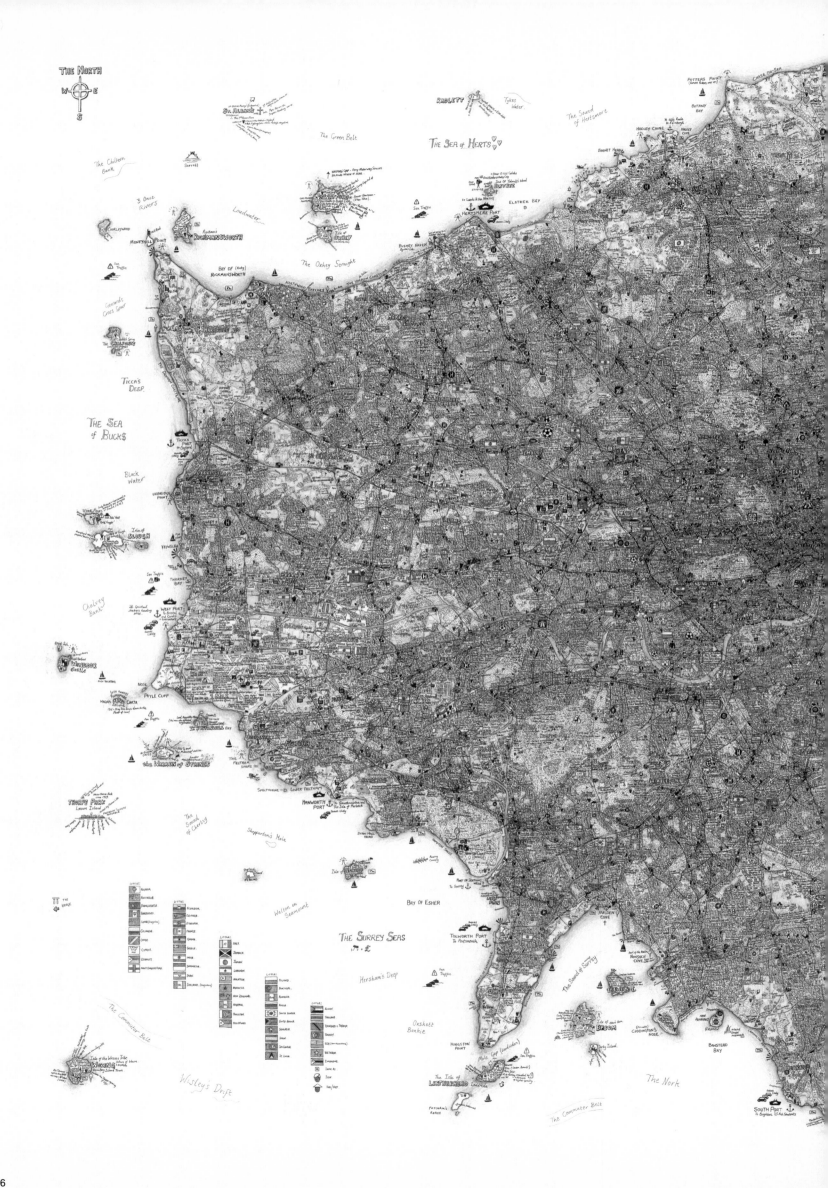

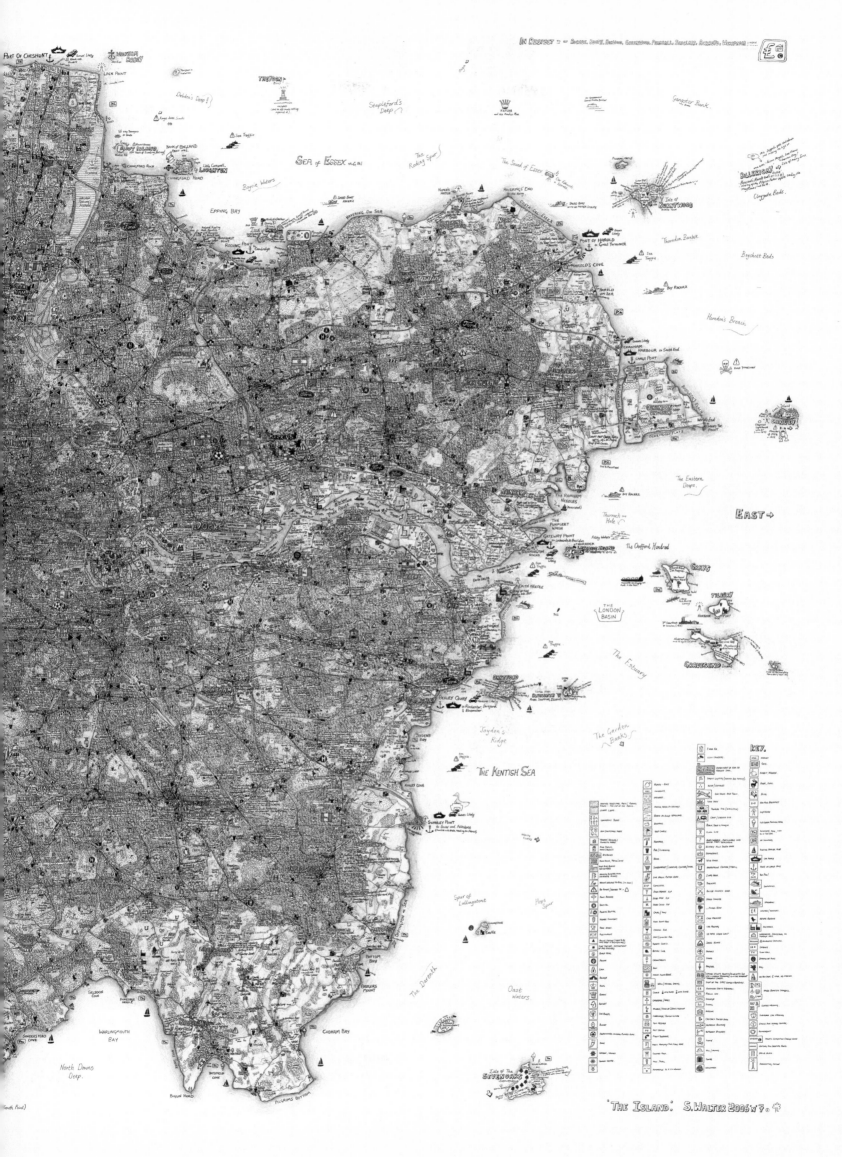

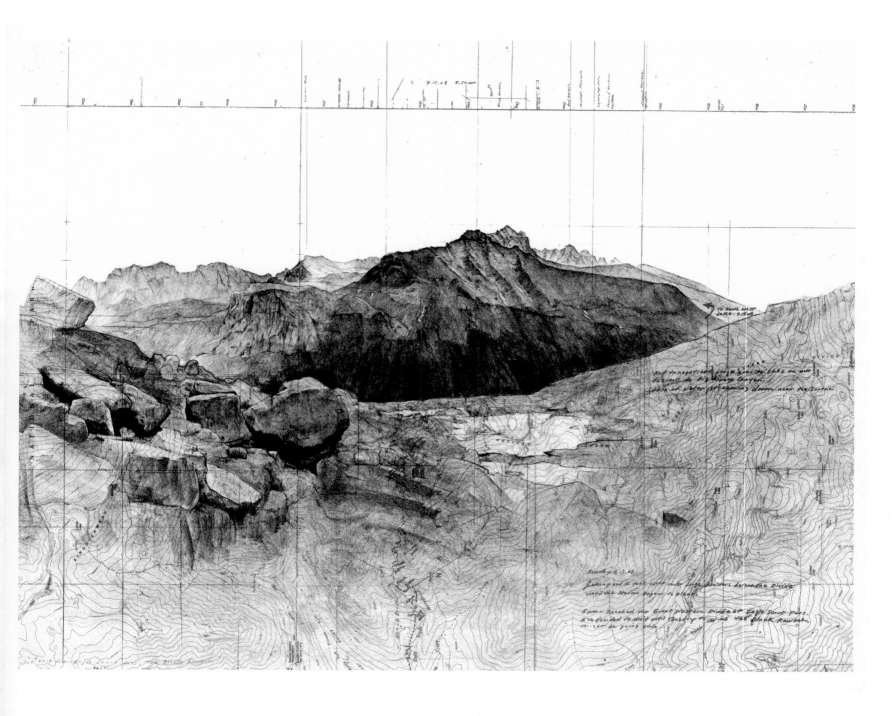

MATTHEW RANGEL

STRONGHOLD — DUE EAST FROM MORO ROCK /
DUE EAST FROM EAGLE SCOUT PASS,
THE BLACK KAWEAH

♦ Based on a seven-day journey across the Sequoia National Park in California, these drawings use a combination of direct observation and official topographic maps to chart the experience of a landscape. The five drawings in the 16-foot long Across the Sierra lithograph correspond to data found in US Geological Survey maps and were printed from west to east on a single sheet of paper.

➥ **SOUTHERN HIGH SIERRA, SEQUOIA NATIONAL PARK, CALIFORNIA / USA**
(2 IMAGES), 2008, PUBL. IN "JOURNEYS BEYOND THE NEATLINE: EXPANDING THE BOUNDARIES OF CARTOGRAPHY" BY THE UNIVERSITY OF ALBERTA LIBRARIES, 2010

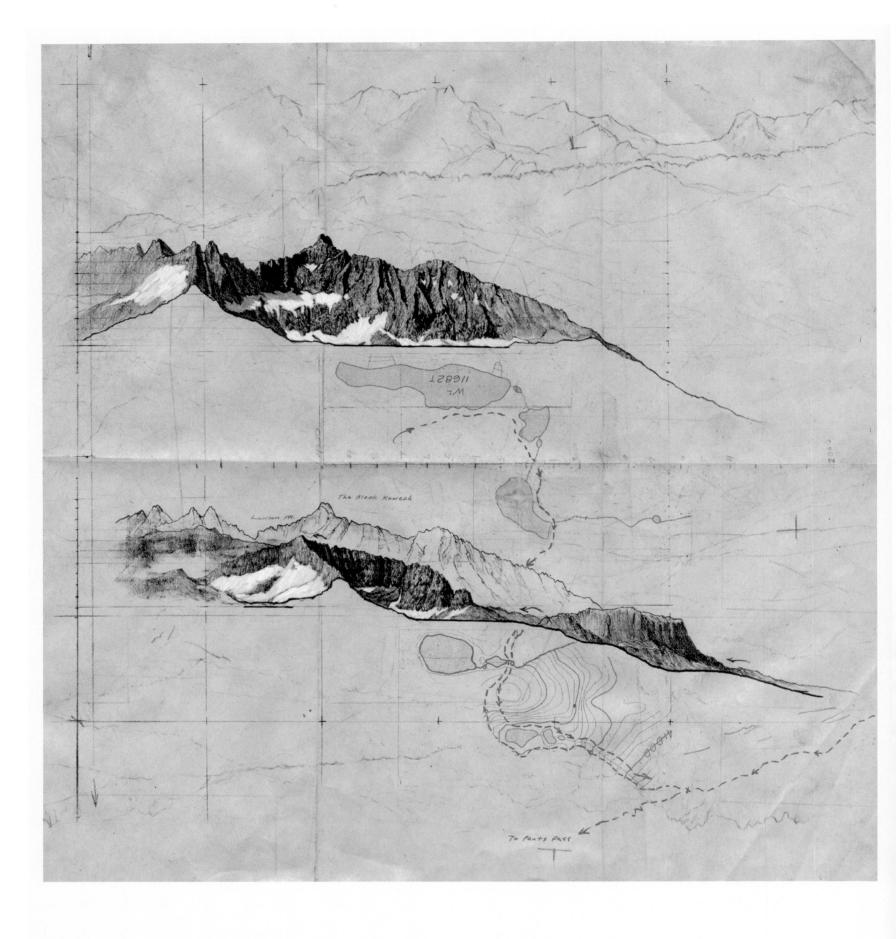

To Pants Pass.

The Black Kaweah

Lawson Mt.

Mt. 11687?

MATTHEW RANGEL

DETOUR / DUE EAST THROUGH ELLIOT RANCH

➡ <u>LEFT PAGE</u>: **KAWEAH PEAKS RANGE, SEQUOIA NATIONAL PARK, CALIFORNIA / USA**, <u>RIGHT PAGE</u>: **SOUTHERN SIERRA FOOTHILLS AND HIGH SIERRA, CALIFORNIA / USA**, 2008, PUBL. IN "JOURNEYS BEYOND THE NEATLINE: EXPANDING THE BOUNDARIES OF CARTOGRAPHY" BY THE UNIVERSITY OF ALBERTA LIBRARIES, 2010

To Sheep Ridge
Trailhea...

7:00 Start
D-6

To Ferry's
Trailhead

x Buckhorn
Cabin

8:30 am

Sunrise
View

S5

Cave

OAMP x
D-6

7:Am D-6
Start

ΙΙ
Corrals

x 7:00 pm

ELLIOTS Consolidated what used to
be small homesteads.

Before I hiked out on his ranch
Ishkic E. told me. "Be aware of
marijuana growers. We call
em mopes."

Antelope

71

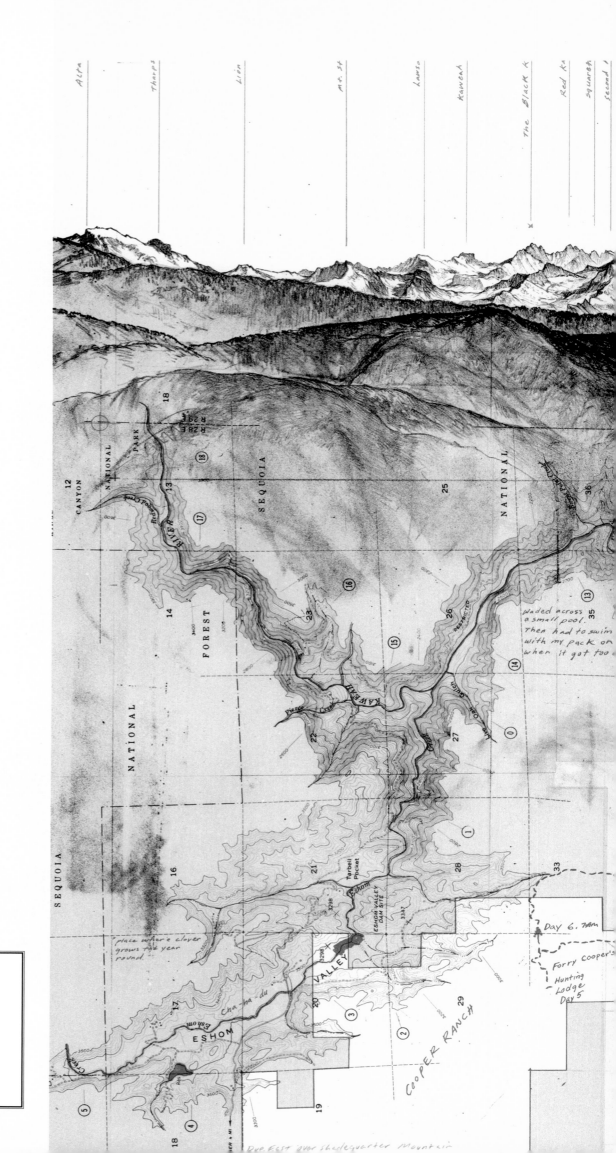

MATTHEW RANGEL
DUE EAST OVER
SHADEQUARTER MOUNTAIN

➡ **SOUTHERN SIERRA FOOTHILLS AND HIGH SIERRA, CALIFORNIA / USA**, 2008, PUBL. IN "JOURNEYS BEYOND THE NEATLINE: EXPANDING THE BOUNDARIES OF CARTOGRAPHY" BY THE UNIVERSITY OF ALBERTA LIBRARIES, 2010

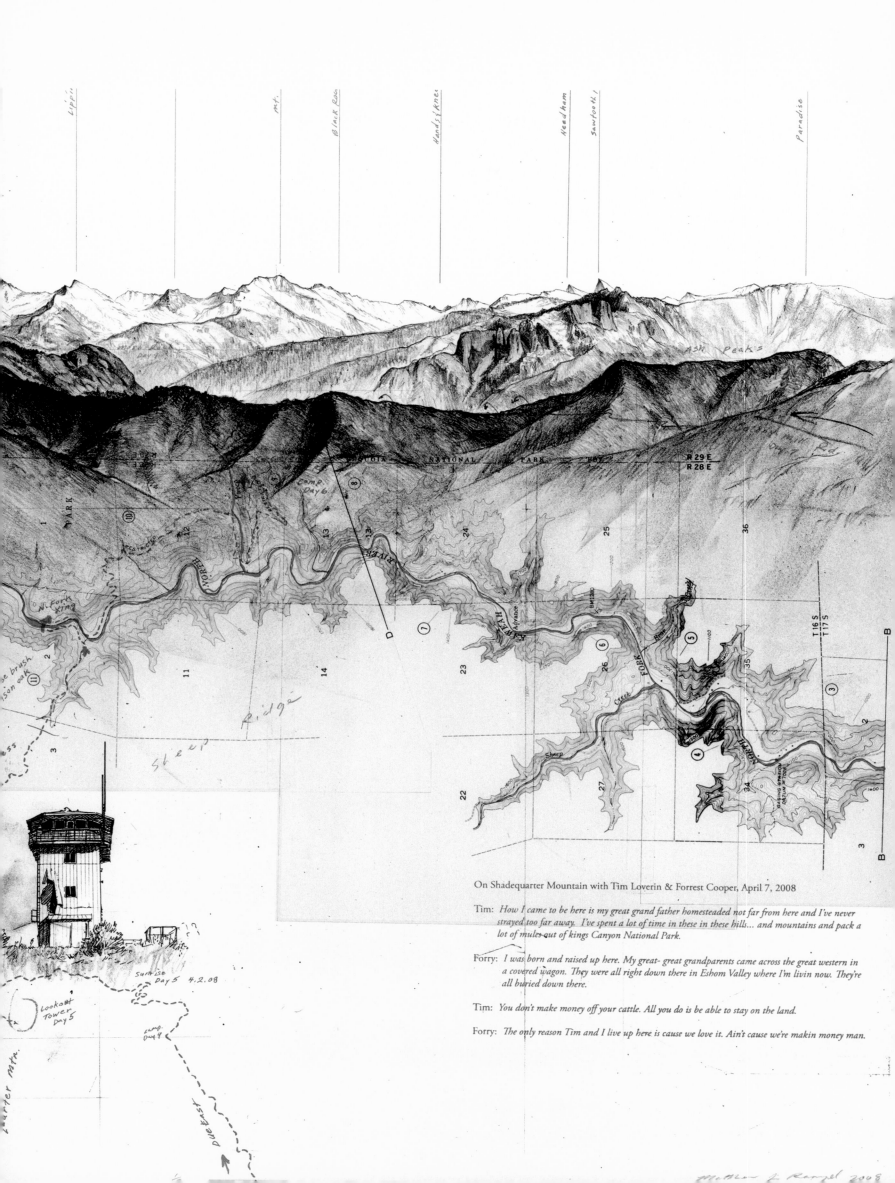

On Shadequarter Mountain with Tim Loverin & Forrest Cooper, April 7, 2008

Tim: *How I came to be here is my great grand father homesteaded not far from here and I've never strayed too far away. I've spent a lot of time in these in these hills... and mountains and pack a lot of mules out of kings Canyon National Park.*

Forry: *I was born and raised up here. My great- great grandparents came across the great western in a covered wagon. They were all right down there in Eshom Valley where I'm livin now. They're all buried down there.*

Tim: *You don't make money off your cattle. All you do is be able to stay on the land.*

Forry: *The only reason Tim and I live up here is cause we love it. Ain't cause we're makin money man.*

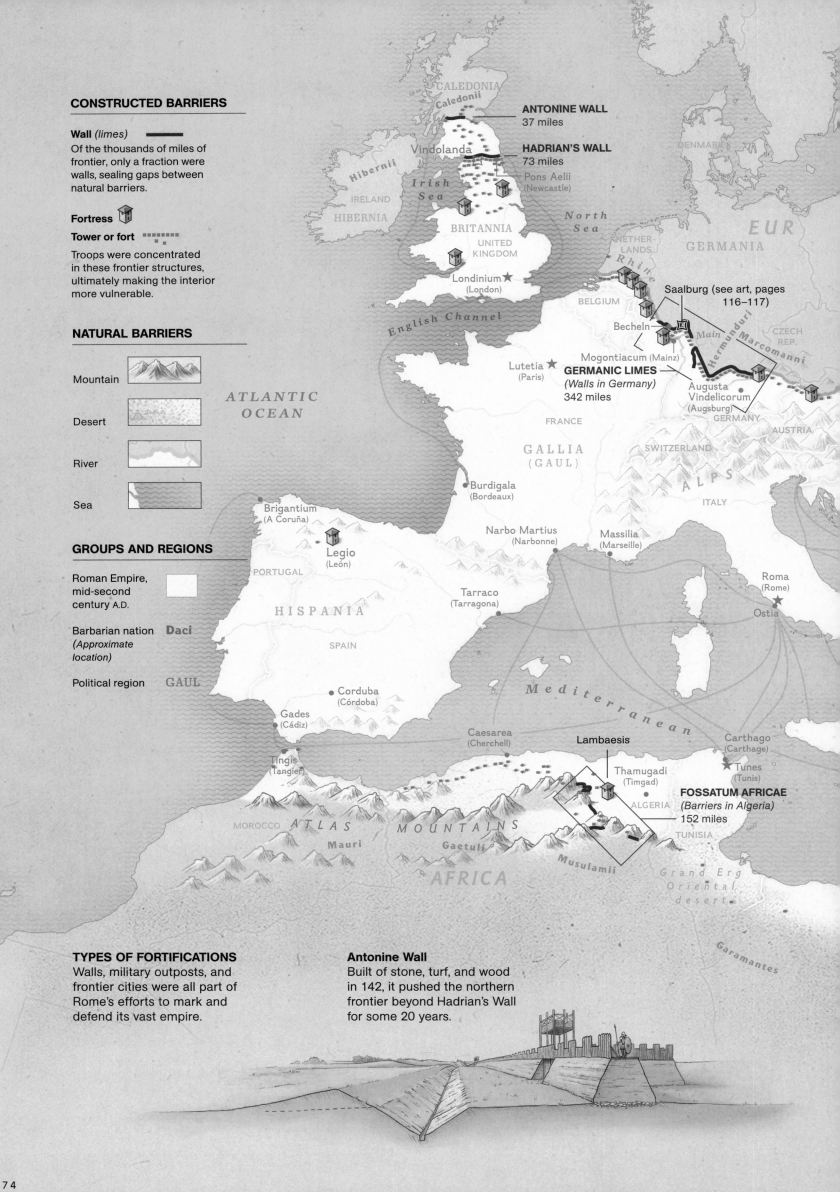

CONSTRUCTED BARRIERS

Wall (limes) ▬▬▬
Of the thousands of miles of frontier, only a fraction were walls, sealing gaps between natural barriers.

Fortress 🏛
Tower or fort ▪▪▪▪▪▪▪
Troops were concentrated in these frontier structures, ultimately making the interior more vulnerable.

NATURAL BARRIERS

Mountain

Desert

River

Sea

GROUPS AND REGIONS

Roman Empire, mid-second century A.D.

Barbarian nation (Approximate location) **Daci**

Political region GAUL

TYPES OF FORTIFICATIONS
Walls, military outposts, and frontier cities were all part of Rome's efforts to mark and defend its vast empire.

Antonine Wall
Built of stone, turf, and wood in 142, it pushed the northern frontier beyond Hadrian's Wall for some 20 years.

CALEDONIA
Caledonii

ANTONINE WALL
37 miles

Vindolanda

HADRIAN'S WALL
73 miles

Pons Aelii
(Newcastle)

Hibernii

IRELAND
HIBERNIA

Irish Sea

BRITANNIA
UNITED KINGDOM

Londinium
(London)

English Channel

North Sea

DENMARK

NETHERLANDS
GERMANIA

EUR

Rhine

BELGIUM

Saalburg (see art, pages 116–117)

Becheln

Mogontiacum (Mainz)

GERMANIC LIMES
(Walls in Germany)
342 miles

Hermunduri

Marcomanni

CZECH REP.

Lutetia
(Paris)

Main

Augusta Vindelicorum
(Augsburg)

GERMANY

AUSTRIA

FRANCE

GALLIA
(GAUL)

SWITZERLAND

ALPS

ITALY

ATLANTIC OCEAN

Burdigala
(Bordeaux)

Narbo Martius
(Narbonne)

Massilia
(Marseille)

Brigantium
(A Coruña)

Legio
(León)

PORTUGAL

HISPANIA

SPAIN

Tarraco
(Tarragona)

Roma
(Rome)

Ostia

Mediterranean

Corduba
(Córdoba)

Gades
(Cádiz)

Tingis
(Tangier)

Caesarea
(Cherchell)

Lambaesis

Thamugadi
(Timgad)

FOSSATUM AFRICAE
(Barriers in Algeria)
152 miles

ALGERIA

Carthago
(Carthage)

Tunes
(Tunis)

MOROCCO

Mauri

ATLAS MOUNTAINS

Gaetuli

Musulamii

TUNISIA

Grand Erg Oriental desert

AFRICA

Garamantes

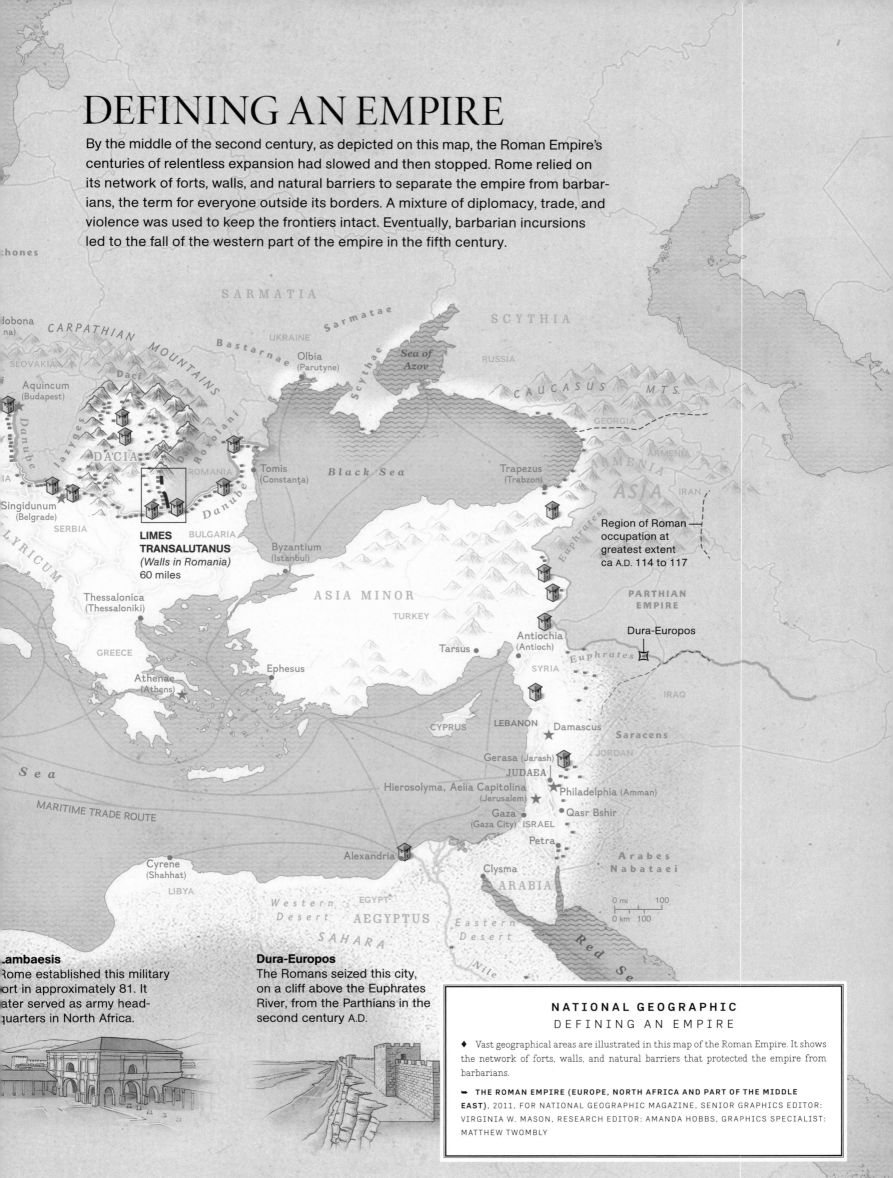

DEFINING AN EMPIRE

By the middle of the second century, as depicted on this map, the Roman Empire's centuries of relentless expansion had slowed and then stopped. Rome relied on its network of forts, walls, and natural barriers to separate the empire from barbarians, the term for everyone outside its borders. A mixture of diplomacy, trade, and violence was used to keep the frontiers intact. Eventually, barbarian incursions led to the fall of the western part of the empire in the fifth century.

SARMATIA

CARPATHIAN MOUNTAINS

Bastarnae

UKRAINE

SCYTHIA

Sarmatae

RUSSIA

Scythae

Olbia
(Parutyne)

Sea of
Azov

CAUCASUS M T S.

GEORGIA

dobona
(na)

SLOVAKIA

Daci

Aquincum
(Budapest)

DACIA

Roxolani

ROMANIA

Danube

Iazyges

Trapezus
(Trabzon)

Black Sea

ARMENIA

ASIA

IRAN

Singidunum
(Belgrade)

SERBIA

Danube

BULGARIA

Tomis
(Constanța)

Region of Roman
occupation at
greatest extent
ca A.D. 114 to 117

PARTHIAN
EMPIRE

**LIMES
TRANSALUTANUS**
(Walls in Romania)
60 miles

Byzantium
(Istanbul)

Euphrates

ILLYRICUM

IA

Thessalonica
(Thessaloniki)

ASIA MINOR

TURKEY

Dura-Europos

GREECE

Ephesus

Tarsus

Antiochia
(Antioch)

Euphrates

SYRIA

IRAQ

Athenae
(Athens)

CYPRUS

LEBANON

Damascus

Saracens

Sea

Gerasa (Jarash)

JORDAN

JUDAEA

MARITIME TRADE ROUTE

Hierosolyma, Aelia Capitolina
(Jerusalem)

Philadelphia (Amman)

Gaza
(Gaza City)

ISRAEL

Qasr Bshir

Petra

Arabes
Nabataei

Cyrene
(Shahhat)

Alexandria

Clysma

ARABIA

0 mi   100

LIBYA

Western
Desert

EGYPT

AEGYPTUS

Eastern
Desert

0 km   100

SAHARA

Nile

Red Sea

Lambaesis
Rome established this military
fort in approximately 81. It
later served as army headquarters in North Africa.

Dura-Europos
The Romans seized this city,
on a cliff above the Euphrates
River, from the Parthians in the
second century A.D.

NATIONAL GEOGRAPHIC
DEFINING AN EMPIRE

♦ Vast geographical areas are illustrated in this map of the Roman Empire. It shows the network of forts, walls, and natural barriers that protected the empire from barbarians.

➡ THE ROMAN EMPIRE (EUROPE, NORTH AFRICA AND PART OF THE MIDDLE EAST), 2011, FOR NATIONAL GEOGRAPHIC MAGAZINE, SENIOR GRAPHICS EDITOR: VIRGINIA W. MASON, RESEARCH EDITOR: AMANDA HOBBS, GRAPHICS SPECIALIST: MATTHEW TWOMBLY

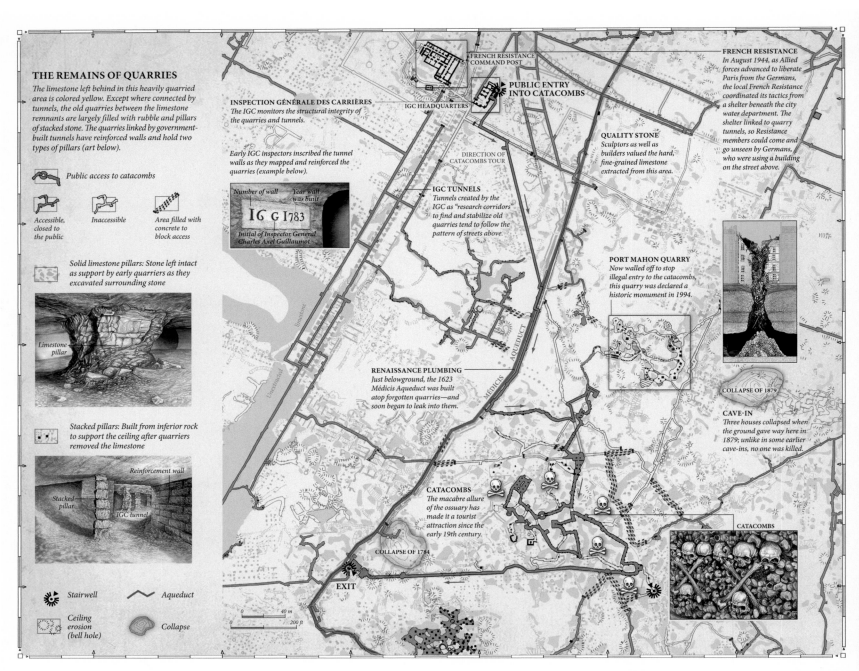

THE REMAINS OF QUARRIES

The limestone left behind in this heavily quarried area is colored yellow. Except where connected by tunnels, the old quarries between the limestone remnants are largely filled with rubble and pillars of stacked stone. The quarries linked by government-built tunnels have reinforced walls and hold two types of pillars (art below).

🪜 Public access to catacombs

Accessible, closed to the public

Inaccessible

Area filled with concrete to block access

Solid limestone pillars: Stone left intact as support by early quarriers as they excavated surrounding stone

Limestone pillar

Stacked pillars: Built from inferior rock to support the ceiling after quarriers removed the limestone

Reinforcement wall

Stacked pillar

IGC tunnel

🪜 Stairwell

〰️ Aqueduct

Ceiling erosion (bell hole)

Collapse

0   40 m
0   200 ft

INSPECTION GÉNÉRALE DES CARRIÈRES
The IGC monitors the structural integrity of the quarries and tunnels.

Early IGC inspectors inscribed the tunnel walls as they mapped and reinforced the quarries (example below).

Number of wall   *Year wall was built*

IG G I783

Initial of Inspector General Charles Axel Guillaumot

IGC TUNNELS
Tunnels created by the IGC as "research corridors" to find and stabilize old quarries tend to follow the pattern of streets above.

RENAISSANCE PLUMBING
Just belowground, the 1623 Médicis Aqueduct was built atop forgotten quarries—and soon began to leak into them.

CATACOMBS
The macabre allure of the ossuary has made it a tourist attraction since the early 19th century.

COLLAPSE OF 1784

EXIT

FRENCH RESISTANCE COMMAND POST

IGC HEADQUARTERS

PUBLIC ENTRY INTO CATACOMBS

DIRECTION OF CATACOMBS TOUR

FRENCH RESISTANCE
In August 1944, as Allied forces advanced to liberate Paris from the Germans, the local French Resistance coordinated its tactics from a shelter beneath the city water department. The shelter linked to quarry tunnels, so Resistance members could come and go unseen by Germans, who were using a building on the street above.

QUALITY STONE
Sculptors as well as builders valued the hard, fine-grained limestone extracted from this area.

PORT MAHON QUARRY
Now walled off to stop illegal entry to the catacombs, this quarry was declared a historic monument in 1994.

COLLAPSE OF 1879

CAVE-IN
Three houses collapsed when the ground gave way here in 1879; unlike in some earlier cave-ins, no one was killed.

CATACOMBS

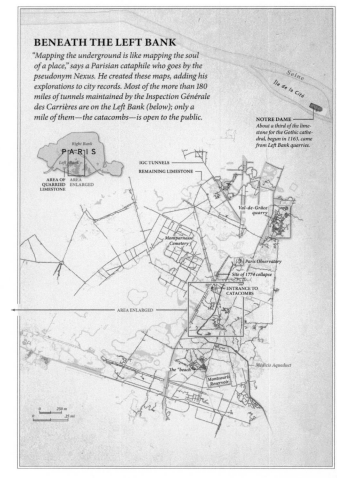

BENEATH THE LEFT BANK

"Mapping the underground is like mapping the soul of a place," says a Parisian cataphile who goes by the pseudonym Nexus. He created these maps, adding his explorations to city records. Most of the more than 180 miles of tunnels maintained by the Inspection Générale des Carrières are on the Left Bank (below); only a mile of them—the catacombs—is open to the public.

Seine

Île de la Cité

P A R I S

Right Bank

Left Bank

AREA OF QUARRIED LIMESTONE

AREA ENLARGED

NOTRE DAME
About a third of the limestone for the Gothic cathedral, begun in 1163, came from Left Bank quarries.

IGC TUNNELS

REMAINING LIMESTONE

Val-de-Grâce quarry

Montparnasse Cemetery

Paris Observatory

Site of 1774 collapse

ENTRANCE TO CATACOMBS

AREA ENLARGED

The "beach"

Montsouris Reservoir

Médicis Aqueduct

0   250 m
0   25 mi

NATIONAL GEOGRAPHIC
BENEATH THE LEFT BANK

♦ Vast geographical areas are illustrated in this map of the Roman Empire. It shows the network of forts, walls, and natural barriers that protected the empire from barbarians.

➥ **PARIS, FRANCE**, 2011, FOR NATIONAL GEOGRAPHIC MAGAZINE, SENIOR GRAPHICS EDITOR: VIRGINIA W. MASON, ILLUSTRATOR : JORGE PORTAZ, ARTIST AND CATAPHILE: NEXUS

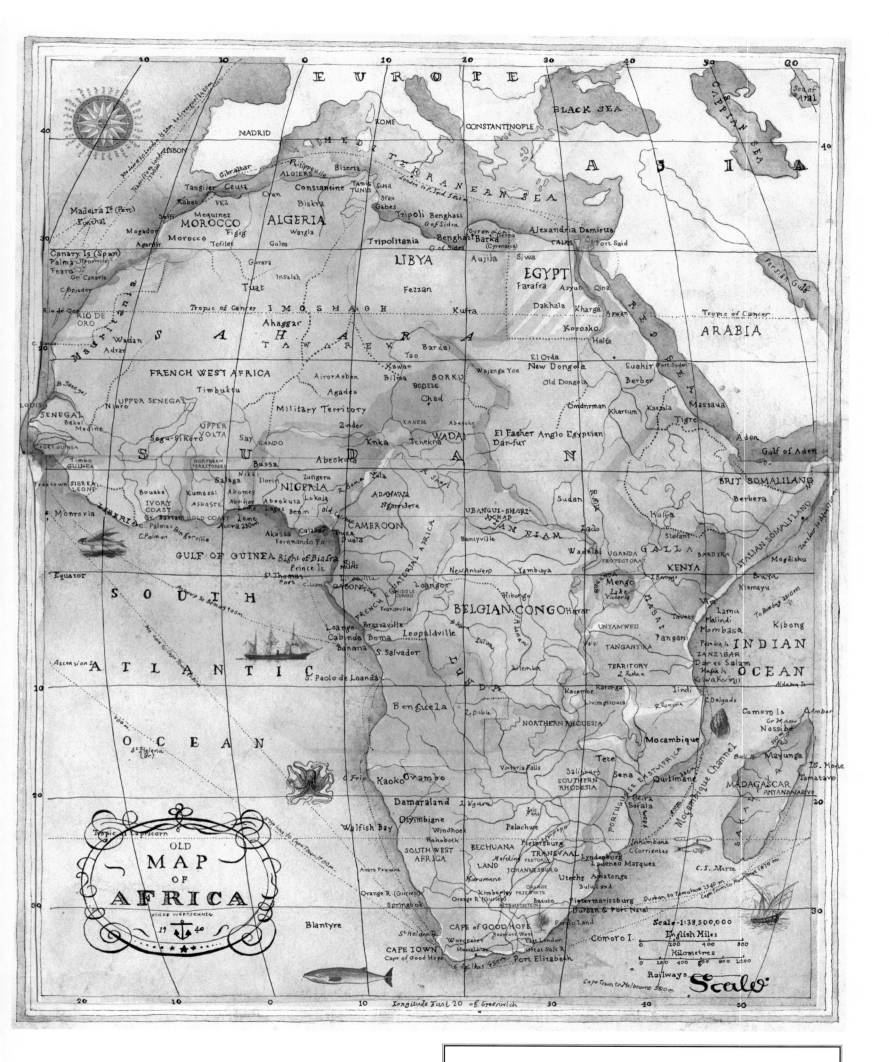

SOIL DESIGN

AFRICA

◆ Recreation of a political map of Africa from the 1940's, in water-colour & fine liner.

➥ **AFRICA**, 2012, ILLUSTRATOR: MIEKE WERTSCHNIG

TAKAYO AKIYAMA
WEST OF ENGLAND
FLANNEL

♦ This map of England was created for ALFRED DUNHILL's West of England flannel, which has been produced in the same Somerset mill for over two centuries. Using a distinctly vintage feel for the drawing, *Takayo Akiyama* evokes the sense of history and tradition associated with the brand.

➥ WEST OF ENGLAND, 2012, FOR ALFRED DUNHILL

YUKO KONDO
W O R L D

♦ Based on found antique maps, these graphics were created to reflect the
name of the record label INTERNATIONAL FEEL RECORDINGS. In keeping with the
vintage feel, the world map was finished with watercolor. The final piece was
printed on vinyl record sleeves with the halved globes echoing the shapes of the
records.

➥ WORLD, 2009, FOR INTL. FEEL RECORDINGS

AUSTRALIA.

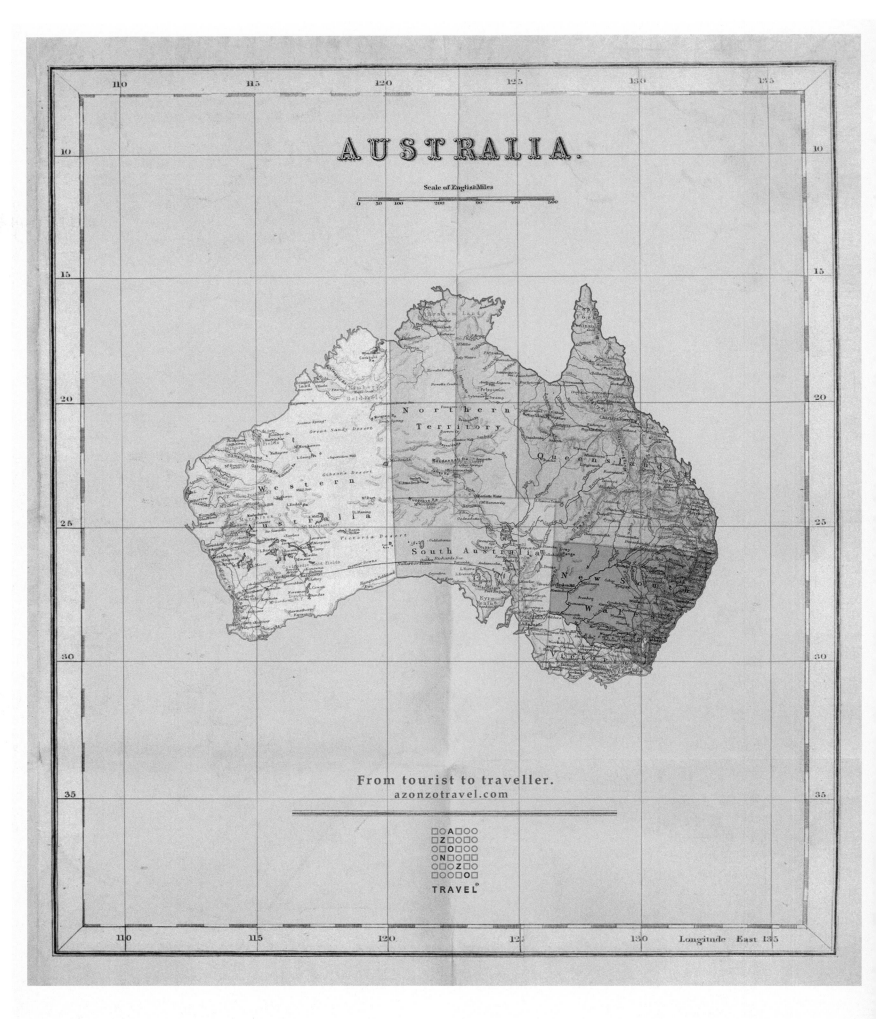

Scale of English Miles

From tourist to traveller.
azonzotravel.com

TRAVEL

AUSTRALIA.

Scale of EnglishMiles

0   50   100   200   90   400   500

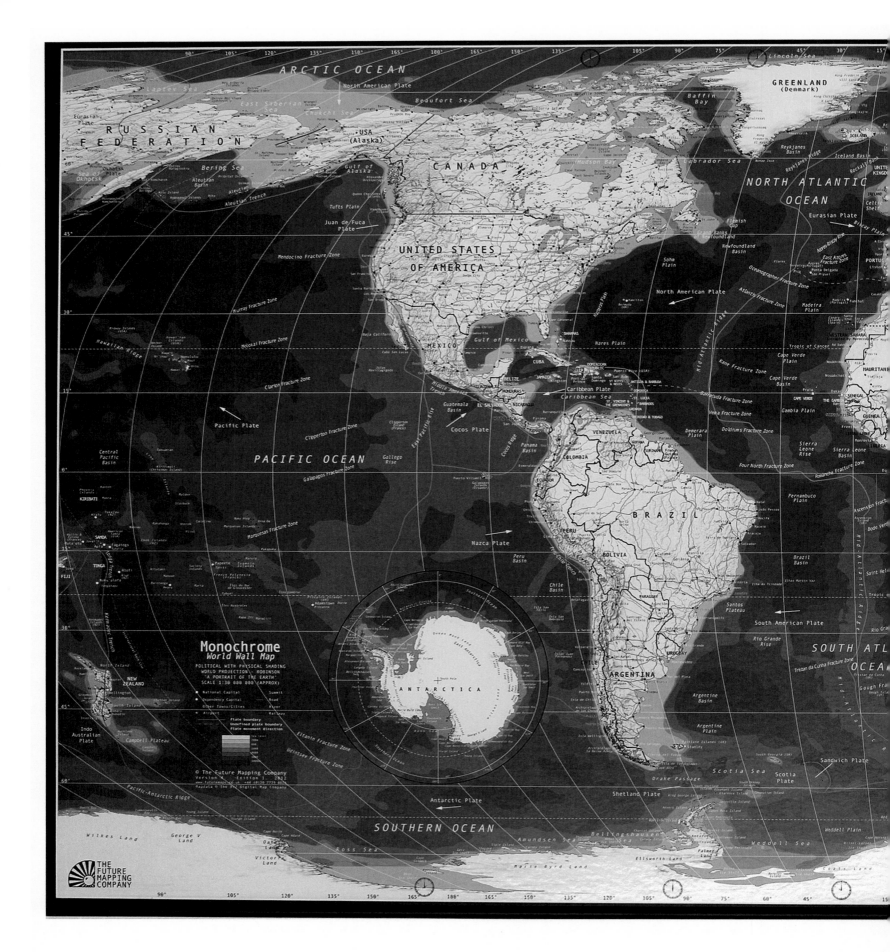

Monochrome
World Wall Map
POLITICAL WITH PHYSICAL SHADING
WORLD PROJECTION - ROBINSON
"A PORTRAIT OF THE EARTH"
SCALE 1:30 000 000 (APPROX)

■ National Capital   ● Summit
● Dependency Capital   Road
● Other Towns/Cities   River
✈ Airport   Railway

Plate boundary
Undefined plate boundary
Plate movement direction

© The Future Mapping Company
Version 4   Edition 1   2012
www.futuremaps.co.uk +44 (0)20 7278 4020
Mapdata © The FMP Digital Map Company

THE
FUTURE
MAPPING
COMPANY

82

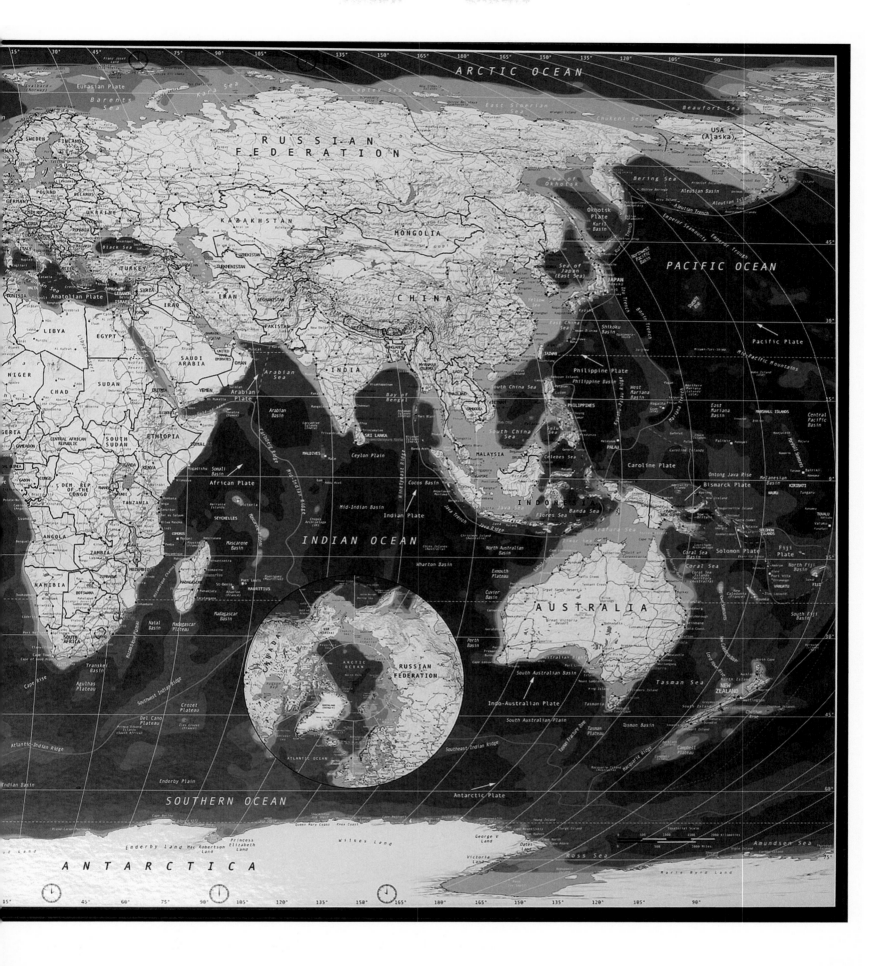

THE FUTURE MAPPING COMPANY
COLOR MAP

♦ The new world reference maps by *The Future Mapping Company* were created for the twenty-first century by combining political and physical information. Although the maps are based on traditional projections (here: Robinson projection), the classic soft pastel hues are abandoned for contemporary color combinations.

➥ <u>THIS / NEXT SPREAD</u>: **WORLD**, 2011, PERSONAL PROJECT

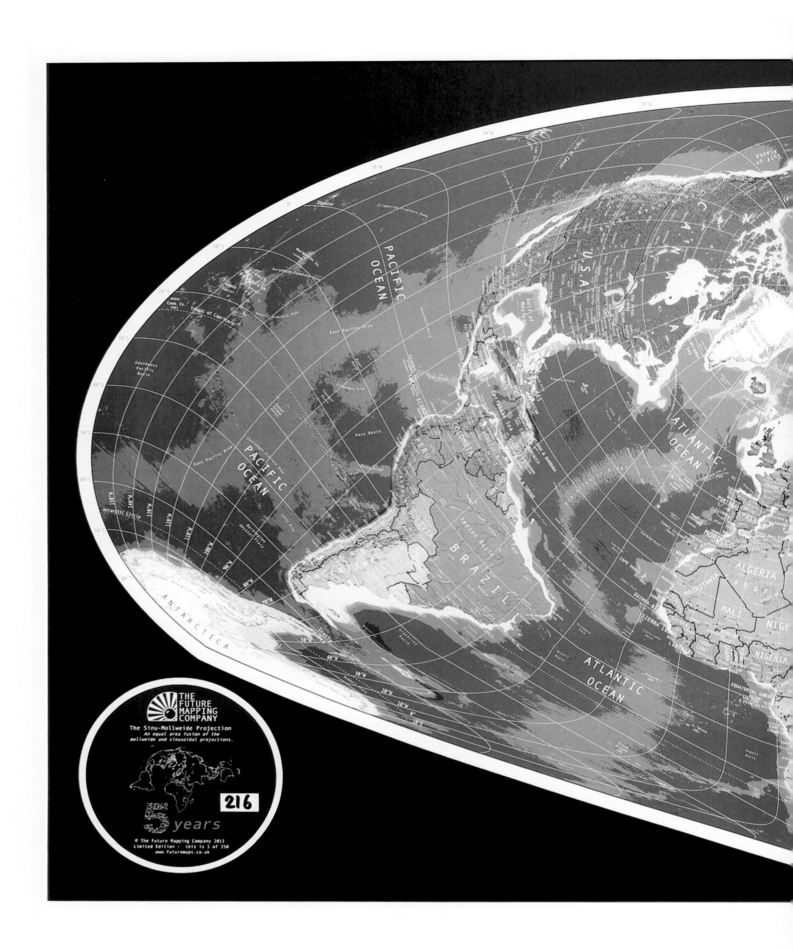

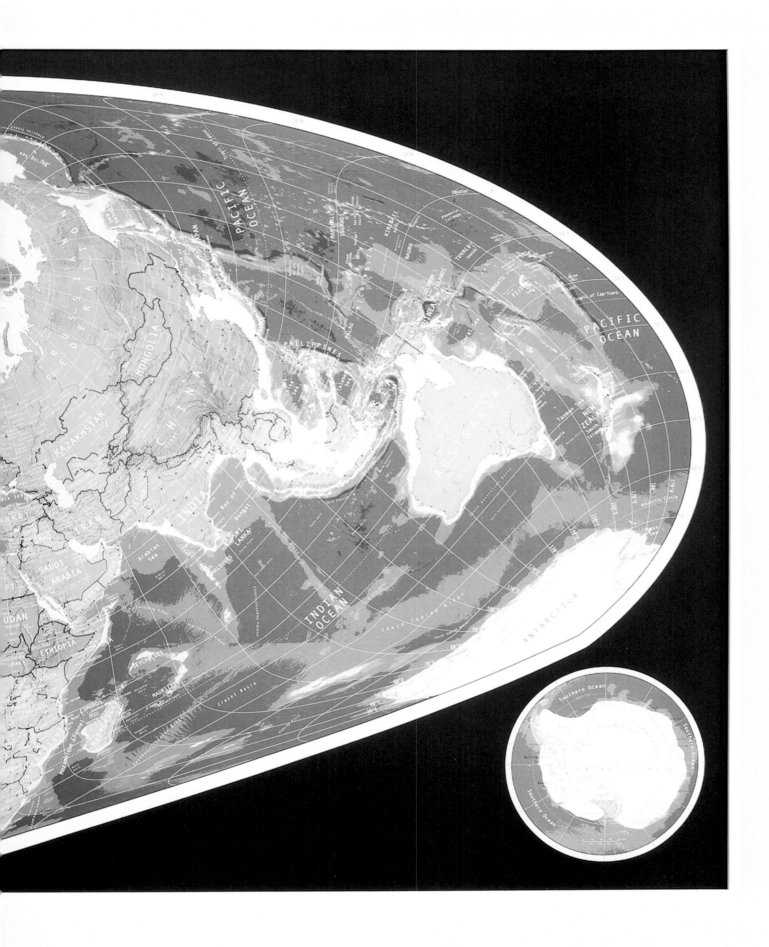

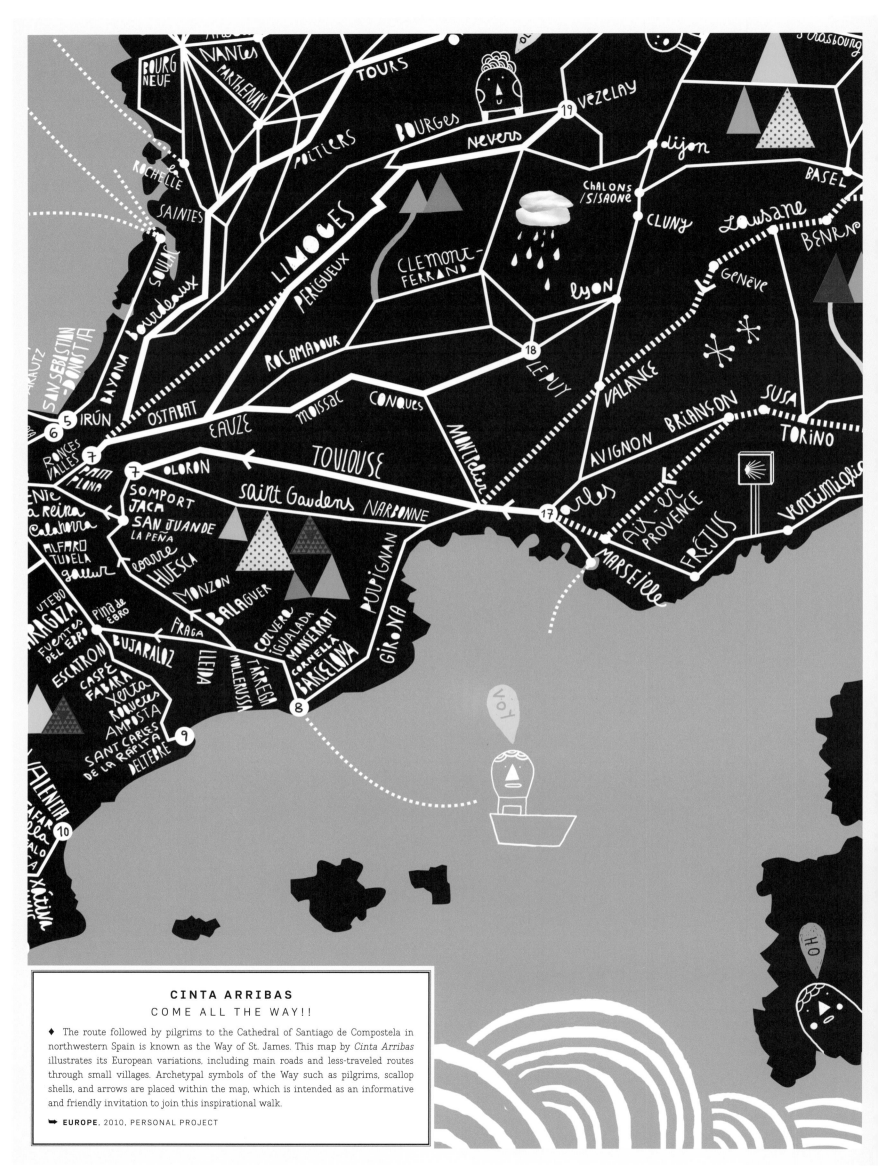

CINTA ARRIBAS

COME ALL THE WAY!!

♦ The route followed by pilgrims to the Cathedral of Santiago de Compostela in northwestern Spain is known as the Way of St. James. This map by *Cinta Arribas* illustrates its European variations, including main roads and less-traveled routes through small villages. Archetypal symbols of the Way such as pilgrims, scallop shells, and arrows are placed within the map, which is intended as an informative and friendly invitation to join this inspirational walk.

➥ EUROPE, 2010, PERSONAL PROJECT

RAYMOND BIESINGER
RISK EUROPE 1919 (UNOFFICIAL)

♦ The compact black-and-white illustrations by *Raymond Biesinger* map the history of places. This is a one-color silkscreened map of Europe circa 1919, made to be simply viewed or played as if it were the classic Risk board game. It is mostly geographically and historically accurate, the result of much research, collaging together five European maps, and hand type-setting each nation's name.

➥ **EUROPE**, 2007, PERSONAL PROJECT

87

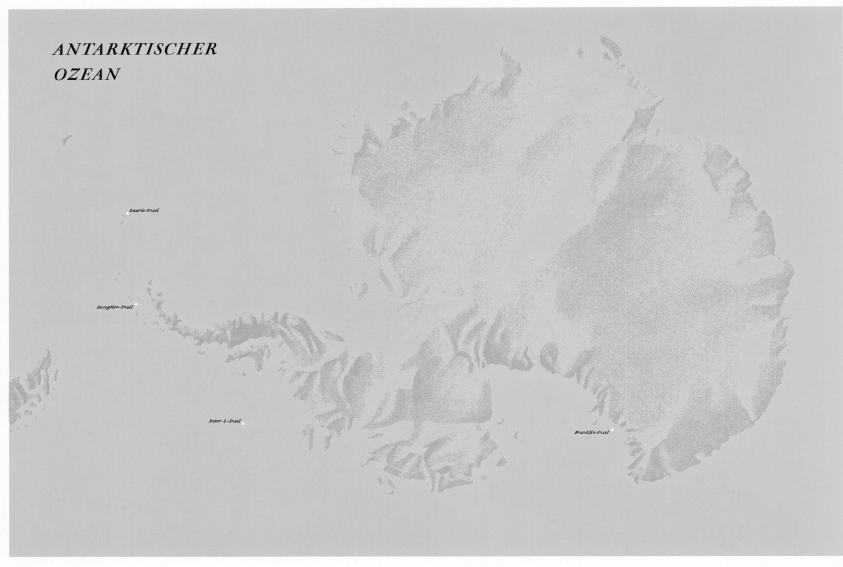

Osterinsel (Chile)

27° 9' S
109° 35' W

SPANISCH *Isla da Pascua* | **RAPANUI** *Rapa Nui*, auch *Te Pit o te Henua* [›Nabel der Welt‹]
163,6 km² | 3791 Einwohner

3690 km
→ Chile

4190 km
→ Tahiti

2970 km
→ Robinsón Crusoe (74)

5. April 1722 (Ostersonntag) entdeckt von Jakob Roggeveen

1687 vermutlich gesichtet von Edward Davis   9. September 1888 annektiert von Chile

Kein Wunder, dass Darwin hier nicht hielt. Flora und Fauna sind dürftig, die Pracht der verwunschenen Galapagosinseln mit dem Kanu Wochenreisen entfernt. // Wie hoch die Riesenpalmen wirklich waren, die diese Insel einmal dicht bewuchsen, weiß heute niemand mehr. Aus dem Stamm floss ein Saft, der zu honigsüßem Wein vergor, aus dem Holz ließen sich Flöße bauen und Seile für den Transport der Statuen machen. // Diese halslosen Ungeheuer aus Stein, hohläugige Wesen mit langen Ohren, bevölkern die Küste, haben verwitterte Haut und den Mund verzogen wie ein trotziges Kind; Wächter aus vulkanischem Tuff, das Meer im moosbewachsenen Rücken. An Festtagen schauen sie mit weißen Korallenaugen auf die Palmenwälder. // Die zwölf Sippen der Osterinsel liefern sich einen Wettstreit, bauen immer größere Riesen aus Stein und stürzen nachts heimlich die der anderen um. Sie betreiben Raubbau mit ihrem Flecken Land, bringen auch die letzten Bäume zu Fall, sägen den Ast ab, auf dem sie sitzen, der Anfang vom Ende: Entweder sterben sie gleich an eingeschleppten Pocken, oder sie werden Sklaven im eigenen Land, Leibeigene der Pächter, die aus ihrer Insel eine riesige Schafsfarm machen. Von Zehntausenden überleben nur 111 Einwohner. Keine Palme steht mehr, die steinernen Wächter liegen am Boden. // Archäologen richten die Ungetüme wieder auf und suchen nach Spuren. Sie graben nach Samen, durchwühlen Abfallhaufen, sammeln Knochen und verkohltes Holz, versuchen die furchenwendigen Zeilen des Rongorongo zu entziffern und in den versteinerten Gesichtern zu lesen, was hier geschah. // Kein Baum wächst heute mehr auf dem öden Land, das entstanden ist aus 70 Vulkanen. Dafür ist das Rollfeld so gewaltig, dass ein Space Shuttle darauf notlanden könnte. Ein Paradefall für das ausgemachte Ende der Erde, eine Kette unglücklicher Umstände, die zur Selbstvernichtung führte, ein Lemming im Stillen Ozean.

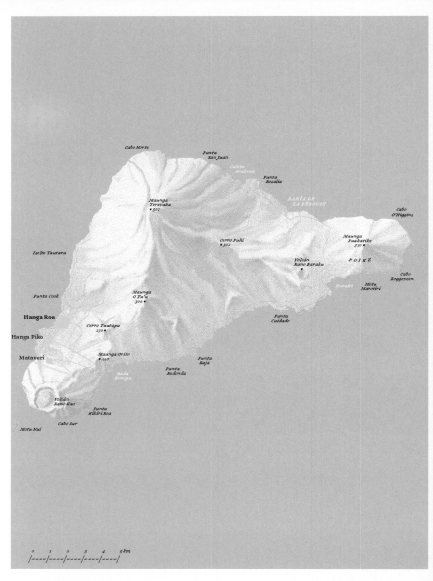

0 1 2 3 4 5 km

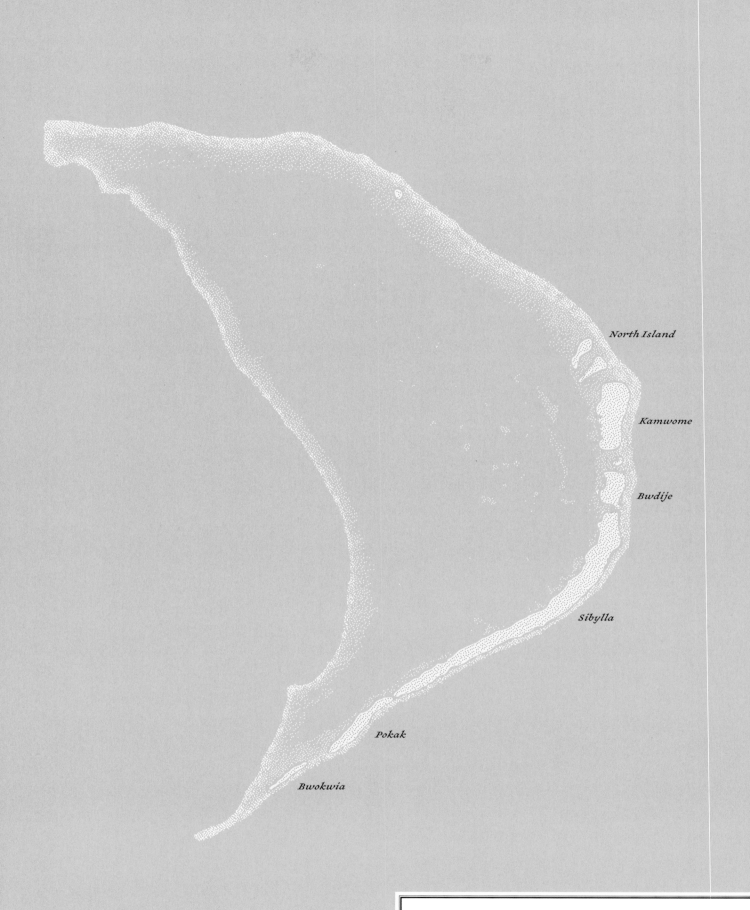

North Island

Kamwome

Bwdije

Sibylla

Pokak

Bwokwia

JUDITH SCHALANSKY
ATLAS OF REMOTE ISLANDS

◆ *Judith Schalansky's* book, Atlas of Remote Islands, presents atlases as works of poetry, interpretations of reality, and attempts to see the world as a whole. Each of its 50 maps are drawn in the same scale and ordered according to the oceans, while the endpapers show two world maps: one Euro-centric and the other Pacific-centric. This book is not a travel guide. It is a book for the armchair explorer, describing places that exist in reality but only come to life in the imagination.

➥ THIS / NEXT SPREAD: **REMOTE ISLANDS**, 2009, IN "ATLAS OF REMOTE ISLANDS", PUBLISHED BY PENGUIN

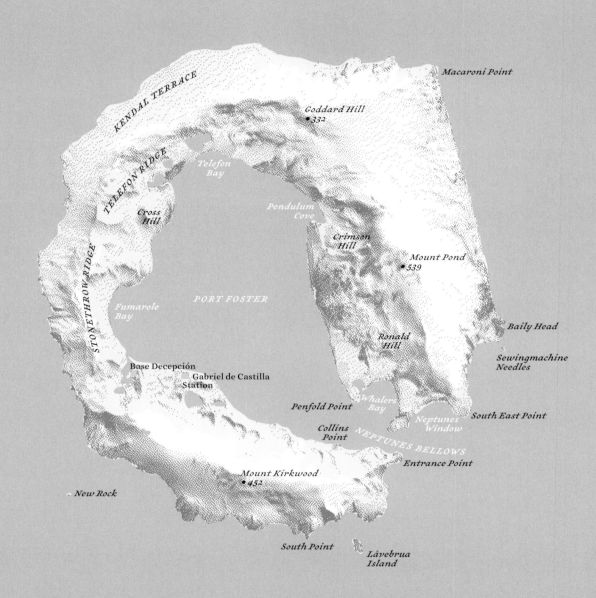

Macaroni Point

KENDAL TERRACE

Goddard Hill
• 332

TELEFON RIDGE

Telefon
Bay

Cross
Hill

Pendulum
Cove

Crimson
Hill

STONETHROW RIDGE

Mount Pond
• 539

PORT FOSTER

Fumarole
Bay

Ronald
Hill

Baily Head

Sewingmachine
Needles

Base Decepción

Gabriel de Castilla
Station

Penfold Point

Whalers
Bay

South East Point

Collins
Point

Neptunes
Window

NEPTUNES BELLOWS

Mount Kirkwood
• 452

Entrance Point

New Rock

South Point

Låvebrua
Island

0   1   2   3   4   5 km
|----|----|----|----|----|

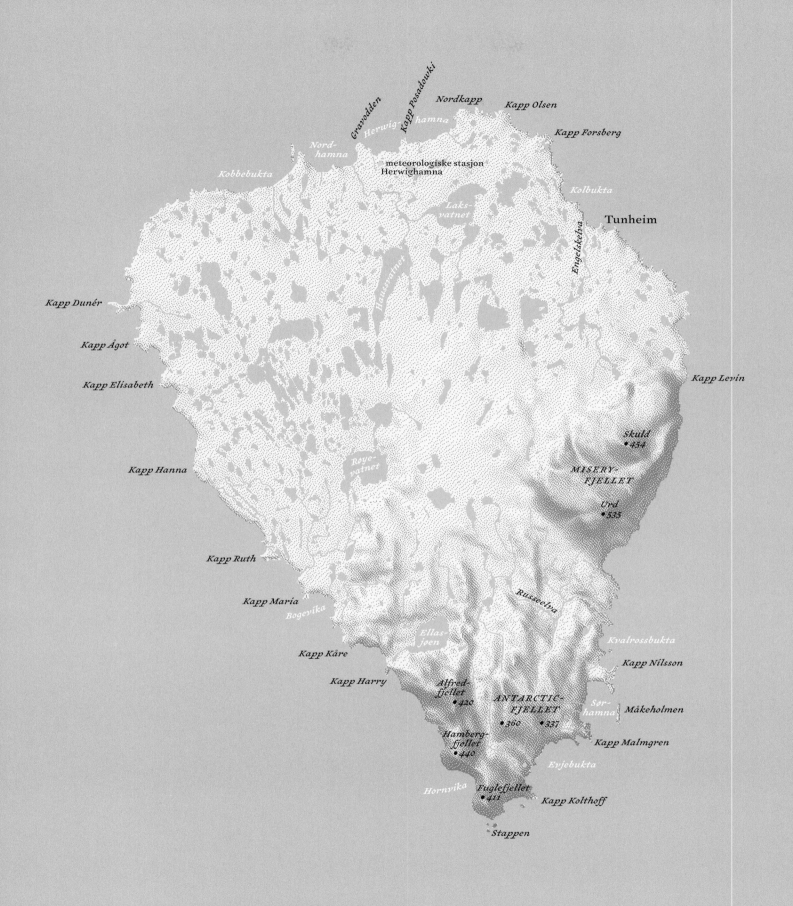

Gravodden

Kapp Posadowki

Herwig-hamna

Nordkapp

Kapp Olsen

Kapp Forsberg

Nord-hamna

Kobbebukta

meteorologiske stasjon
Herwighamna

Kolbukta

Laks-
vatnet

Tunheim

Engelskelva

Kapp Dunér

Kapp Ågot

Kapp Elisabeth

Kapp Levin

Skuld
• 454

MISERY-
FJELLET

Kapp Hanna

Røye-
vatnet

Urd
• 535

Kapp Ruth

Kapp Maria

Russeelva

Bogevika

Kvalrossbukta

Ellas-
jøen

Kapp Kåre

Kapp Nilsson

Kapp Harry

Alfred-
fjellet
• 420

ANTARCTIC-
FJELLET

Sør-
hamna

Måkeholmen

• 360   • 337

Hamberg-
fjellet
• 440

Kapp Malmgren

Evjebukta

Hornvika

Fuglefjellet
• 411

Kapp Kolthoff

• Stappen

0   1   2   3   4   5 km
|----|----|----|----|----|

SOUTH
ATLANTIC OCEAN

60° W

PALMER STATION
(US)

WEDDELL
SEA

Antarctic Peninsula

90° W

ANTARCTIC CIRCLE

*Ellsworth
Highland*

120° W

SOUTH PACIFIC
OCEAN

150° W

100 JAHRE ENTDECKUNG DES SÜDPOLS
// 100 YEARS OF EXPLORING THE SOUTHPOLE

WETTLAUF
BIS ANS ENDE DER WELT
// RACING TO THE END OF THE WORLD

**Der Norweger Roald Amundsen und sein Team waren vor
100 Jahren die ersten Menschen am Südpol. Sie gewan-
nen das ruhmreiche Rennen nur knapp vor Robert Falcon
Scott aus Großbritannien. Er und sein Team trafen nur
einen Monat später auf den südlichsten Punkt der Erde
ein. Leider wurde ihnen die beschwerliche Rückreise zum
Verhängnis und sie bezahlten den Wettlauf mit dem Tod.
Doch schon vorher hatten Forscher versucht, die
Antarktis zu ergründen. James Cook umsegelte sie
1773/74 als erster und legte somit den Grundstein für die
Erschließung des Kontinents.** // The Norwegian Roald
Amundsen and his team in 1911 were the first people to reach
the South Pole. They won the race for glory just a month
before Robert Falcon Scott from Great Britain and his team
who also reached the most southern point in the world.
Unfortunately they didn't survive the arduous journey back
and died in the cold. For a long time people tried to fathom
out the Antarctic. James Cook was the first to circuit the
continent 1773/74 and established its exploration.

AUSWAHL VON EXPEDITIONEN
// SELECTED EXPLORATIONS

1770	1775

JAMES COOK (UK)
1773-74
**kreuzte als erster Mensch
den antarktischen
Wendekreis und umsegelte
die Antarktis**
*// the first man to cross
the Antarctic Circle
and to circumnavigate
the Antarctic continent*

1820	1825

**FABIAN GOTTLIEB VON
BELLINGSHAUSEN** (RU)
1820-21
**der erste Mensch, der
den antarktischen Kontinent
zu Gesicht bekommt**
*// the first person to
see the Antarctic land mass*

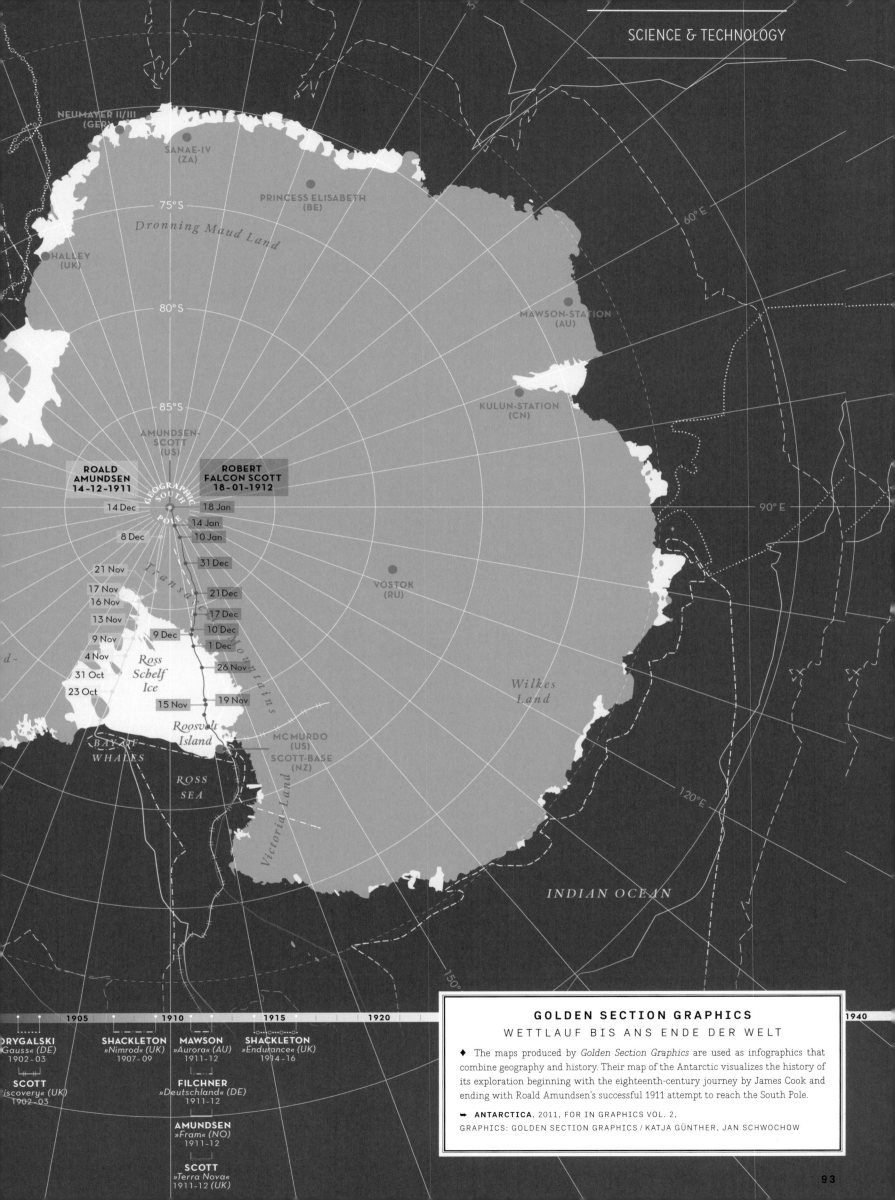

NEUMAYER II/III
(GER)

SANAE-IV
(ZA)

PRINCESS ELISABETH
(BE)

75°S

Dronning Maud Land

HALLEY
(UK)

80°S

MAWSON-STATION
(AU)

85°S

KULUN-STATION
(CN)

AMUNDSEN-
SCOTT (US)

**ROALD
AMUNDSEN
14-12-1911**

**ROBERT
FALCON SCOTT
18-01-1912**

GEOGRAPHIC
SOUTH
POLE

14 Dec | 18 Jan

14 Jan

8 Dec | 10 Jan

31 Dec

21 Nov

17 Nov | 21 Dec

16 Nov | 17 Dec

13 Nov | 10 Dec

9 Nov | 9 Dec | 1 Dec

4 Nov | 26 Nov

31 Oct

23 Oct

15 Nov | 19 Nov

*Ross
Schelf
Ice*

Transantarctic Mountains

VOSTOK
(RU)

90° E

60° E

*Wilkes
Land*

*Roosvelt
Island*

BAY OF
WHALES

MCMURDO
(US)

SCOTT-BASE
(NZ)

*ROSS
SEA*

Victoria Land

120° E

INDIAN OCEAN

150°

1905 | 1910 | 1915 | 1920 | 1940

DRYGALSKI
»Gauss« (DE)
1902–03

SHACKLETON
»Nimrod« (UK)
1907–09

MAWSON
»Aurora« (AU)
1911–12

SHACKLETON
»Endurance« (UK)
1914–16

SCOTT
»Discovery« (UK)
1902–03

FILCHNER
»Deutschland« (DE)
1911–12

AMUNDSEN
»Fram« (NO)
1911–12

SCOTT
»Terra Nova«
1911–12 (UK)

GOLDEN SECTION GRAPHICS
WETTLAUF BIS ANS ENDE DER WELT

♦ The maps produced by *Golden Section Graphics* are used as infographics that combine geography and history. Their map of the Antarctic visualizes the history of its exploration beginning with the eighteenth-century journey by James Cook and ending with Roald Amundsen's successful 1911 attempt to reach the South Pole.

➥ **ANTARCTICA**, 2011, FOR IN GRAPHICS VOL. 2,
GRAPHICS: GOLDEN SECTION GRAPHICS / KATJA GÜNTHER, JAN SCHWOCHOW

Geteilte Inseln

Ab auf die Insel – das klingt nach grenzenloser Freiheit. Aber es gibt Landstücke im Meer, durch die eine Grenze verläuft. Oft ist diese Gegenstand heftiger Kämpfe

N°
164

THEMA:
GEOGRAFIE

Die Themen der letzten Grafiken:

163
Olympia

162
Dschungelcamp

161
Rolling Stones

Weitere Grafiken im Internet:
www.zeit.de/grafik

PAZIFISCHER OZEAN

INDONESIEN
49 %

Jayapura

BISMARCKSEE

PAPUA-NEUGUINEA
51 %

ARAFURASEE

SALOMONENSEE

GOLF VON PAPUA

NEUGUINEA

Port Moresby

KORALLENSEE

OSTTIMOR
47,9 %

Dili

SAWUSEE

Kupang

TIMORSEE

TIMOR

INDONESIEN
52,1 %

HISPANIOLA

ATLANTIK

HAITI
35,2 %

DOMINI-
KANISCHE
REPUBLIK
64,8 %

Port-au-Prince

Santo Domingo

KARIBISCHES MEER

Bandar Seri Begawan

BRUNEI
0,6 %

SÜDCHINESISCHES MEER

CELEBESSEE

MALAYSIA
26,8 %

Kuching

INDONESIEN
72,6 %

BORNEO

STRASSE VON MAKASSAR

JAVASEE

Banjarmasin

Sind das alle?

Wir zeigen alle geteilten Meeresinseln, die größer als 100 Quadratkilometer sind. Es gibt noch ein paar kleinere, meist unbewohnte Meeresinseln sowie Inseln, die zwischen zwei Ländern in einem See oder Fluss liegen.

ZYPERN

REPUBLIK
ZYPERN
57,2 %

Nikosia

NORD-
ZYPERN
42,8 %

MITTELMEER

DEUTSCHLAND
89,5 %

OSTSEE

POLEN
10,5 %

USEDOM

CELEBESSEE

MALAYSIA
42,7 %

INDONESIEN
57,3 %

SEBATIK

Usedom

Swine-
münde

VENEZUELA
88,7 %

ATLANTIK

GUYANA
11,3 %

RIO BARIMA
(FLUSS)

COROCORO

USEDOM

dünn besiedelt

SEBATIK

IRLAND

NORD
KANAL

VEREINIGTES
KÖNIGREICH
17,3 %

Belfast

IRISCHE
SEE

ATLANTIK

IRLAND
82,7 %

Dublin

SANKT-GEORGS-KANAL

TIERRA DEL FUEGO
(FEUERLAND)

CHILE
57,2 %

Porvenir

ATLANTIK

Rio Grande

ARGENTINIEN
42,8 %

PAZIFISCHER OZEAN

COROCORO

unbewohnt

Neuguinea	Borneo	Irland	Hispaniola	Tierra del Fuego	Timor	Zypern	Corocoro	Sebatik	Usedom
Indonesien / Papua-Neuguinea	Indonesien / Malaysia / Brunei	Irland / Vereinigtes Königreich	Haiti / Dominikanische Republik	Chile / Argentinien	Indonesien / Osttimor	Republik Zypern / Nordzypern	Venezuela / Guyana	Indonesien / Malaysia	Deutschland / Polen
785 753 km²	748 168 km²	81 638 km²	73 929 km²	47 992 km²	28 418 km²	9 234 km²	690 km²	452 km²	445 km²

Nach der Kolonialzeit besetzte Indonesien 1963 den Westen, der Osten wurde 1975 unabhängig.

Die einzige Insel, die sich drei Länder teilen, darunter das unabhängige Sultanat Brunei.

Als Irland 1921 unabhängig wurde, teilte man die Insel. Frieden herrscht erst seit einigen Jahren.

Die Grenze zwischen dem bettelarmen Westen und dem touristischen Osten ist undurchlässig.

In der argentinischen Hälfte der Insel leben zehnmal so viele Menschen wie in der chilenischen.

Nach einem langen, blutigen Krieg wurde Osttimor, ehemals portugiesisch, im Jahr 2002 unabhängig.

Ist Zypern geteilt oder nicht? De facto ja, aber nur die Türkei erkennt Nordzypern an.

Eine unbewohnte Insel in der Mündung des Barima River, die beide Staaten für sich beanspruchen.

Der Grenzverlauf auf der Insel im Nord-osten Borneos ist umstritten – es geht um Erdöl und Erdgas.

Die bei Touristen beliebte Ostseeinsel wurde 1945 durch das Potsdamer Abkommen geteilt.

Illustration:
Golden Section Graphics;
Katharina Stipp,
Dirk Aschoff

Recherche:
Katharina Stipp

Quellen:
islands.unep.ch,
wikipedia.de,
eigene Recherche

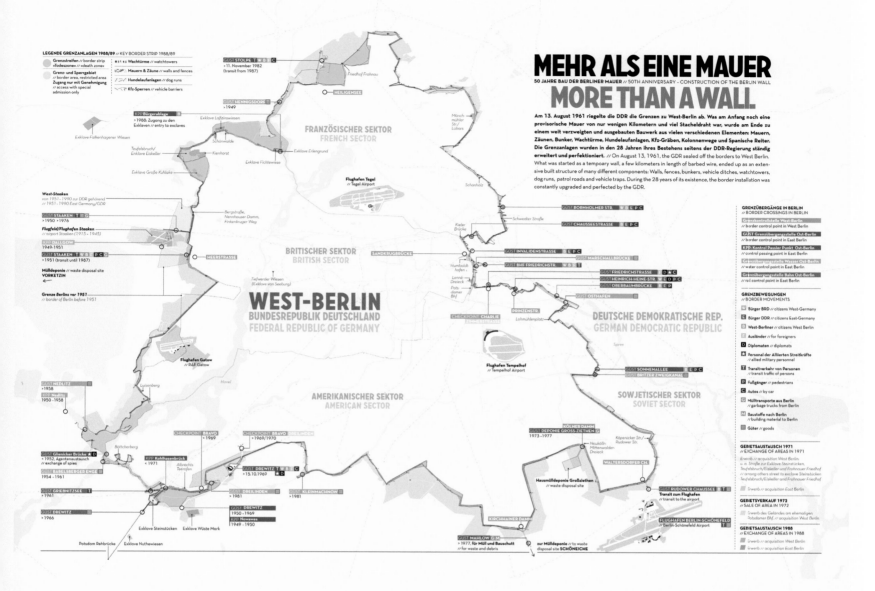

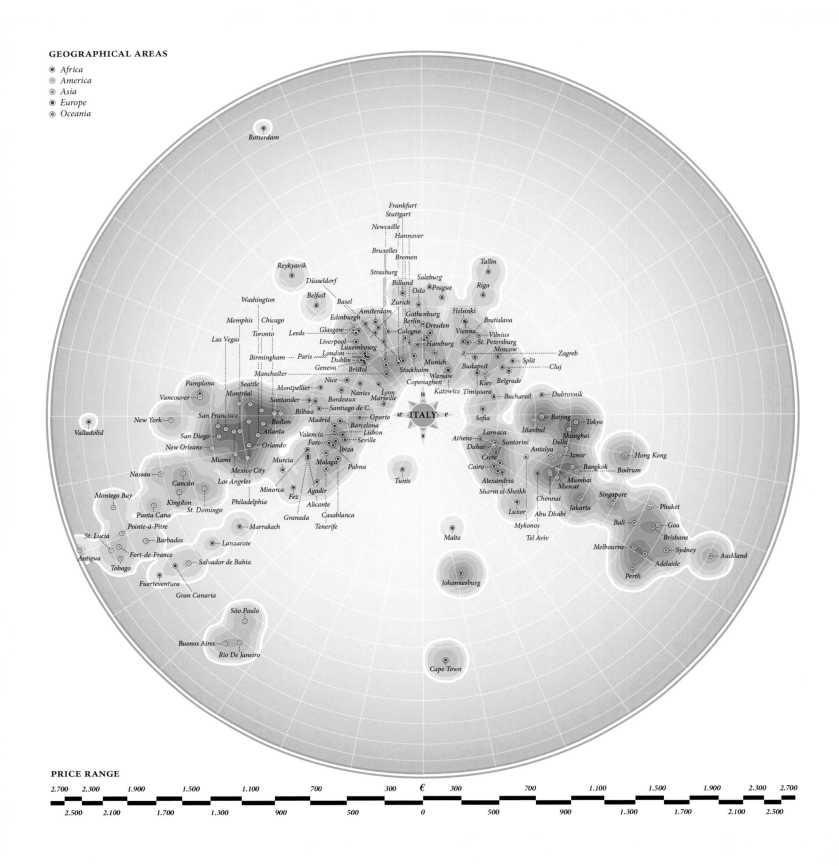

GEOGRAPHICAL AREAS
◉ Africa
◉ America
◉ Asia
◉ Europe
◉ Oceania

PRICE RANGE

| 2.700 | 2.300 | 1.900 | 1.500 | 1.100 | 700 | 300 | € | 300 | 700 | 1.100 | 1.500 | 1.900 | 2.300 | 2.700 |

| 2.500 | 2.100 | 1.700 | 1.300 | 900 | 500 | 0 | 500 | 900 | 1.300 | 1.700 | 2.100 | 2.500 |

DENSITY DESIGN
VACANZE PER TUTTE LE TASCHE /
LE ALTRE ITALIE LONTANO DALL'ITALIA

♦ Density Design, a research lab in the design department of the Politecnico di Milano, created a map depicting an Italo-centric geography based on last minute flights. The visualization displays flight offers from Italy for New Year's Eve 2011/2012 by Kayak, a travel metasearch engine. The other map seeks to remind Italians of their history as immigrants to other countries by presenting comparative figures on Italian expats and culture around the world. By combining data from the registry of Italians abroad with overseas Italian newspapers, radio, and television, the map emphasizes the presence of the Italian community abroad.

➥ WORLD, 2011/2012, BOTH FOR CORRIERE DELLA SERA / LA LETTURA

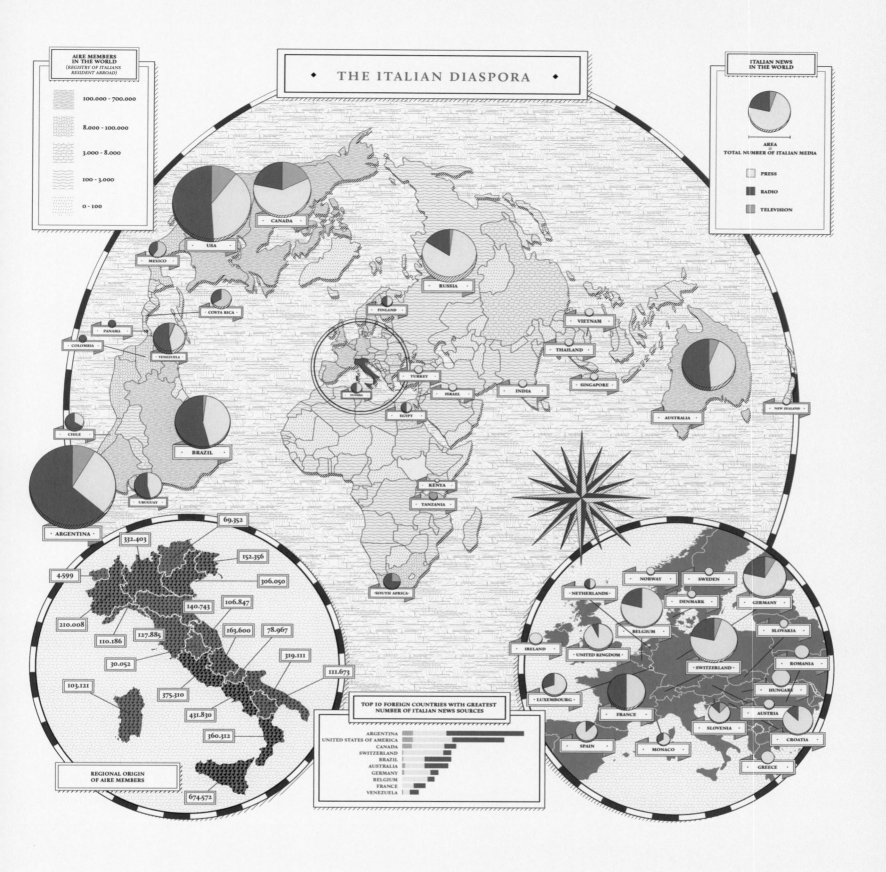

THE ITALIAN DIASPORA

ITALIAN NEWS
IN THE WORLD

AREA
=
TOTAL NUMBER OF ITALIAN MEDIA

PRESS
RADIO
TELEVISION

CANADA

USA

MEXICO

COSTA RICA

PANAMA

COLOMBIA

VENEZUELA

CHILE

BRAZIL

URUGUAY

ARGENTINA

FINLAND

RUSSIA

TUNISIA

TURKEY

ISRAEL

EGYPT

VIETNAM

THAILAND

SINGAPORE

INDIA

KENYA

TANZANIA

SOUTH AFRICA

AUSTRALIA

NEW ZEALAND

REGIONAL ORIGIN OF AIRE MEMBERS

69.352
332.403
152.356
4.599
306.050
140.743
106.847
210.008
110.186
127.885
163.600
78.967
30.052
319.111
103.121
375.310
431.830
111.673
360.312
674.572

TOP 10 FOREIGN COUNTRIES WITH GREATEST NUMBER OF ITALIAN NEWS SOURCES

ARGENTINA
UNITED STATES OF AMERICA
CANADA
SWITZERLAND
BRAZIL
AUSTRALIA
GERMANY
BELGIUM
FRANCE
VENEZUELA

NORWAY
SWEDEN
NETHERLANDS
DENMARK
GERMANY
BELGIUM
SLOVAKIA
IRELAND
UNITED KINGDOM
SWITZERLAND
ROMANIA
LUXEMBOURG
HUNGARY
FRANCE
AUSTRIA
SPAIN
SLOVENIA
MONACO
CROATIA
GREECE

97

MAKE YOURSELF AT HOME

19 SET./14H00
CALOIRO
DE MOLHO

ATÉ 21 SET.
(INSCRIÇÕES)
TROFÉU
AAUM

18 BRAGA
20 GUIMARÃES
DÁDIVA DE
SANGUE

18 SET./15H00
RUMA
AO CENTRO

18 SET./18H00
ACTIVIDADE
CEJ
(PROMOVIDA PELA
CAPITAL EUROPEIA
DA JUVENTUDE)

17 SET.
12H00 ÀS 14H00
ALMOÇO OFERECIDO
PELO REITOR

17 SET.
14H30 ÀS 16H00
CERIMÓNIA DE BOAS
VINDAS DO REITOR

10 A 14 SET.
SEMANA DE
MATRÍCULAS

18 SET./21H00
SARAU
CULTURAL

17 SET.
20H00 ÀS 24H00
ARRAIAL
AZEITEIRO

17 SET.
09H30 ÀS 12H00
SESSÃO DE BOAS
VINDAS NAS UOEI

18 SET./10H00
PEDDY PAPER
@ UM

Acolhimento

PREPARA-TE PARA TE SENTIRES EM CASA COM A PRIMEIRA
SEMANA DEDICADA ÀS MATRÍCULAS E A SEGUNDA SEMANA
DEDICADA A ACTIVIDADES PARA CONHECERES OS CANTOS À CASA

aaum
associação académica
da universidade do minho

PATROCINADORES

		DATAS	ANO	LOCALIZAÇÃO	DESIGN
		DE 10 A 21 SETEMBRO	**2012**	**BRG/GMR**	**gen**

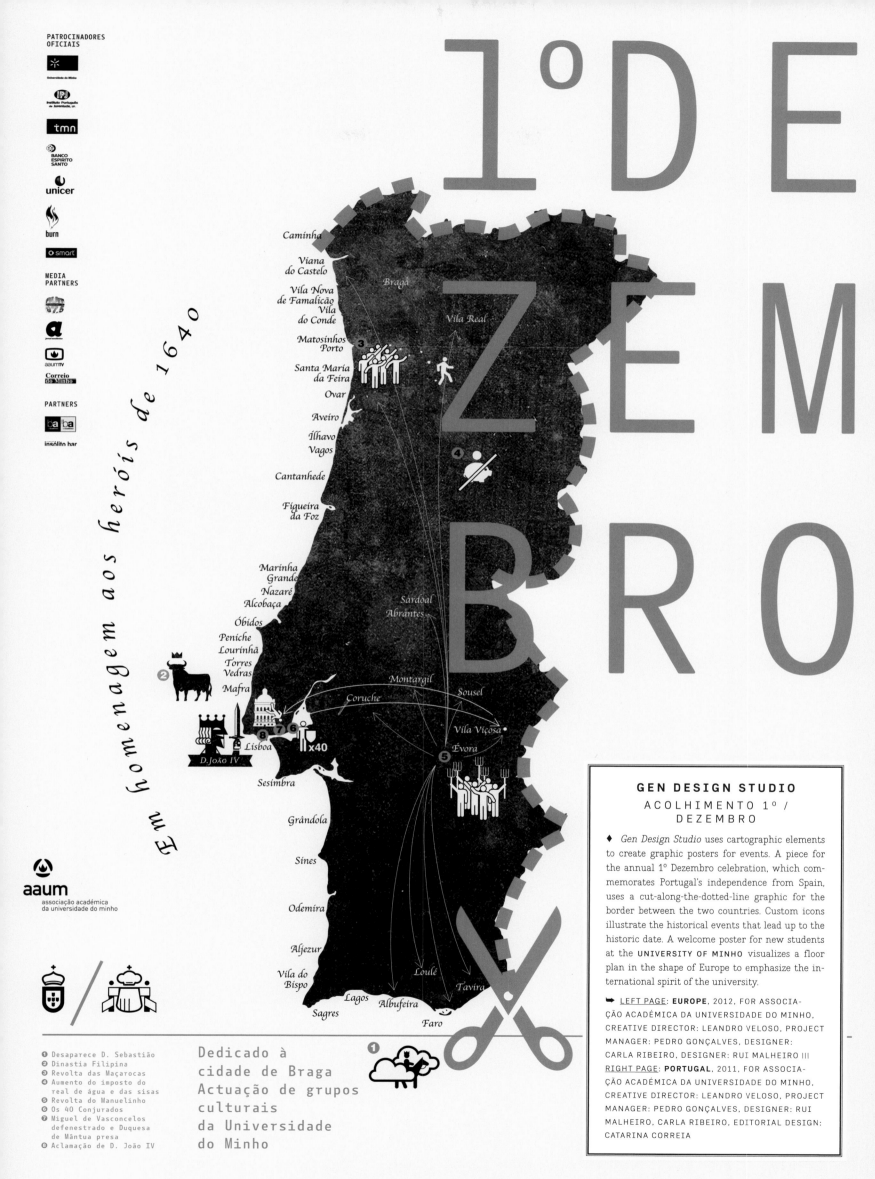

GEN DESIGN STUDIO
ACOLHIMENTO 1º / DEZEMBRO

♦ *Gen Design Studio* uses cartographic elements to create graphic posters for events. A piece for the annual 1º Dezembro celebration, which commemorates Portugal's independence from Spain, uses a cut-along-the-dotted-line graphic for the border between the two countries. Custom icons illustrate the historical events that lead up to the historic date. A welcome poster for new students at the **UNIVERSITY OF MINHO** visualizes a floor plan in the shape of Europe to emphasize the international spirit of the university.

➥ LEFT PAGE: **EUROPE**, 2012, FOR ASSOCIA-ÇÃO ACADÉMICA DA UNIVERSIDADE DO MINHO, CREATIVE DIRECTOR: LEANDRO VELOSO, PROJECT MANAGER: PEDRO GONÇALVES, DESIGNER: CARLA RIBEIRO, DESIGNER: RUI MALHEIRO III RIGHT PAGE: **PORTUGAL**, 2011, FOR ASSOCIA-ÇÃO ACADÉMICA DA UNIVERSIDADE DO MINHO, CREATIVE DIRECTOR: LEANDRO VELOSO, PROJECT MANAGER: PEDRO GONÇALVES, DESIGNER: RUI MALHEIRO, CARLA RIBEIRO, EDITORIAL DESIGN: CATARINA CORREIA

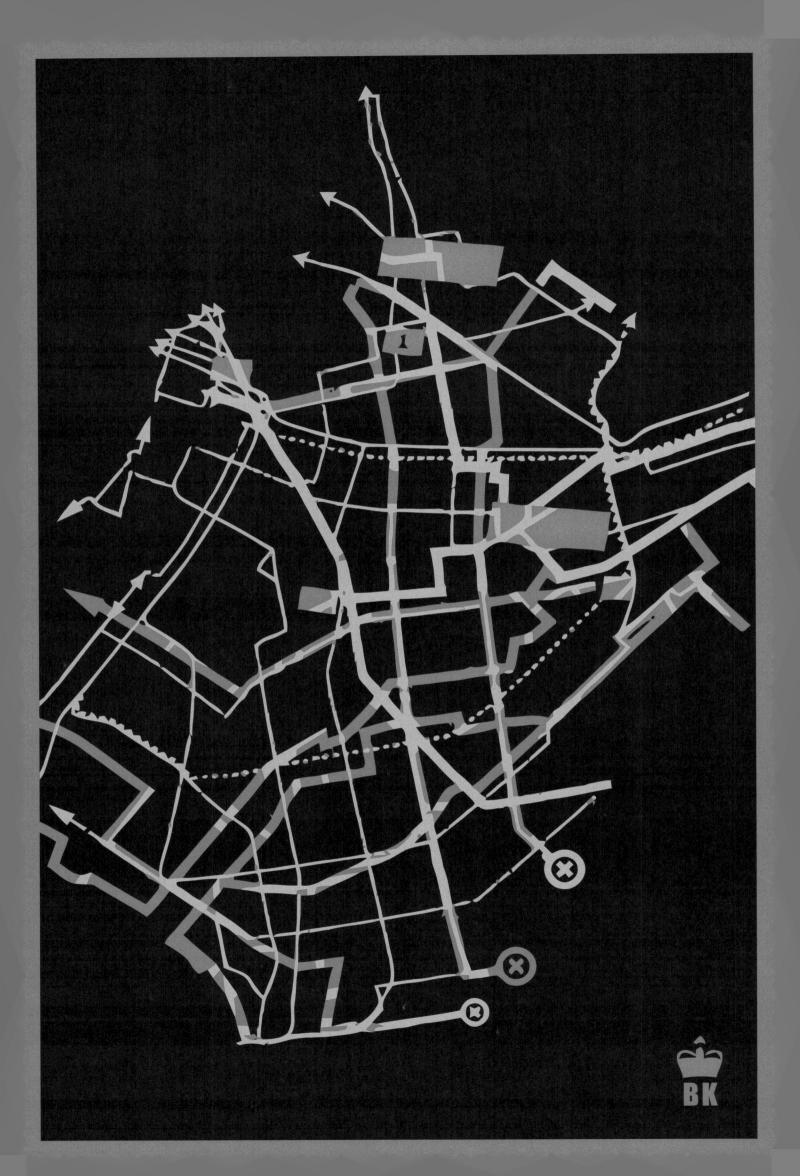

VIGILISM
ARTERIAL BROOKLYN
#01 & #05

♦ The Brooklyn maps by *Vigilism* are shape and color studies of the borough. Each map examines boundaries from various angles and plays with light and dark backgrounds to emphasize the linear qualities of neighborhood streets.

➥ **NEW YORK / USA**, 2012, PERSONAL PROJECT

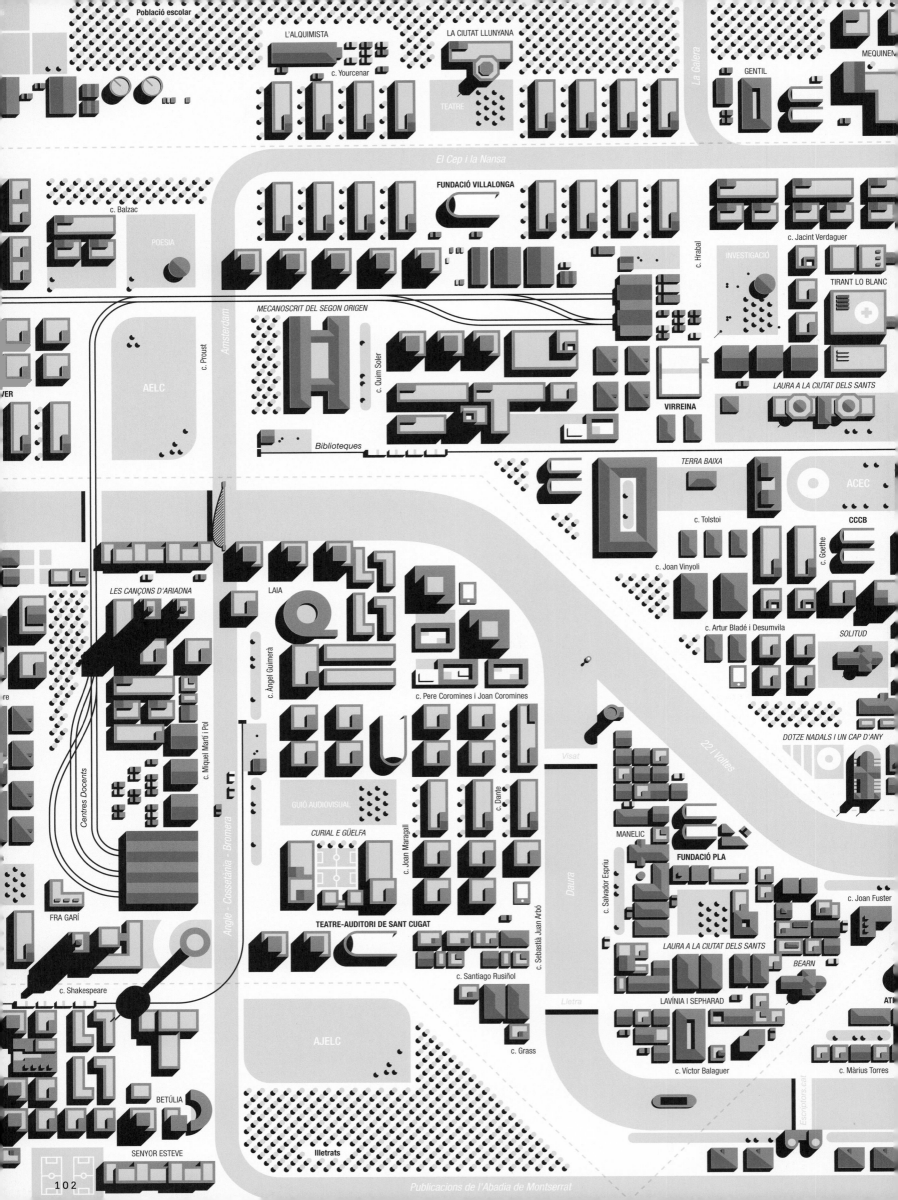

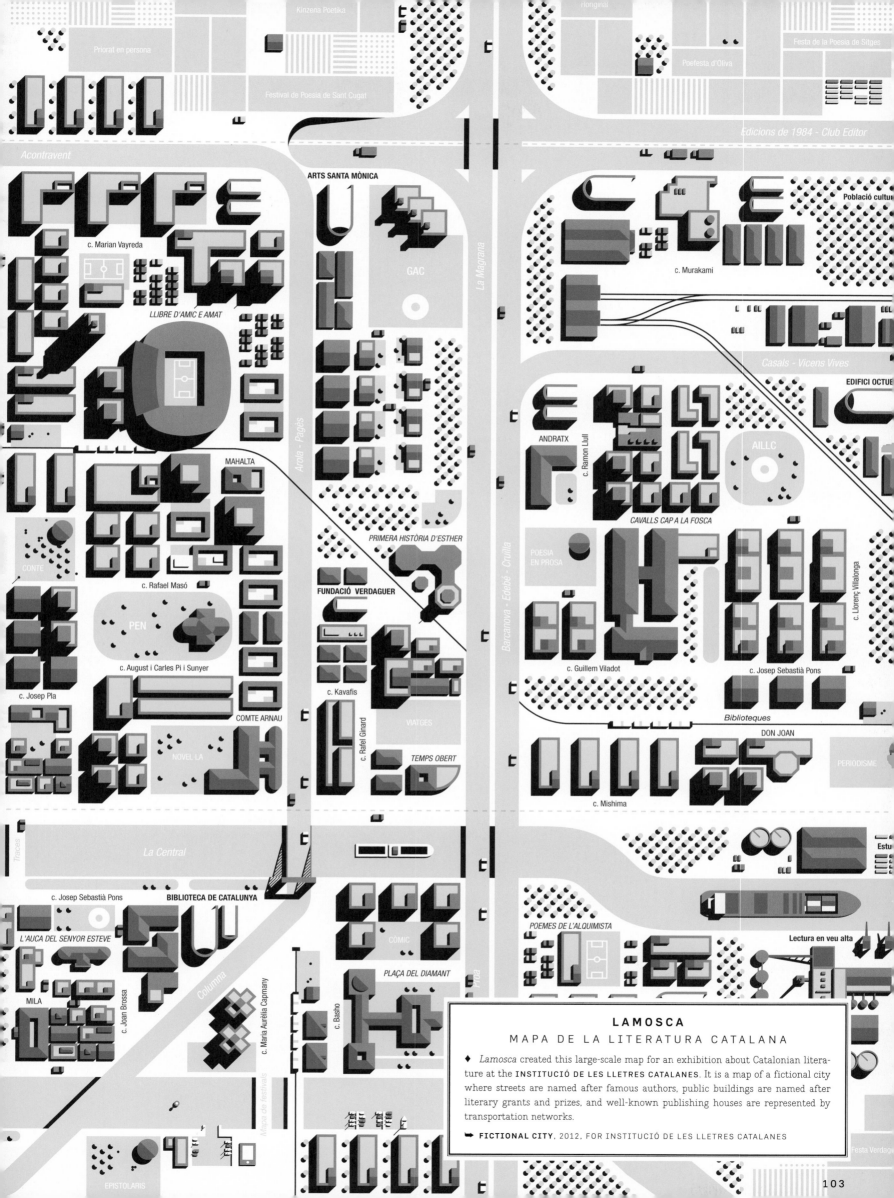

Priorat en persona

Kinzena Poetika

Festival de Poesia de Sant Cugat

Honginal

Festa de la Poesia de Sitges

Poefesta d'Oliva

Edicions de 1984 - Club Editor

Acontravent

ARTS SANTA MÒNICA

Població cultur

c. Marian Vayreda

GAC

c. Murakami

La Magrana

LLIBRE D'AMIC E AMAT

Casals - Vicens Vives

EDIFICI OCTUE

Arola - Pagès

MAHALTA

ANDRATX

AILLC

c. Ramon Llull

c. Rafael Masó

PRIMERA HISTÒRIA D'ESTHER

CAVALLS CAP A LA FOSCA

CONTE

POESIA EN PROSA

c. Llorenç Villalonga

PEN

FUNDACIÓ VERDAGUER

Barcanova - Edebé - Cruïlla

c. August i Carles Pi i Sunyer

c. Guillem Viladot

c. Josep Sebastià Pons

c. Josep Pla

c. Kavafis

Biblioteques

COMTE ARNAU

VIATGES

DON JOAN

c. Rafel Ginard

NOVEL·LA

TEMPS OBERT

PERIODISME

c. Mishima

Traces

La Central

Estu

c. Josep Sebastià Pons

BIBLIOTECA DE CATALUNYA

POEMES DE L'ALQUIMISTA

L'AUCA DEL SENYOR ESTEVE

Lectura en veu alta

CÒMIC

Columna

MILA

c. Joan Brossa

PLAÇA DEL DIAMANT

c. Maria Aurèlia Capmany

c. Basho

Frida

Mapa de festivals

EPISTOLARIS

LAMOSCA
MAPA DE LA LITERATURA CATALANA

♦ *Lamosca* created this large-scale map for an exhibition about Catalonian literature at the INSTITUCIÓ DE LES LLETRES CATALANES. It is a map of a fictional city
where streets are named after famous authors, public buildings are named after
literary grants and prizes, and well-known publishing houses are represented by
transportation networks.

➥ FICTIONAL CITY, 2012, FOR INSTITUCIÓ DE LES LLETRES CATALANES

Festa Verdag

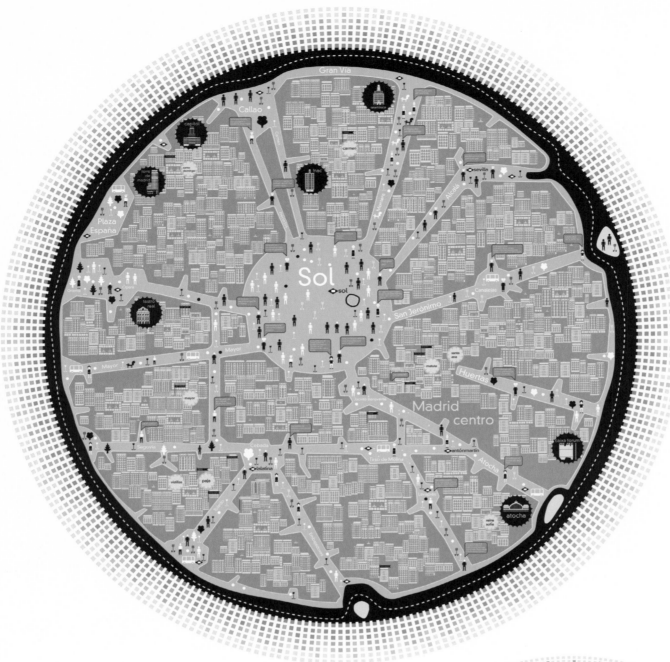

CARLOS ROMO MELGAR
COSMOGRAPHIES

♦ The Cosmographies project maps locations using personal experiences as a way to contribute to the understanding of place. The project is based on medieval mapping systems created by monks, which reflect personal visions of cities and routes by focusing on the circumstantial details of place.

➥ MADRID DOWNTOWN & MADRID / SPAIN,
2010, PERSONAL PROJECT

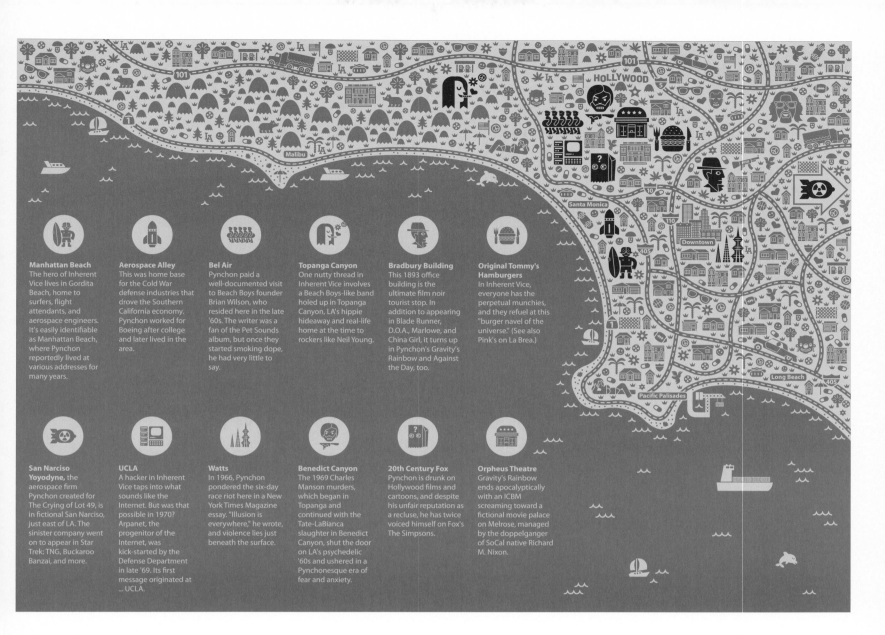

Manhattan Beach
The hero of Inherent Vice lives in Gordita Beach, home to surfers, flight attendants, and aerospace engineers. It's easily identifiable as Manhattan Beach, where Pynchon reportedly lived at various addresses for many years.

Aerospace Alley
This was home base for the Cold War defense industries that drove the Southern California economy. Pynchon worked for Boeing after college and later lived in the area.

Bel Air
Pynchon paid a well-documented visit to Beach Boys founder Brian Wilson, who resided here in the late '60s. The writer was a fan of the Pet Sounds album, but once they started smoking dope, he had very little to say.

Topanga Canyon
One nutty thread in Inherent Vice involves a Beach Boys-like band holed up in Topanga Canyon, LA's hippie hideaway and real-life home at the time to rockers like Neil Young.

Bradbury Building
This 1893 office building is the ultimate film noir tourist stop. In addition to appearing in Blade Runner, D.O.A., Marlowe, and China Girl, it turns up in Pynchon's Gravity's Rainbow and Against the Day, too.

Original Tommy's Hamburgers
In Inherent Vice, everyone has the perpetual munchies, and they refuel at this "burger navel of the universe." (See also Pink's on La Brea.)

San Narciso
Yoyodyne, the aerospace firm Pynchon created for The Crying of Lot 49, is in fictional San Narciso, just east of LA. The sinister company went on to appear in Star Trek: TNG, Buckaroo Banzai, and more.

UCLA
A hacker in Inherent Vice taps into what sounds like the Internet. But was that possible in 1970? Arpanet, the progenitor of the Internet, was kick-started by the Defense Department in late '69. Its first message originated at ... UCLA.

Watts
In 1966, Pynchon pondered the six-day race riot here in a New York Times Magazine essay. "Illusion is everywhere," he wrote, and violence lies just beneath the surface.

Benedict Canyon
The 1969 Charles Manson murders, which began in Topanga and continued with the Tate-LaBianca slaughter in Benedict Canyon, shut the door on LA's psychedelic '60s and ushered in a Pynchonesque era of fear and anxiety.

20th Century Fox
Pynchon is drunk on Hollywood films and cartoons, and despite his unfair reputation as a recluse, he has twice voiced himself on Fox's The Simpsons.

Orpheus Theatre
Gravity's Rainbow ends apocalyptically with an ICBM screaming toward a fictional movie palace on Melrose, managed by the doppelganger of SoCal native Richard M. Nixon.

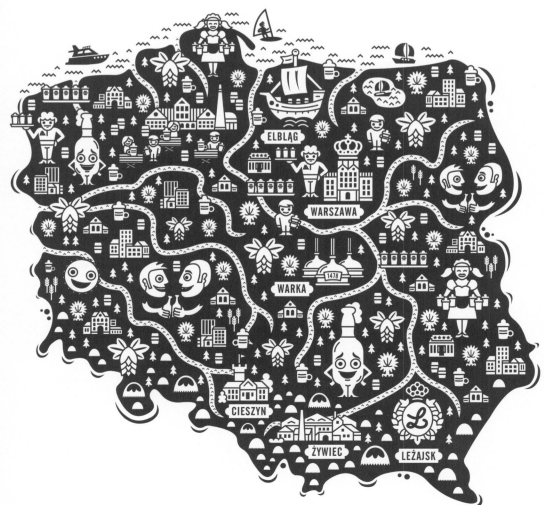

JAN FELIKS KALLWEJT

LOS ANGELES / POLAND

♦ Using an abstract style, *Jan Feliks Kallwejt* maps places and routes. His Los Angeles map illustrates the places and events in Los Angeles related to Thomas Pynchon and his books, while his map of Poland is a guide to Polish breweries.

➦ TOP: **LOS ANGELES / USA**, 2008, FOR WIRED MAGAZINE ‖ BOTTOM: **POLAND**, 2011, FOR ZYWIEC, AGENCY: WALK THE LINE

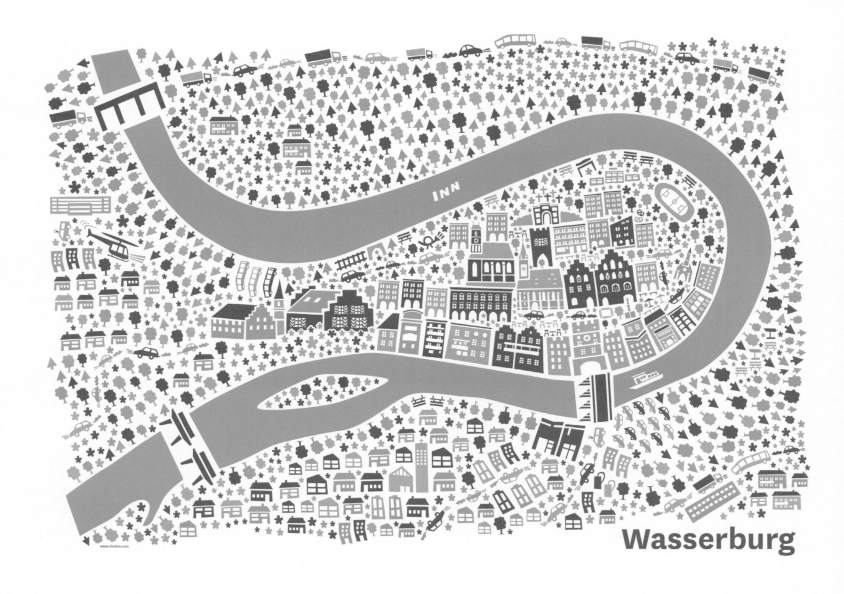

Wasserburg

NINA WILSMANN

VIANINA — GUTE KARTEN HABEN

♦ *Nina Wilsmann's* maps attempt to portray cities in an emotional way as if they are being experienced for the first time. She seeks to recreate how it feels to be somewhere new and unfamiliar, when details are overwhelming and unorganized. The resulting maps are drawn to approximate shapes of the districts they portray.

➦ LEFT PAGE: **WASSERBURG AM INN / GERMANY**. RIGHT PAGE: **VIENNA / AUSTRIA**, 2010, POSTERS FOR THE VIANINA WEBSHOP

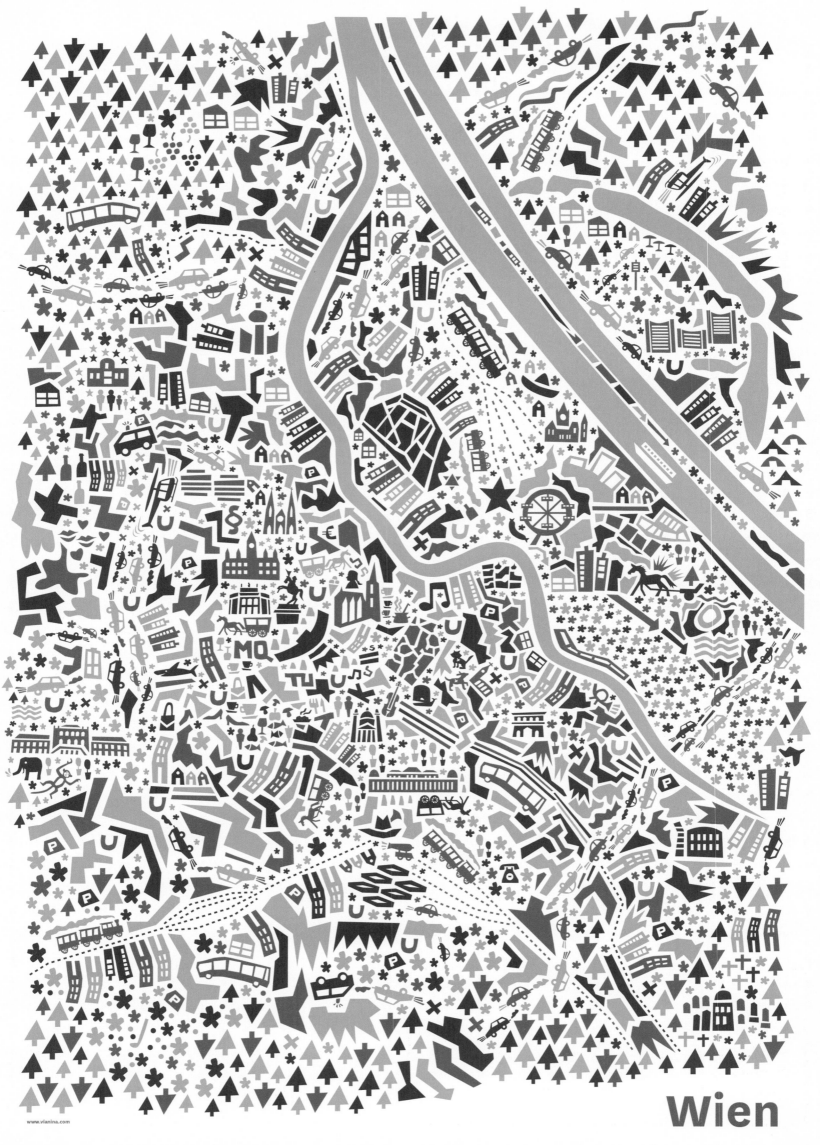

Wien

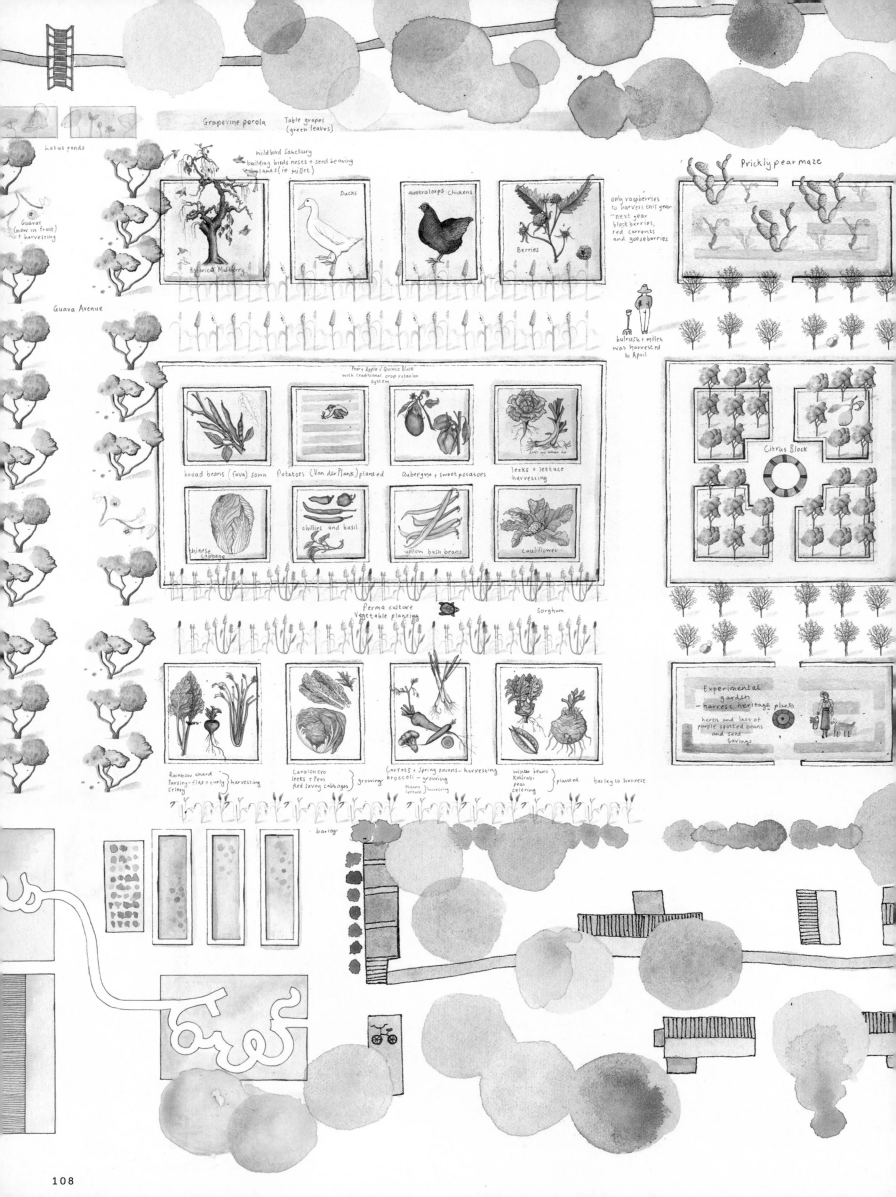

Grapevine pergola   Table grapes
(green leaves)

Lotus ponds

wildbird sanctury
building birds nests + seed bearing
plants (ie millet)

Prickly pear maze

Guavas
(now in fruit)
+ harvesting

Ducks   australorps Chickens

Berries

only raspberries
to harvest this year
- next year
black berries,
red currents
and gooseberries

Historical Mulberry

Guava Avenue

bulrush + millet
was harvested
in April

Pear, Apple + Quince Block
with traditional crop rotation
system

broad beans (fava) sown   Potatoes (Van der Plank) planted   Aubergyne + sweet potatoes   leeks + lettuce
harvesting

Leeks and lettuce bar

Citrus Block

chinese
cabbage   chillies and basil   yellow bush beans   cauliflower

Perma culture
Vegetable planting   Sorghum

Experimental
garden
- harvest heritage plants

herbs and last of
purple spotted beans
and seed
savings

Rainbow chard
Parsley - flat + curly } harvesting
Celery

Cavalonero
leeks + Peas } growing
Red savoy cabbages

Carrots + Spring onions - harvesting
broccoli - growing
Mizuna } harvesting
lettuce

winter beans
Kohlrabi } planted
peas
celering

barley to harvest

barley

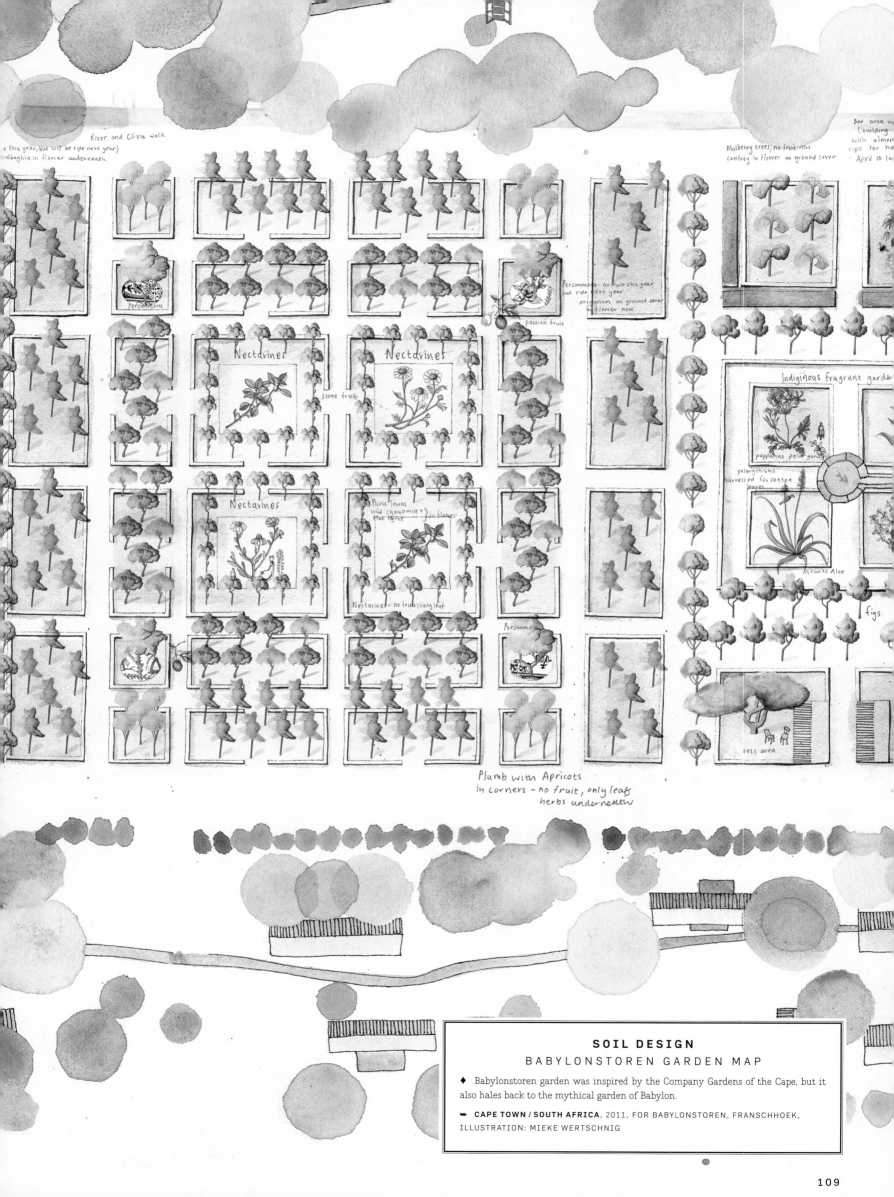

River and Clivia walk

e this year, but will be ripe next year)
ulbaghia in flower underneath.

Mulberry trees, no fruit now
comfrey in flower as ground cover

Bee area w
C building
with almon
ripe for ho
- April to la

Persimmons

Persimmons - no fruit this year
but ripe next year
origanum as ground cover
in flower now

passion fruit

Nectarines

Nectarines

stone fruit

Indigenous fragrant garden

poppermint pelargoniu

pelargoniums
harvested for scented
leaves

Krantz Aloe

Nectarines

Picnic lawns
wild chamomile +
flax thistle   in flower

Nectarines - no fruit, only leaf

figs

Persimmons

rest area

Plumb with Apricots
in corners - no fruit, only leaf
herbs underneath

SOIL DESIGN
BABYLONSTOREN GARDEN MAP

♦ Babylonstoren garden was inspired by the Company Gardens of the Cape, but it also hales back to the mythical garden of Babylon.

➡ **CAPE TOWN / SOUTH AFRICA**, 2011, FOR BABYLONSTOREN, FRANSCHHOEK, ILLUSTRATION: MIEKE WERTSCHNIG

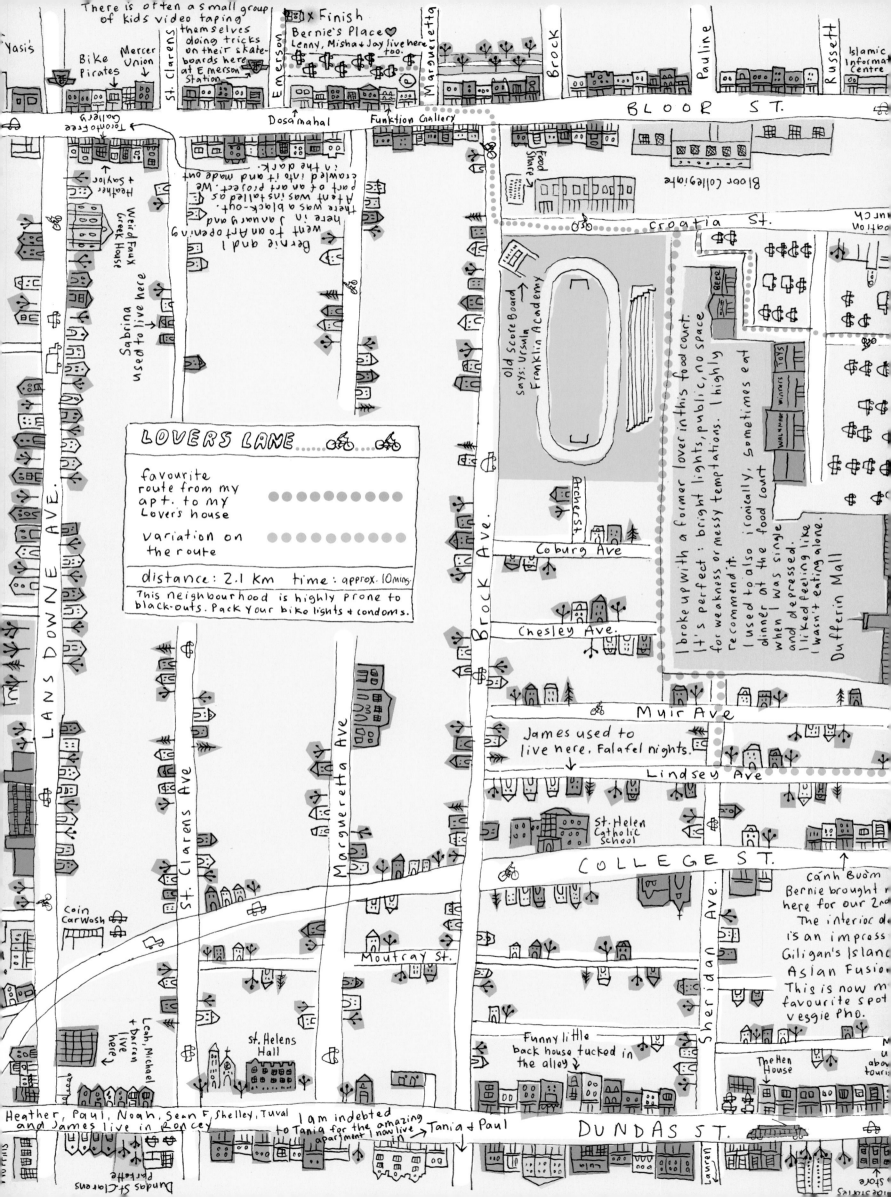

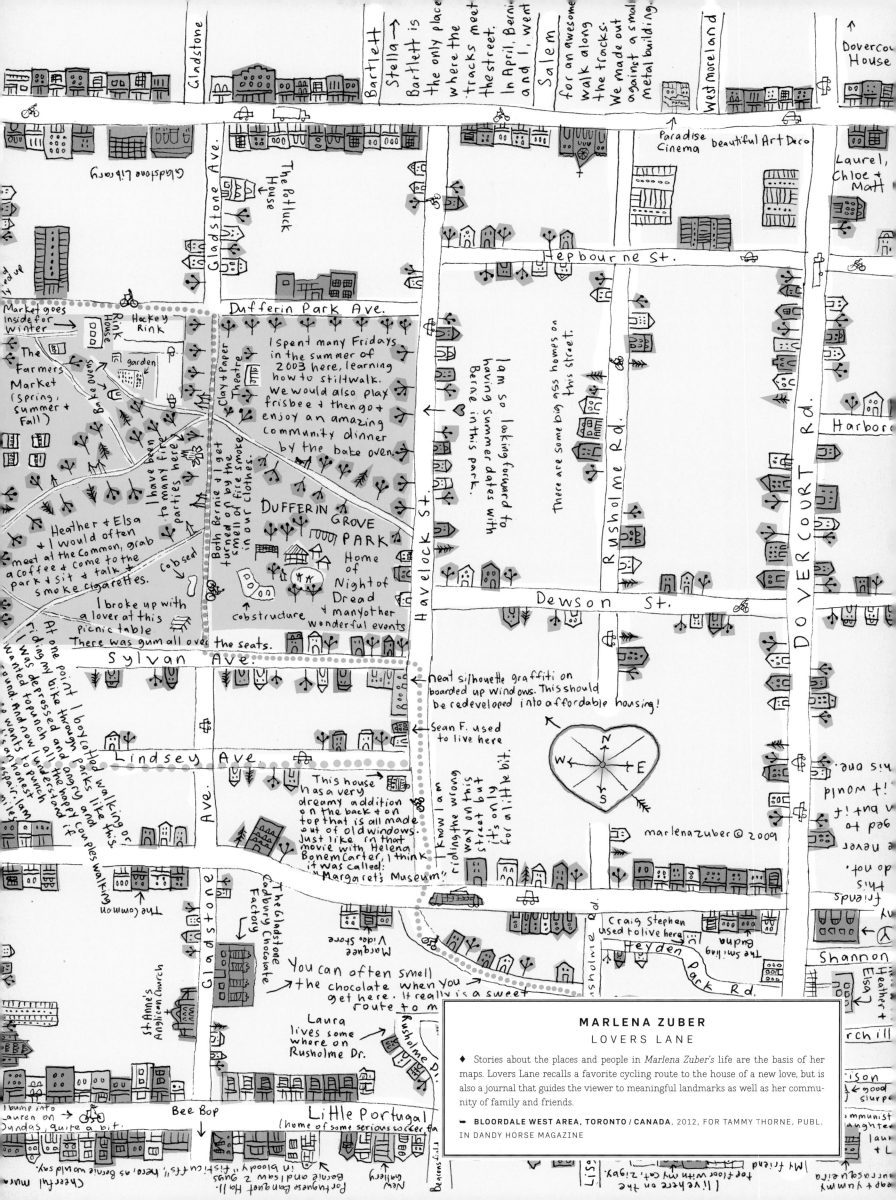

Gladstone

Bartlett

Stella

Bartlett is the only place where the tracks meet the street. In April, Bernie and I, went

Salem

for an awesome walk along the tracks. We made out against a small metal building.

West moreland

↑ Dovercourt House

Paradise Cinema beautiful Art Deco

Laurel, Chloe + Matt

Gladstone Library

Gladstone Ave.

The Potluck House

Hepbourne St.

Market goes inside for winter →

Rink House

Hockey Rink

garden

Dufferin Park Ave.

I spent many Fridays in the summer of 2003 here, learning how to stiltwalk. We would also play frisbee + then go + enjoy an amazing community dinner by the bake oven.

I am so looking forward to having summer dates with Bernie in this park.

There are some big ass homes on this street.

The Farmers Market (spring, summer + Fall)

Bike Lane

Clay + Paper Theatre

I have been to many fire parties here

Both Bernie + I get turned on by the smell of fire smoke in our clothes.

Rusholme Rd.

Heather + Elsa + I would often meet at the Common, grab a coffee + come to the park + sit + talk + smoke cigarettes.

Cob seat

DUFFERIN GROVE PARK

Home of Night of Dread + many other wonderful events

I broke up with a lover at this picnic table. There was gum all over the seats.

cob structure

Dewson St.

Sylvan Ave.

Havelock St.

neat silhouette graffiti on boarded up windows. This should be redeveloped into affordable housing!

At one point I boycotted riding my bike through parks like this. I was depressed and angry and wanted to punch all the happy couples walking around. And now I understand it wants to punch... is an honest... repair, I am... smiles.

Sean F. used to live here

Lindsey Ave.

Ave.

This house has a very dreamy addition on the back + on top that is all made out of old windows. Just like in that movie with Helena Bonem Carter, I think it was called: "Margaret's Museum"

I know I am riding the wrong way on this street but it's only a little bit for a big big

N W E S

marlenazuber © 2009

Dovercourt Rd.

Harbor...

this one would t. would t. put it to bed t never up not. this friends top floor... lisa...

The common

Gladstone

St. Anne's Anglican Church

The Gladstone Cadbury Chocolate Factory

Marquee Video Store

Craig Stephen used to live here

Heyden Park Rd.

The smiling...

Shannon

Heather + Elsa...

You can often smell the chocolate when you get here. It really is a sweet route to m...

Laura lives some where on Rusholme Dr.

Rusholme Rd.

I bump into Lauren on → Dundas, quite a bit.

Bee Bop

Little Portugal (home of some serious soccer fa...

Cheerful mur...

Bernie and I saw 2 guys in bloody fish cut fis... Portuguese Banquet Hall. Irene, as Bernie would say.

New Gallery

Beaconsfield...

Lisa...

My friend... rous... laur... t...

I live... top floor... with my cat, ziggy.

MARLENA ZUBER

LOVERS LANE

◆ Stories about the places and people in *Marlena Zuber's* life are the basis of her maps. Lovers Lane recalls a favorite cycling route to the house of a new love, but is also a journal that guides the viewer to meaningful landmarks as well as her community of family and friends.

➥ **BLOORDALE WEST AREA, TORONTO / CANADA,** 2012, FOR TAMMY THORNE, PUBL. IN DANDY HORSE MAGAZINE

MARLENA ZUBER

UTOPIA

♦ A fantastical, dreamy, visionary Toronto.

➥ **TORONTO**, 2005, FOR ALANA WILCOX, PUBLISHED IN UTOPIA, TOWARDS A NEW TORONTO

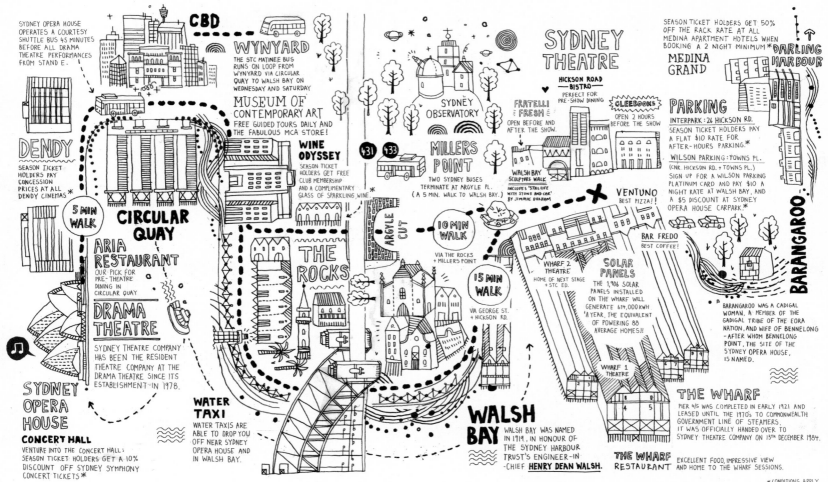

JAMES GULLIVER HANCOCK

SYDNEY THEATRE COMPANY /
WILLIAMSBURG

➡ TOP: CIRCULAR QUAY, SYDNEY, AUSTRALIA, 2009, FOR SYDNEY THEATRE COMPANY
SEASON CATALOGUE III BOTTOM: WILLIAMSBURG, BROOKLYN, 2010, SELF PUBLISHED

KATE HYDE

WALKING THE PAGE —
AN EXPLORER'S GUIDE TO HACKNEY

♦ Designed with the 2012 London Olympic Games in mind, this guide to the East London neighborhood of Hackney uses illustrated walking tours to introduce visitors to the artistic, lively, and unusual aspects of the area. Created as a celebratory pack, it contains posters, fold-out maps, and postcards that can be kept as souvenirs after use.

➥ **HACKNEY, LONDON / UK**, 2011, PERSONAL PROJECT

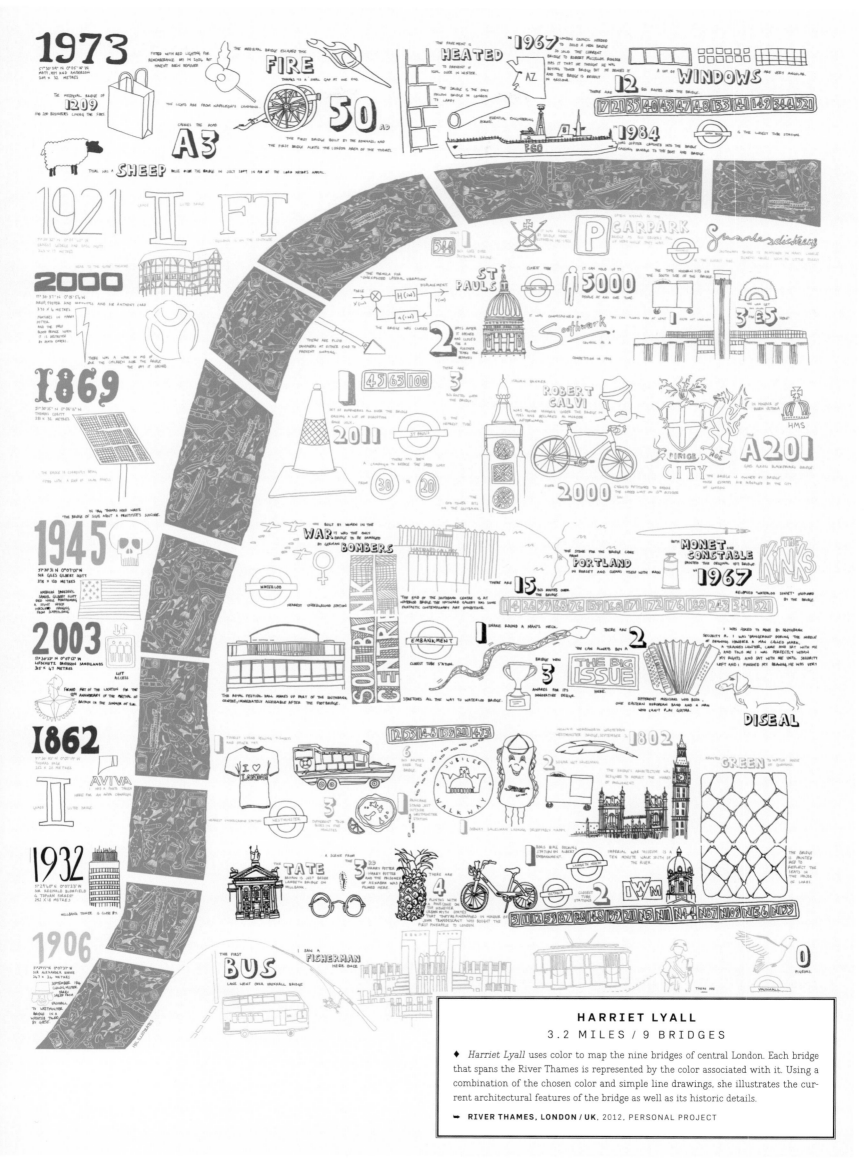

HARRIET LYALL

3.2 MILES / 9 BRIDGES

♦ *Harriet Lyall* uses color to map the nine bridges of central London. Each bridge that spans the River Thames is represented by the color associated with it. Using a combination of the chosen color and simple line drawings, she illustrates the current architectural features of the bridge as well as its historic details.

→ RIVER THAMES, LONDON / UK, 2012, PERSONAL PROJECT

Chiltern St, London

There are more reasons to visit this elegant area than its impressive architecture – luxury boutiques, unique new interiors stores and tempting interiors stores and tempting

Words HELEN BROWN *Illustration* ZOE MORE O'FERRALL

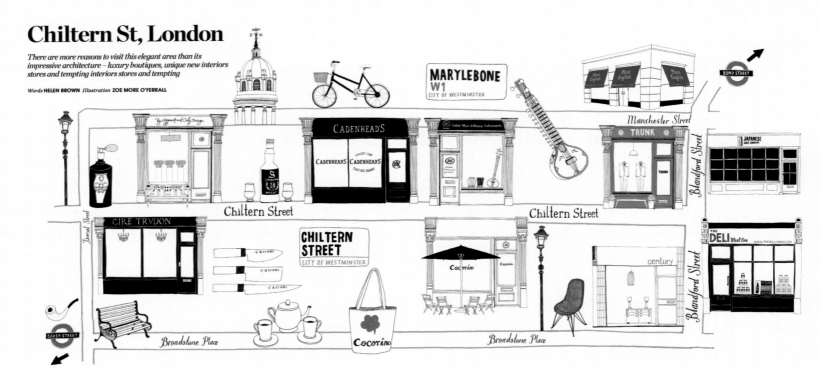

① TOMTOM COFFEE HOUSE
For the best cup of coffee in town, head to Tomtom Coffee House. The vibe is cosy and relaxed, while the ethically sourced beans, never served more than two weeks after being roasted, brim with flavour. You can also buy loose teas, roasts and paraphernalia for a delicious brew at home. cosy and relaxed, while the ethically sourced beans, never served more than two weeks after being roasted, brim with flavour. You can 114 Ebury Street, SW1W (020 7730

① TOMTOM COFFEE HOUSE
For the best cup of coffee in town, head to Tomtom Coffee House. The vibe is cosy and relaxed, while the ethically sourced beans, never served more than two weeks after being roasted, brim with flavour. You can also buy loose teas, roasts and paraphernalia for a delicious brew at home. cosy and relaxed, while the ethically sourced beans, never served more than two weeks after being roasted, brim with flavour. You can 114 Ebury Street, SW1W (020 7730

① TOMTOM COFFEE HOUSE
For the best cup of coffee in town, head to Tomtom Coffee House. The vibe is cosy and relaxed, while the ethically sourced beans, never served more than two weeks after being roasted, brim with flavour. You can also buy loose teas, roasts and paraphernalia for a delicious brew at home. cosy and relaxed, while the ethically sourced beans, never served more than two weeks after being roasted, brim with flavour. You can 114 Ebury Street, SW1W (020 7730

① TOMTOM COFFEE HOUSE
For the best cup of coffee in town, head to Tomtom Coffee House. The vibe is cosy and relaxed, while the ethically sourced beans, never served more than two weeks after being roasted, brim with flavour. You can also buy loose teas, roasts and paraphernalia for a delicious brew at home. cosy and relaxed, while the ethically sourced beans, never served more than two weeks after being roasted, brim with flavour. You can 114 Ebury Street, SW1W (020 7730

① TOMTOM COFFEE HOUSE
For the best cup of coffee in town, head to Tomtom Coffee House. The vibe is cosy and relaxed, while the ethically sourced beans, never served more than two weeks after being roasted, brim with flavour. You can also buy loose teas, roasts and paraphernalia for a delicious brew at home. cosy and relaxed, while the ethically sourced beans, never served more than two weeks after being roasted, brim with flavour. You can 114 Ebury Street, SW1W (020 7730

① TOMTOM COFFEE HOUSE
For the best cup of coffee in town, head to Tomtom Coffee House. The vibe is cosy and relaxed, while the ethically sourced beans, never served more than two weeks after being roasted, brim with flavour. You can also buy loose teas, roasts and paraphernalia for a delicious brew at home. cosy and relaxed, while the ethically sourced beans, never served more than two weeks after being roasted, brim with flavour. You can 114 Ebury Street, SW1W (020 7730

① TOMTOM COFFEE HOUSE
For the best cup of coffee in town, head to Tomtom Coffee House. The vibe is cosy and relaxed, while the ethically sourced beans, never served more than two weeks after being roasted, brim with flavour. You can also buy loose teas, roasts and paraphernalia for a delicious brew at home. cosy and relaxed, while the ethically sourced beans, never served more than two weeks after being roasted, brim with flavour. You can 114 Ebury Street, SW1W (020 7730

① TOMTOM COFFEE HOUSE
For the best cup of coffee in town, head to Tomtom Coffee House. The vibe is cosy and relaxed, while the ethically sourced beans, never served more than two weeks after being roasted, brim with flavour. You can also buy loose teas, roasts and paraphernalia for a delicious brew at home. cosy and relaxed, while the ethically sourced beans, never served more than two weeks after being roasted, brim with flavour. You can 114 Ebury Street, SW1W (020 7730

Bermondsey's village vibe

If you walk south over Tower Bridge on a Saturday morning, you'll find a thriving village scene in the heart of London. Once an industrial borough, Bermondsey is fast gaining a reputation for its foodie community, artisanal stores and galleries

Words ROHINI WAHI *Illustration* ZOE MORE O'FERRALL

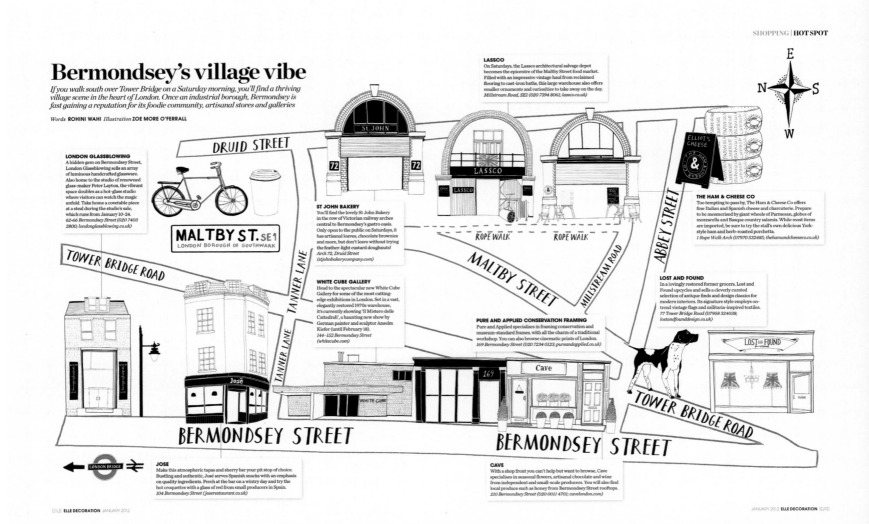

LONDON GLASSBLOWING
A hidden gem on Bermondsey Street, London Glassblowing sells an array of luminous handcrafted glassware. Also home to the studio of renowned glass-maker Peter Layton, the vibrant space doubles as a hot-glass studio where visitors can watch the magic unfold. Take home a covetable piece at a steal during the studio's sale, which runs from January 10-24.
62-66 Bermondsey Street (020 7403 2800; londonglassblowing.co.uk)

ST JOHN BAKERY
You'll find the lovely St John Bakery in the row of Victorian railway arches central to Bermondsey's gastro oasis. Only open to the public on Saturdays, it has artisanal loaves, chocolate brownies and more, but don't leave without trying the feather-light custard doughnuts!
Arch 72, Druid Street (stjohnbakerycompany.com)

WHITE CUBE GALLERY
Head to the spectacular new White Cube Gallery for some of the most cutting-edge exhibitions in London. Set in a vast, elegantly restored 1970s warehouse, it's currently showing 'Il Mistero delle Cattedrali', a haunting new show by German painter and sculptor Anselm Kiefer (until February 18).
144-152 Bermondsey Street (whitecube.com)

PURE AND APPLIED CONSERVATION FRAMING
Pure and Applied specialises in framing conservation and museum-standard frames, with all the charm of a traditional workshop. You can also browse cinematic prints of London.
169 Bermondsey Street (020 7234 0123; pureandapplied.co.uk)

LASSCO
On Saturdays, the Lassco architectural salvage depot becomes the epicentre of the Maltby Street food market. Filled with an impressive vintage haul from reclaimed flooring to cast-iron baths, this large warehouse also offers smaller ornaments and curiosities to take away on the day.
Millstream Road, SE1 (020 7394 8061; lassco.co.uk)

THE HAM & CHEESE CO
Too tempting to pass by, The Ham & Cheese Co offers fine Italian and Spanish cheese and charcuterie. Prepare to be mesmerised by giant wheels of Parmesan, globs of mozzarella and Basque country salamis. While most items are imported, be sure to try the stall's own delicious York-style ham and herb-roasted porchetta.
1 Rope Walk Arch (07970 532485; thehamandcheeseco.co.uk)

LOST AND FOUND
In a lovingly restored former grocers, Lost and Found upcycles and sells a cleverly curated selection of antique finds and design classics for modern interiors. Its signature style employs on-trend vintage flags and militaria-inspired textiles.
77 Tower Bridge Road (07988 324038; lostandfounddesign.co.uk)

JOSE
Make this atmospheric tapas and sherry bar your pit stop of choice. Bustling and authentic, José serves Spanish snacks with an emphasis on quality ingredients. Perch at the bar on a wintry day and try the hot croquettes with a glass of red from small producers in Spain.
104 Bermondsey Street (joserestaurant.co.uk)

CAVE
With a shop front you can't help but want to browse, Cave specialises in seasonal flowers, artisanal chocolate and wine from independent and small-scale producers. You will also find local produce such as honey from Bermondsey Street rooftops.
210 Bermondsey Street (020 0011 4701; cavelondon.com)

PARK LANE

GROSVENOR SQ

GROSVENOR STREET

GROSVENOR STREET

CONDUIT STREET

REGENT'S STREET

W ✦ E
N
S

MAYFAIR
W1
CITY OF WESTMINSTER

CORK STREET

MOUNT STREET

BERKELEY SQ

BOND STREET

NOBU

Royal Academy of Arts

PICCADILLY CIRCUS

PARK LANE

CURZON
CURZON STREET

Burger + Lobster

GREEN PARK

PICCADILLY

HYDE PARK CORNER

PICCADILLY

Green Park

THE RITZ

DUKE OF YORK STEPS

PALL MALL

ICA

CONSTITUTION HILL

THE MALL

ZOE MORE O'FERRALL

ELLE DECORATION / HARRODS

♦ The shops, landmarks, and attractions of several London boroughs are visualized in these place maps by *Zoe More O'Ferrall*. Each drawing shows the locations of underground stations and landmarks, providing orientation as well as illustrating the special flair of each area.

➥ LEFT PAGE: **MARYLEBONE, BERMONDSEY, LONDON / UK**, 2012, FOR ELLE DECORATION
‖‖ RIGHT PAGE: **MAYFAIR, LONDON / UK**, 2012, FOR HARRODS ESTATES MAGAZINE

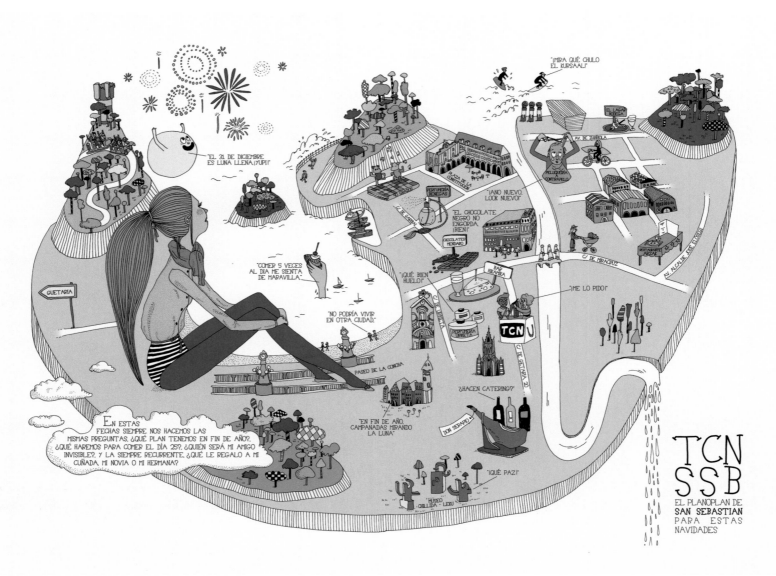

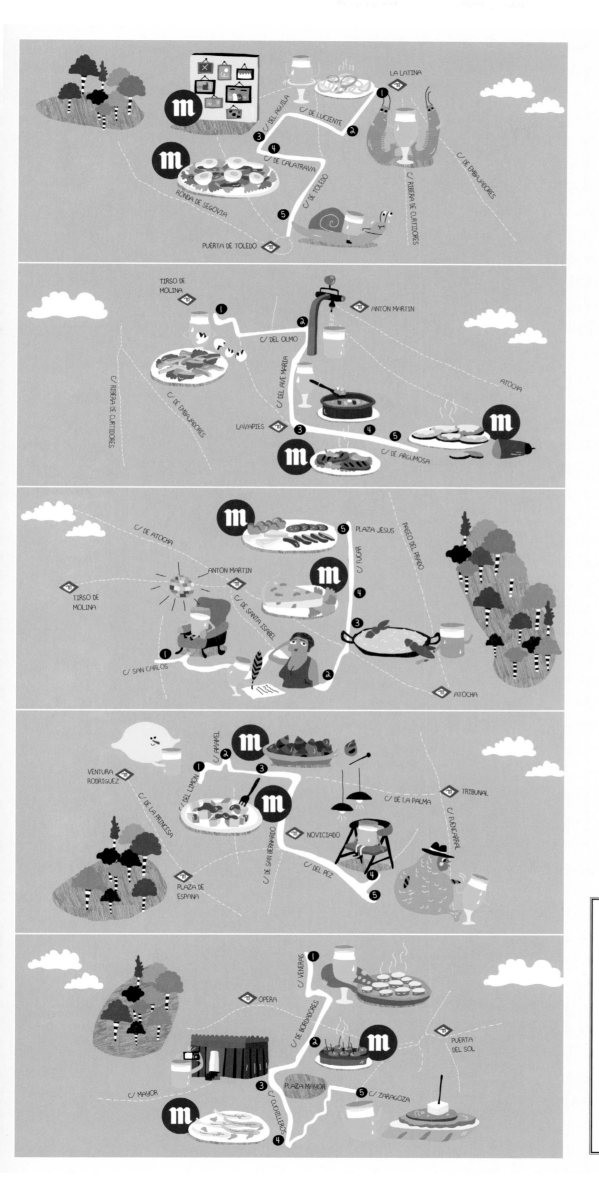

CAROLINE SELMES
TCN PLANOPLAN /
MADRID TAPAS ROUTES

♦ Amusing details, interesting places, and helpful information come together in the maps of *Caroline Selmes*. Her illustrations of detailed walking tours of Madrid guide pedestrians to the city's tapas bars. She also created maps of various Spanish cities for a clothing company that not only showed their store locations, but nearby hotels, restaurants, and attractions.

➥ <u>LEFT PAGE</u>: **VALENCIA & SAN SEBASTIAN / SPAIN**, 2009, FOR TCN, AGENCY: WWW.SANTA-MARTA. COM ‖ <u>RIGHT PAGE</u>: **AREA OF MADRID**, 2011, FOR MAHOU, AGENCY: WEB.SOCIALNOISE.COM

PETER OUMANSKI

NEW JERSEY BEACHES / UNITED STATES OF INNOVATION / WORLD TRIPS

♦ *Peter Oumanski* communicates large amounts of information in relatively small drawings. His map of the United States locates the country's most innovative companies and projects and illustrates what they do, while his map of the New Jersey shoreline lists the state's best beaches and what they are known for. A series of compact illustrations depicts trips taken all around the world.

➡ <u>TOP</u>: **USA**, 2011, FOR FAST COMPANY MAGAZINE, CREATIVE DIRECTOR: FLORIAN BACHLEDA, ART DIRECTOR: ALICE ALVES III <u>BOTTOM</u>: **WORLD**, 2011, FOR HEMISPHERES MAGAZINE, CREATIVE DIRECTOR: ROB HEWITT III <u>RIGHT PAGE</u>: **NEW JERSEY / USA**, 2011, PUBL. IN NEW JERSEY MONTHLY

Sandy Hook

Asbury Park

Pt. Pleasant Beach

Seaside Heights
Island Beach

Beach Haven

Atlantic City

Ocean City

The Wildwoods
Cape May

HALLO JORDA!

ANNA FISKE

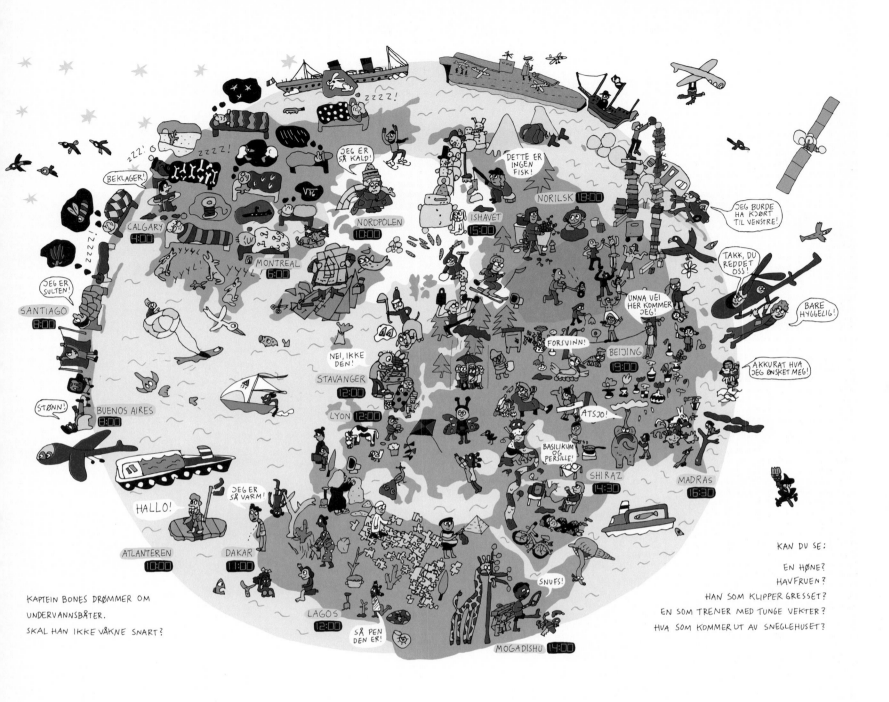

ANNA FISKE

HELLO EARTH!

◆ The book *Hello Earth!* asks readers to search for and find as many details as they can within its complex illustrations. The story follows six people for 16 hours, illustrating the things that happen or change from one hour to the next.

➜ WORLD (2 IMAGES), 2007, FOR CAPPELEN DAMM

ANDY COUNCIL
PLANET BRISTOL / DESIGN MAP OF BRITAIN

♦ The magazine **COMPUTER ARTS PROJECTS** asked *Andy Council* to draw a map of Britain for an article on the country's top design studios. The final piece populates the UK with major landmarks from the natural and built environment including Stonehenge and the White Cliffs of Dover.

➥ LEFT PAGE: **BRISTOL, UK**, 2010, FOR BRISTOL GREEN DOORS ||| RIGHT PAGE: **UK**, 2009, FOR FUTURE PUBLISHING, PUBL. IN COMPUTER ARTS PROJECTS MAGAZINE

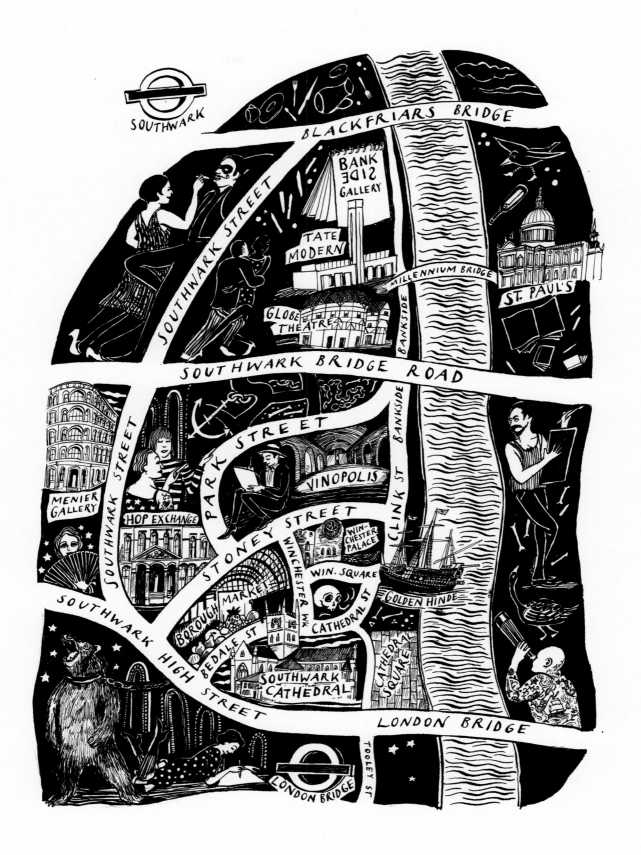

STEPHANIE VON REISWITZ
ISLAY / BANKSIDE

♦ *Stephanie von Reiswitz's hand drawn maps are loosely drawn but offer detailed information about the locations they illustrate. Her map of Islay shows the island's most popular destinations for the tourists who come to visit its many world class malt whisky distilleries. The playfully functional map of Bankside shows the venues of an all ages drawing event while also highlighting the area's unique landmarks and history.*

➥ LEFT PAGE: **ISLAY, INNER HEBRIDES / SCOTLAND,** 2010, FOR THE SCOTCH MALT WHISKY SOCIETY, PUBL. IN UNFILTERED / SMWS MAGAZINE ||| RIGHT PAGE: **LONDON / UK,** 2009, FOR THE CAMPAIGN FOR DRAWING / PUBL. AS BIG DRAW SKETCHBOOKS COVER

OLIVER JEFFERS
PLACES IN AMERICA /
NEW BRITANNIA / EVERYWHERE ON EARTH

♦ Painted with oil on wood, these maps by Oliver Jeffers are uncomplicated depictions of vast places. TED Prize winner and artist JR commissioned the illustrator to create Everywhere on Earth for the completion of his Inside Out project, a global participatory art project about personal identity. New Britannia was created for Morgan Spurlock's television show of the same name, which humorously compares American and British culture.

➥ LEFT PAGE: **USA**, 2009, PERSONAL PROJECT ||| RIGHT PAGE: **GREAT BRITAIN AND IRELAND**, 2011, MORGAN SPURLOCK / SKY ATLANTIC ||| NEXT SPREAD: **WORLD**, 2011, JR

NEW BRITANNia

The NORTH
SEA

The ATLANTIC
OCEAN

SCOT-
LAND

NORTHern
IRELAND

ENgland

IRELand

the IRISH sea

WALES

the CELTIC
SEA

the ENGLISH channel

VERONA FROM THE SKY

RUDE

VERONA FROM THE SKY

♦ *Rude's* abstract maps serve as posters that advertise a variety of events. The posters designed for several exhibitions leave out words entirely, relying instead on shapes and lines.

➥ **VERONA, ITALY**, 2009, FOR FEDRIGONI PAPER EXHIBITION, ADD.: RUPERT MEATS

ANNA HÄRLIN
BARCELONA MAP

♦ When the German magazine CUT asked *Anna Härlin* to design a map of Barcelona, she based her materials and concept on the magazine's content, which focuses on DIY, design, fashion, and crafting. Each element of the map is cut from paper, then folded into shapes to create a handmade, three-dimensional representation of the city.

➥ BARCELONA / SPAIN, 2010,
FOR CUT MAGAZINE

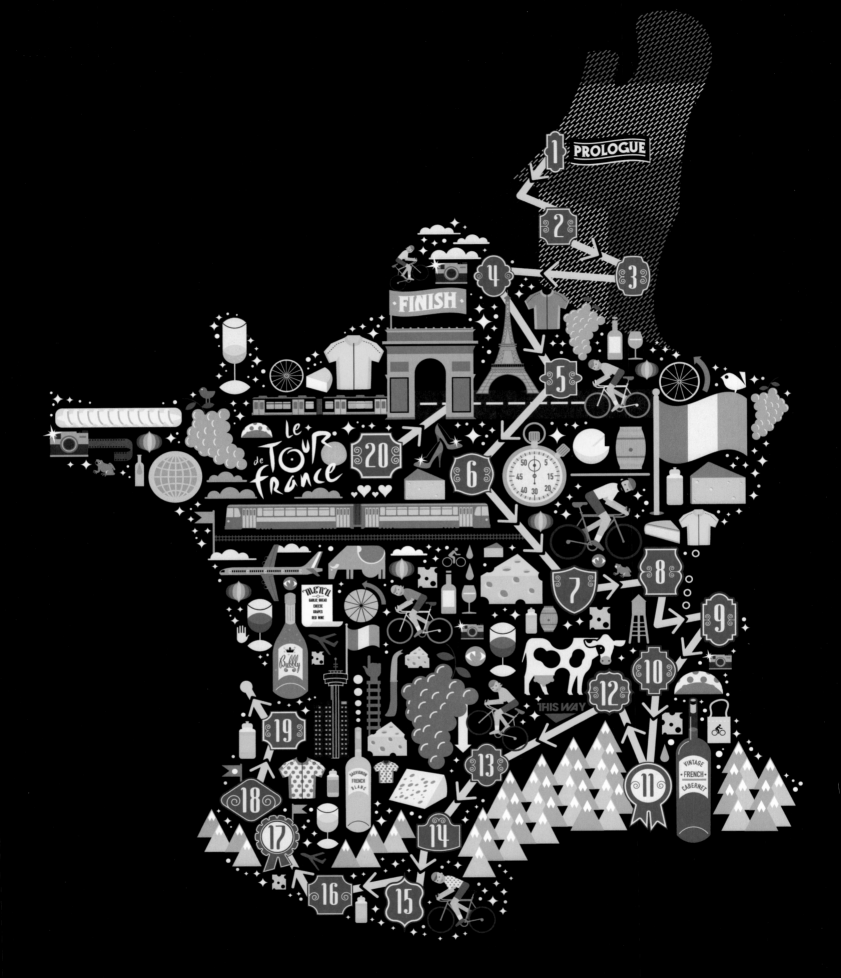

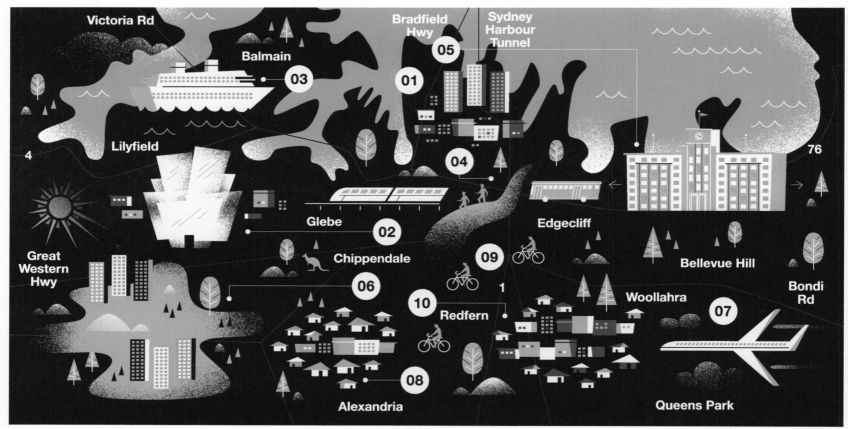

BRENT COUCHMAN

SAO PAULO / SYDNEY

➥ TOP: **SAO PAULO / BRAZIL**, BOTTOM: **SYDNEY / AUSTRALIA**, 2010, BOTH FOR MONOCLE, ADD.: TY WILKINS

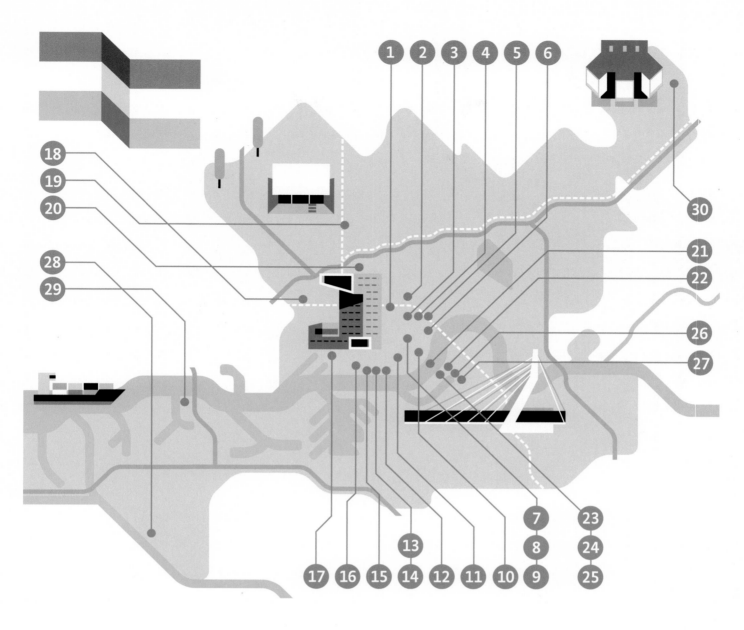

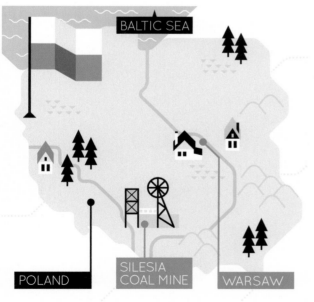

BALTIC SEA

POLAND

SILESIA
COAL MINE

WARSAW

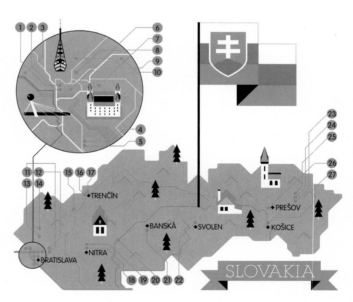

TRENČÍN

PREŠOV

BANSKÁ

SVOLEN

KOŠICE

NITRA

BRATISLAVA

SLOVAKIA

LOULOU & TUMMIE

MAPS FOR SPOON / A10

➥ TOP: **ROTTERDAM / NETHERLANDS**, 2012, FOR A10 MAGAZINE #43 JAN / FEB
2012 ||| BOTTOM LEFT: **COAL MINE / POLAND**, 2012, FOR SPOON MAGAZINE ||| BOT-
TOM RIGHT: **SLOVAKIA**, 2011, FOR A10 MAGAZINE #40 JUL/AUG 2011

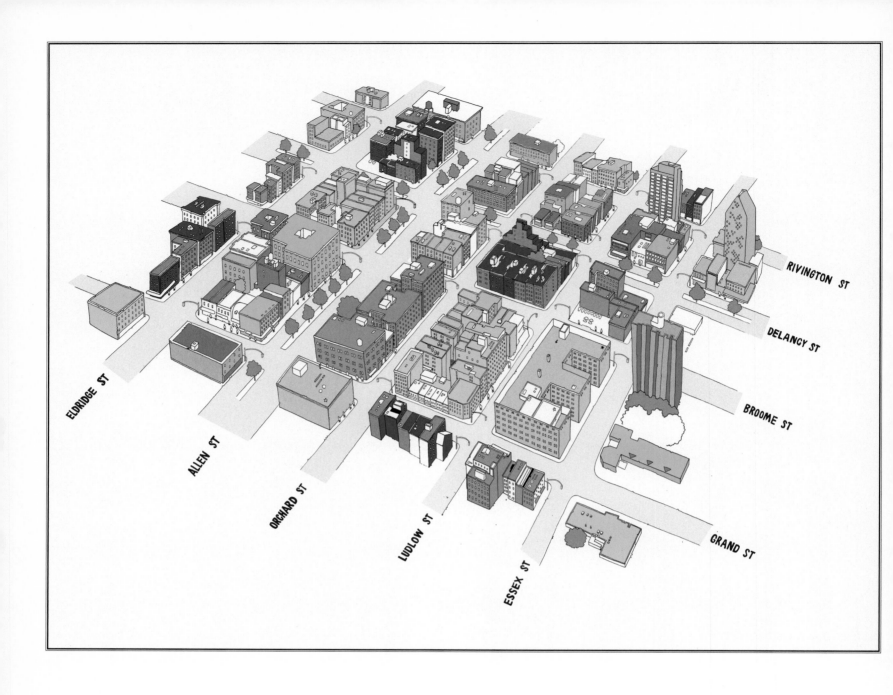

RIVINGTON ST

DELANCY ST

BROOME ST

GRAND ST

ELDRIDGE ST

ALLEN ST

ORCHARD ST

LUDLOW ST

ESSEX ST

CHRIS DENT

LOWER EAST SIDE

♦ *Chris Dent's* pared down map of New York City's Lower East Side gives a clear, color-coded overview of the area that highlights various locations for an article in New York Magazine.

➥ **NEW YORK CITY / USA**, 2009, PUBL. IN NEW YORK MAGAZINE

NEW LITTLES

New York is often celebrated because of its diversity of ethnic groups and cultures. We are all familiar with Little Italy as a small settlement nestled into the complex structure of Manhattan. This map depicts the twenty-five other ethnic groups that help to form the fabric of the five boroughs of New York City. Public radio station WNYC provided a database defining the locations of these enclaves, and the drawing defines each boundary with a collection of architectural icons associated with each culture. The buildings are numbered and labeled with flags of their origin countries. Overlapping neighborhoods create new hybrids, such as where the Great Wall of China runs through the Greek Islands.

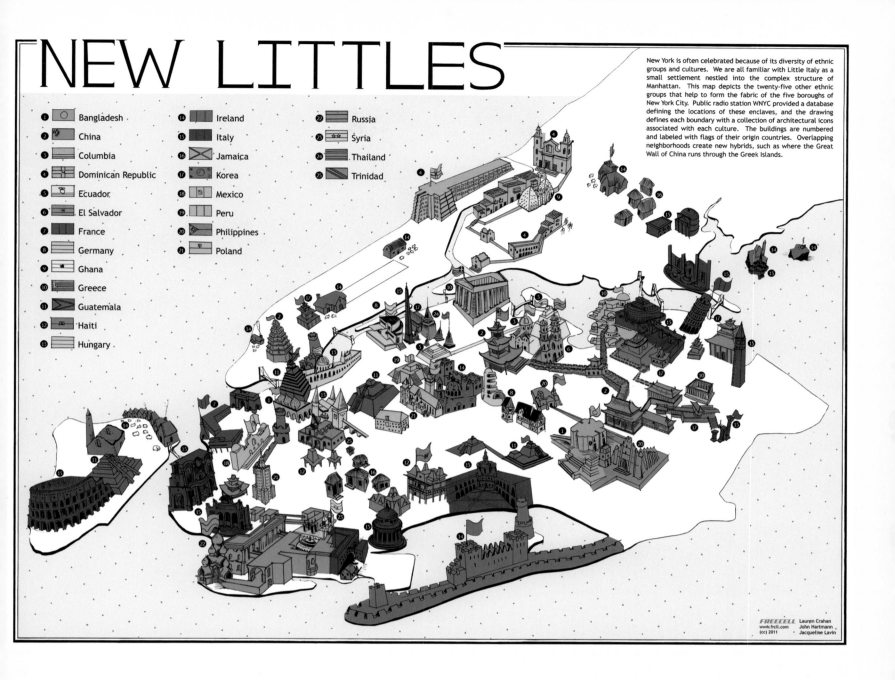

Legend:

① Bangladesh
② China
③ Columbia
④ Dominican Republic
⑤ Ecuador
⑥ El Salvador
⑦ France
⑧ Germany
⑨ Ghana
⑩ Greece
⑪ Guatemala
⑫ Haiti
⑬ Hungary
⑭ Ireland
⑮ Italy
⑯ Jamaica
⑰ Korea
⑱ Mexico
⑲ Peru
⑳ Philippines
㉑ Poland
㉒ Russia
㉓ Syria
㉔ Thailand
㉕ Trinidad

FREECELL Lauren Crahan
www.frcll.com John Hartmann
(cc) 2011 Jacqueline Lavin

FREECELL

NEW LITTLES

♦ Using architectural icons, the New Littles map represents the ethnic diversity found throughout the five boroughs of New York. Each ethnic neighborhood is depicted with vernacular or contemporary architecture from the home country. The buildings are color-coded and labeled with flags that can be read and identified in the key at the top of the map.

➡ **NEW YORK CITY / USA**, 2011, MAP SUBMISSION FOR THE "NEW LITTLES" SERIES ON THE BRIAN LEHRER SHOW, WNYC.

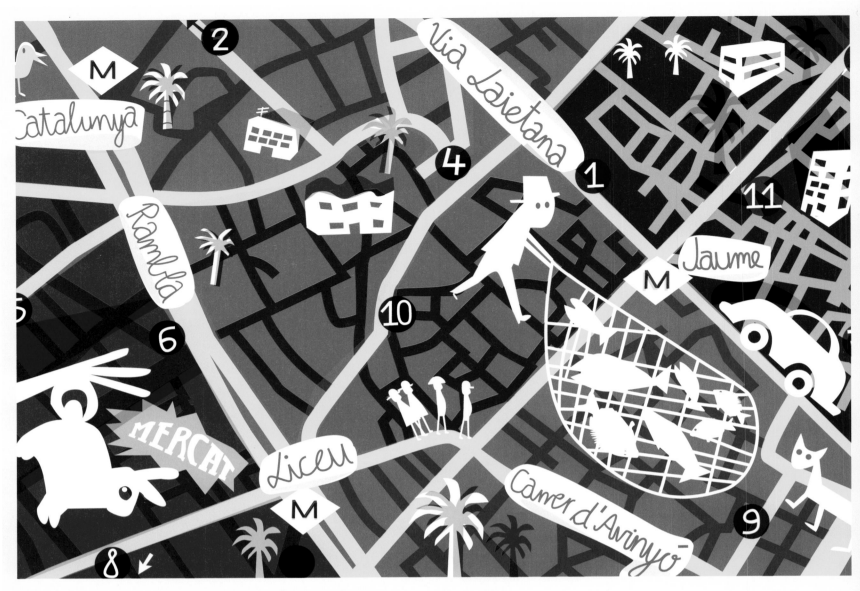

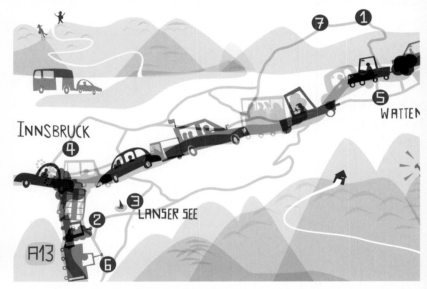

HELLO YELLOW
STUDIO

THE PERFECT PLAN

♦ Maps showcasing the best spots in town.

➥ TOP: **BARCELONA / SPAIN,** BOTTOM LEFT: **KREUZBERG – BERLIN / GERMANY,**
BOTTOM RIGHT: **INNTAL / GERMANY**, 2009, FOR SÜDDEUTSCHE ZEITUNG MAGAZIN,
ART DIRECTOR: BIRTHE STEINBECK / ZSUZSANNA ILIJIN

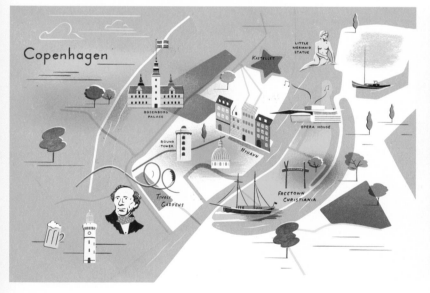

OWEN GATLEY

PARIS / COPENHAGEN / LONDON

◆ Famous cities are distilled by *Owen Gatley* into bold colors and vibrant drawings that map famous landmarks, people, and attractions.

➥ TOP: **PARIS / FRANCE**, BOTTOM LEFT: **COPENHAGEN / DENMARK**, BOTTOM RIGHT: **LONDON / UK**, 2012, FOR YCN, PUBL. IN IDEAS ILLUSTRATED

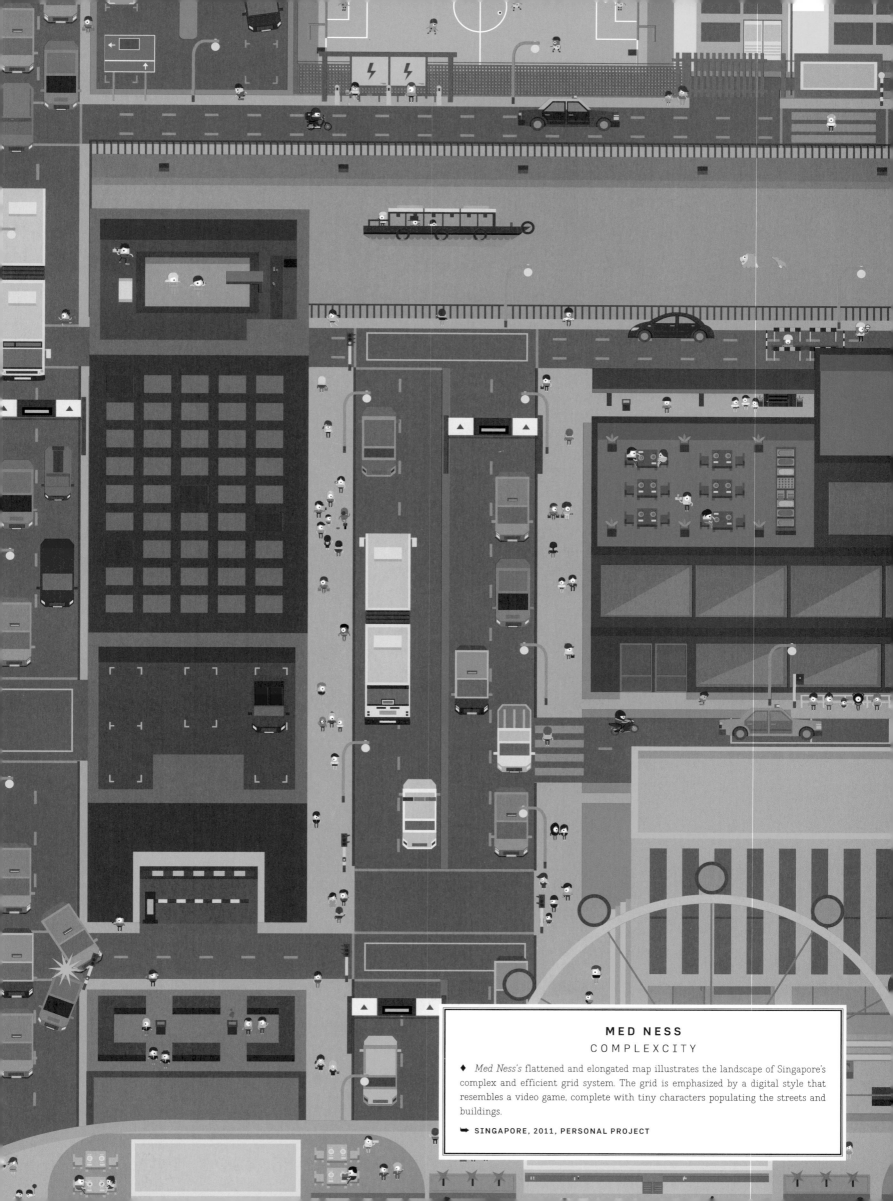

MED NESS
COMPLEXCITY

♦ *Med Ness's* flattened and elongated map illustrates the landscape of Singapore's complex and efficient grid system. The grid is emphasized by a digital style that resembles a video game, complete with tiny characters populating the streets and buildings.

➡ SINGAPORE, 2011, PERSONAL PROJECT

TEAMLAB
THE TOKYO SKYTREE MURAL

♦ Thirteen monitors are embedded in *teamLab's* 40-meter long mural of the Tokyo metropolis. The content on the monitors blends in with the mural itself, reflecting the Japanese tradition of including imaginary content, the four seasons, and time within one picture. The mural includes old town Tokyo, the vogue and fashions of the past, and stories from history.

➡ **TOKYO / JAPAN**, 2012, FOR TOBU RAILWAY COMPANY, TOBU TOWER SKYTREE COMPANY

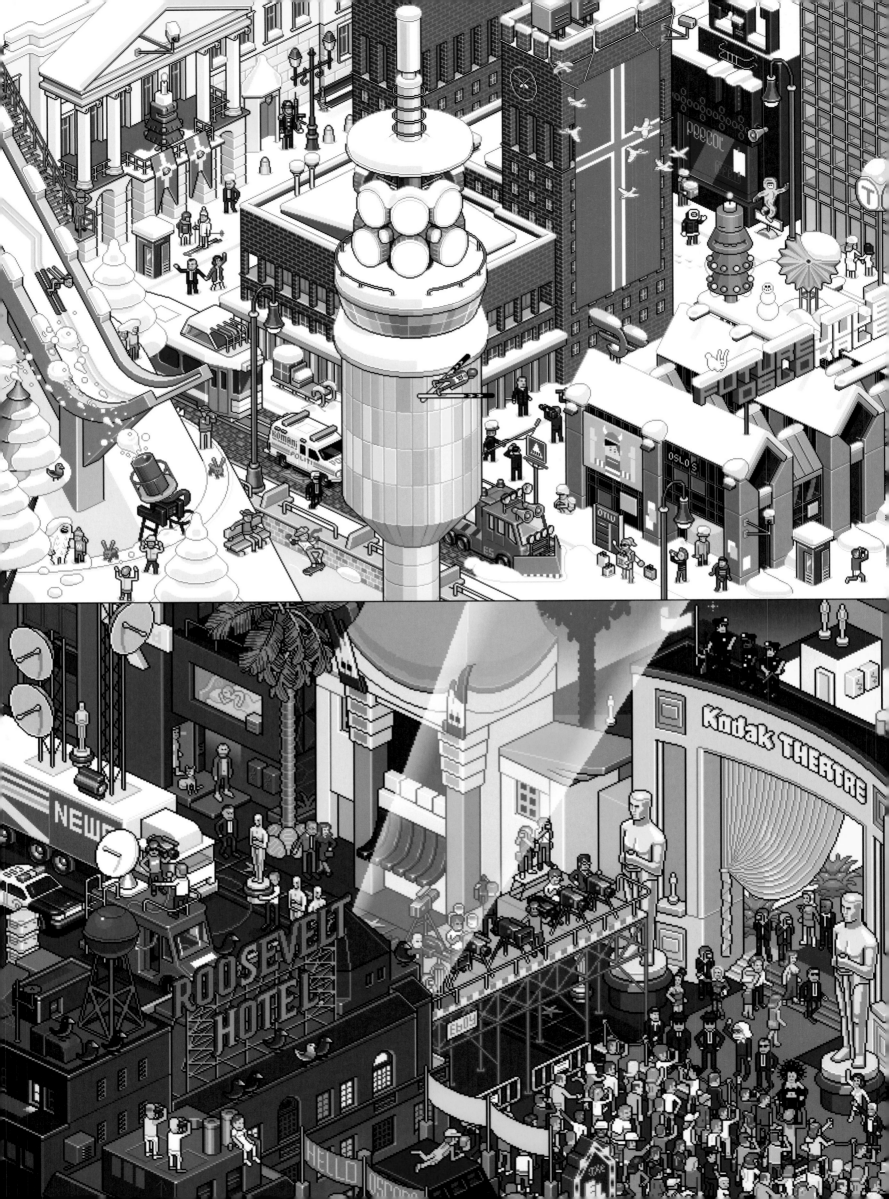

EBOY

OSLO / OSCARS

♦ The isometric illustrations created by the members of *eBoy* are complex spaces that draw on childhood memories of popular culture, video games, and toys for their structure and style. Current events and iconic locations fuse together in their work, creating narrative portraits of the places they depict.

➡ TOP: **OSLO / NORWAY**, 2007, FOR ROOM FOR ART, ADD.: KULTURBYRÅET MESÉN (AGENCY), PUBL. AS BILLBOARD IN OSLO CENTRAL STATION ‖‖ BOTTOM: **LOS ANGELES / USA**, 2009, PUBL. IN THE LOS ANGELES TIMES MAGAZINE

NILS-PETTER EKWALL
SNOWFALL TO OUTFALL

➥ CALIFORNIA / USA, SAN FRANCISCO, SANTA CLARA, SILICON VALLEY, SAN FRANCISCO BAY, PALO ALTO, TRACY, MODESTO, PACIFIC OCEAN, MODESTO, YOSEMITE NATIONAL PARK, SACRAMENTO / USA, 2012, FOR OBSCURA DIGITAL AND SAN FRANCISCO PUBLIC UTILITIES, PRODUCER: MARIA WALCUTT, ART DIRECTION: MARC MELZER FROM OBSCURA DIGITAL, PUBL. ON / AS INTERACTIVE DIGITAL CANVAS ESTRID MAGAZINE

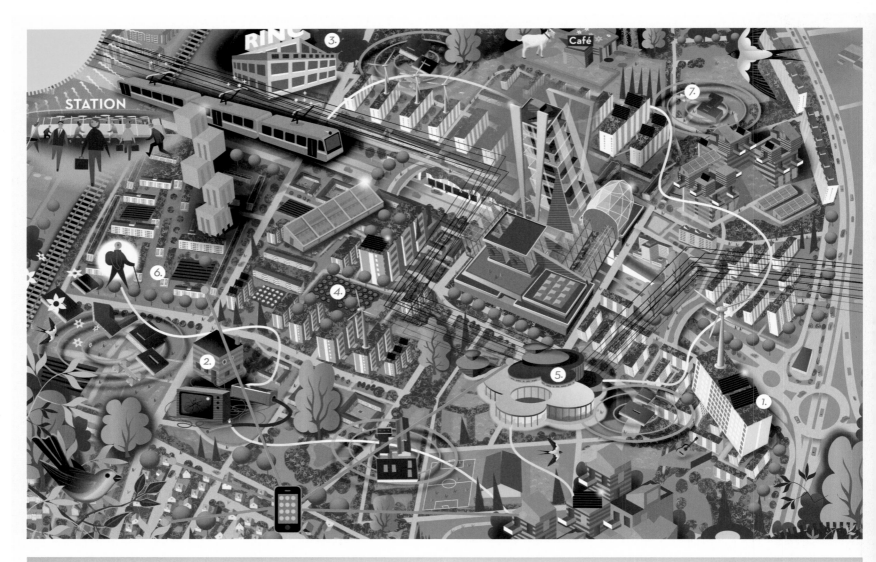

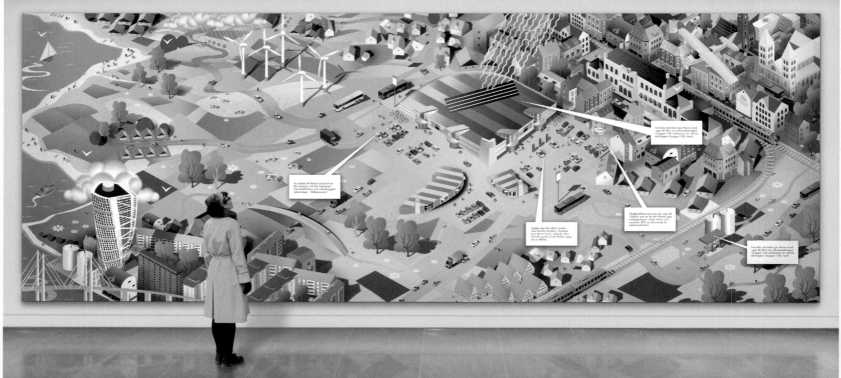

NILS-PETTER EKWALL
ROSENGÅRD / NOVA LUND

♦ The large scale maps by Nils-Petter Ekwall are detailed views of vast spaces. A map created for the city of Malmö playfully highlights environmentally friendly improvements to an impoverished neighborhood. His 9-meter mural of a shopping center in Sweden distorts the region's geography so that the building appears to be at the center of a neighboring town.

➥ TOP: **ROSENGÅRD CITY DISTRICT, MALMÖ / SWEDEN**, 2008, FOR MALMÖ CITY PLANNING OFFICE, PUBL. IN BROSCHURE ‖‖ BOTTOM: **SKÅNE/SCANIA: LUND, MALMÖ, ØRESUND BRIDGE / SWEDEN**, 2011, FOR NOVA LUND, UNIBAIL-RODAMCO

ROD HUNT

CIRCLE LINE SIGHTSEEING CRUISES 101
NEW YORK ATTRACTIONS

◆ The vibrant and detailed maps created by *Rod Hunt* for tourism clients reflect the
fun and leisurely nature of the tourism business. The maps encompass large areas,
such as the 101 sights on the Circle Line cruise around Manhattan.

➥ **NEW YORK CITY / USA**, 2012, FOR NEW YORK CRUISE LINES, INC.,
DESIGN DIRECTOR: NOBLE CUMMING, NEW YORK CRUISE LINES, INC.

SAVONLINNA

RIGA

OSLO

EDINBURGH

BERLIN

CORK

LONDON

BRESLAU

RUHR-
GEBIET

BAYREUTH
MÜNCHEN

BORDEAUX

SALZBURG

WIEN

GUCA

RAVENNA

AVIGNON

SSABON

ARANJUEZ

BARCELONA

PALERMO

ATHEN

155

MALUNG

OCKELBO
12

HÖGBO 6
GÄVLE
E4
SANDVIKEN 14
Cu
FALUN
STORVIK 16

1
2 3 BORLÄNGE

19 ULFSHYTTAN

SÄFSEN 18
LUDVIKA 8

GRÄNGESBERG 5
15 SMEDJEBACKEN

10 11 NORBERG

4 FAGERSTA
Fe

13 RIDDARHYTTAN
Ag
VÄSTERÅS
17 20 GALLERY ASTLEY
STRÅSSA 21

LOKA BRUNN 7

NORA 9

E18 KARLSKOGA
ÖREBRO
E20

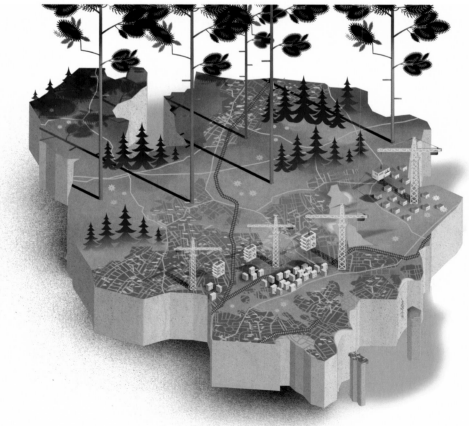

NILS-PETTER EKWALL
FINLAND /
BERGSLAGEN / TÄBY

♦ Many of Nils-Petter Ekwall's maps focus on topics relating to the Scandinavian countries, including the unusual attractions of the Bergslagen mining district and the abandonment of Sweden by Swedish-Finnish authors for the greater European market.

➡ LEFT PAGE: FINLAND, SWEDEN, BALTIC SEA, 2010, FOR VI MAGAZINE ||| TOP: BERGSLAGEN: ÖREBRO, KARLSTAD, GÄVLE, OCKELBO, VÄSTERÅS / SWEDEN, 2010, FOR FILTER MAGAZINE & INTEREST GROUP BERGSLAGET, PUBL. IN URKRAFT MAGAZINE ||| BOTTOM: TÄBY, SWEDEN, 2010, FOR CLINTON AGENCY AND TÄBY MUNICIPALITY, PUBL. IN ESTRID MAGAZINE

Santiago de Compostela
Gijón
Santander
Bilbao
Picos de Europa
Girona
Salamanca
Segovia
Barcelona
Madrid
Valencia
Palma
Seville
Málaga
Cádiz
Santa Cruz de Tenerife
Las Palmas de Gran Canaria

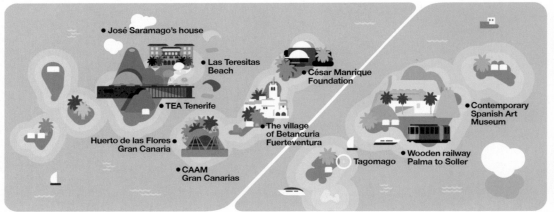

José Saramago's house
Las Teresitas Beach
César Manrique Foundation
TEA Tenerife
Contemporary Spanish Art Museum
Huerto de las Flores Gran Canaria
The village of Betancuria Fuerteventura
CAAM Gran Canarias
Tagomago
Wooden railway Palma to Soller

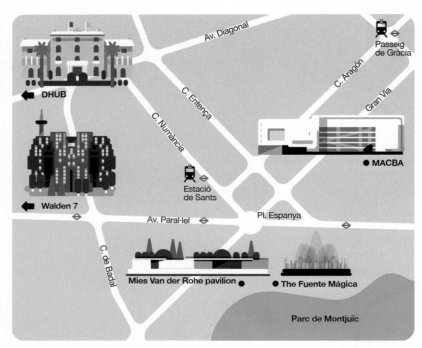

Av. Diagonal
Passeig de Gràcia
C. Aragón
Gran Via
DHUB
C. Entença
C. Numància
MACBA
Estació de Sants
Walden 7
Av. Paral·lel
Pl. Espanya
C. de Badal
Mies Van der Rohe pavilion
The Fuente Mágica
Parc de Montjuïc

Museum of Fine Arts
Casa de Pilatos
Av. Menéndez Pelayo
Casa de la Memoria
Av. de la República de Argentina
Av. Maria Luisa
Maria Luisa Park
Paseo de las Delicias
Av. Juan Pablo II
Itálica

HEY STUDIO
THAILAND / SPAIN

♦ Drawing on their multidisciplinary background, Hey Studio fuses infographics, maps, and iconic illustrations. Their work for special travel editions of Monocle Magazine illustrates the most important sights, buildings, cities, and beaches in Spain and Thailand.

➥ LEFT PAGE: **SPAIN**, 2011, RIGHT PAGE: **THAILAND**, 2012, BOTH FOR MONOCLE MAGAZINE

KHUAN + KTRON
FRANCE / ITALY

➡ LEFT PAGE: **FRANCE**, 2010, RIGHT PAGE: **ITALY**, 2010, BOTH FOR WEEKEND MAGAZINE

KHUAN + KTRON

ICELAND / AUSTRALIA / WESTERN EUROPE

♦ The vintage illustration style of the design collective *KHUAN+KTRON* depicts worlds with stylized geographical elements that are recognizable but idealized. Their maps tackle a broad range of issues from cultural stereotypes to classic tourist attractions.

➥ LEFT PAGE: **ICELAND**, 2010, FOR WEEKEND KNACK ⫴ TOP: **AUSTRALIA**, 2010, FOR COMMONWEALTH BANK, ART DIRECTION: BMF, PUBL. IN SEPARATE PUBLICATION ⫴ BOTTOM: **WESTERN EUROPE**, 2011, FOR THE GOOD LIFE MAGAZINE

KHUAN + KTRON
GOOD TOYS EUROPE

➡ EUROPE, 2011, PUBL. IN THE GOOD LIFE MAGAZINE

MASERATI

NOSTRUM

HELLO YELLOW STUDIO
MUSIC MAP

➥ WORLD, 2007, PERSONAL PROJECT

LOULOU & TUMMIE
SMART ELECTRIQUE DRIVE

♦ Lingering between fiction and reality, *Loulou & Tummie's* maps represent idealized versions of the places they depict. Their city map of Paris became an online game used to promote the launch of an electric car.

➡ **FRANCE**, 2012, FOR BBDO PARIS – MERCEDES BENZ SMART, AGENT: SHOP AROUND

LOTTA NIEMINEN

NEW YORK CITY / LISBON

➥ LEFT: **CENTRAL PARK, NEW YORK CITY / USA**, RIGHT: **LISBON / PORTUGAL**, 2011,
FOR TATE PUBLISHING

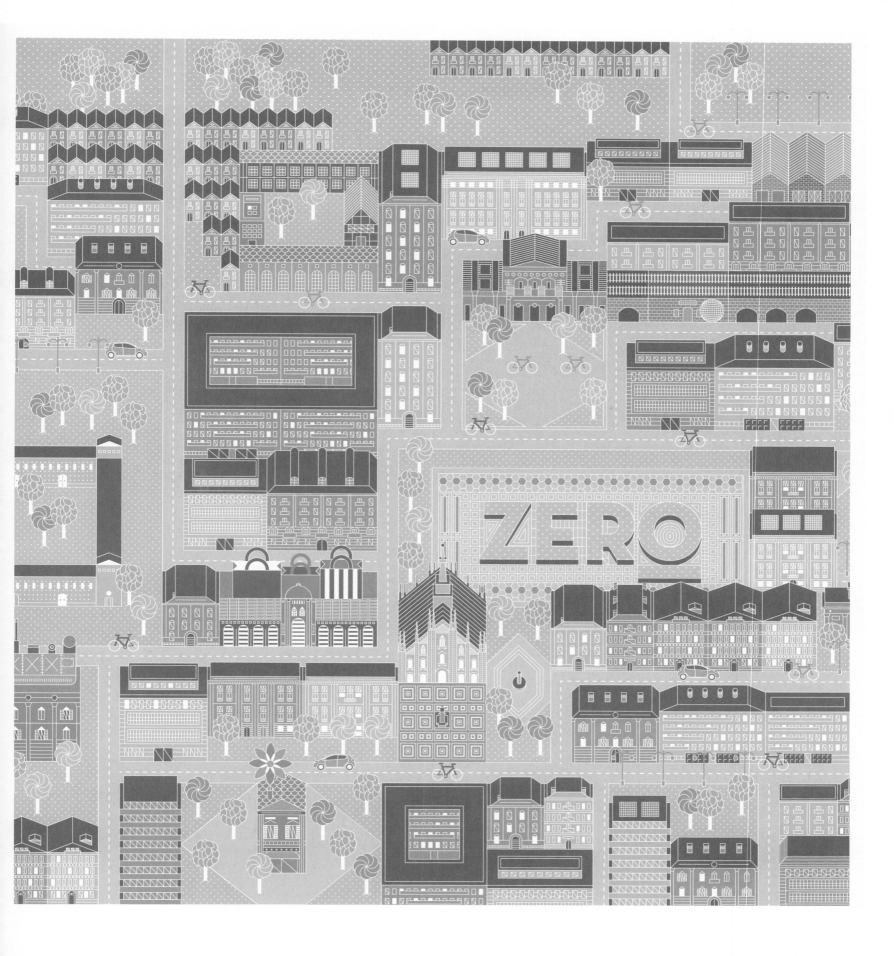

LA TIGRE
ZERO MAP COVERS

♦ *La Tigre* designed two map covers for the Italian magazine **ZERO** for its issue devoted to the Yaris hybrid car. The map of Milan combines a concise graphic style with detailed content to transform city maps into a dense pattern. Each location is emphasized with a color palette of complementary colors.

➥ **MILAN / ITALY**, 2012, FOR ZERO MAGAZINE, ART DIRECTION: STEFANO TEMPORIN & ALESSANDRO BUSSENI

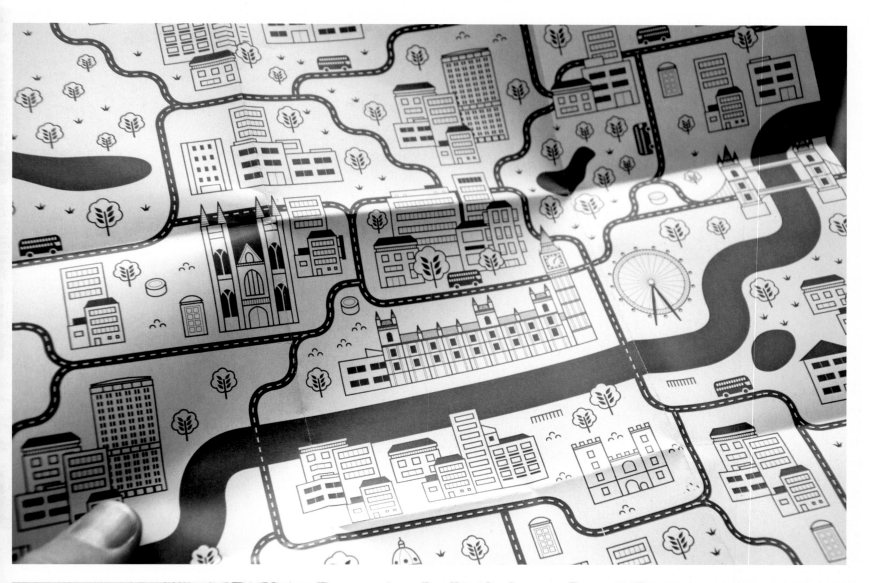

DEEAIT X CREATES
LONDON CITY MAP

◆ The London City Map relies solely on graphic representations of popular land-marks to orient the viewer within the city of London. It comes in a variety of sizes from small postcards and notebooks to large posters.

➥ **LONDON / UK**, 2011, PERSONAL PROJECT

VESA SAMMALISTO
FEX FELLINI — CITIES EP

➡ TOP: **LONDON / UK, 2010,** BOTTOM: **HELSINKI /
FINLAND**, 2010, FOR FEX FELLINI / GLOBELLE
RECORD LABEL

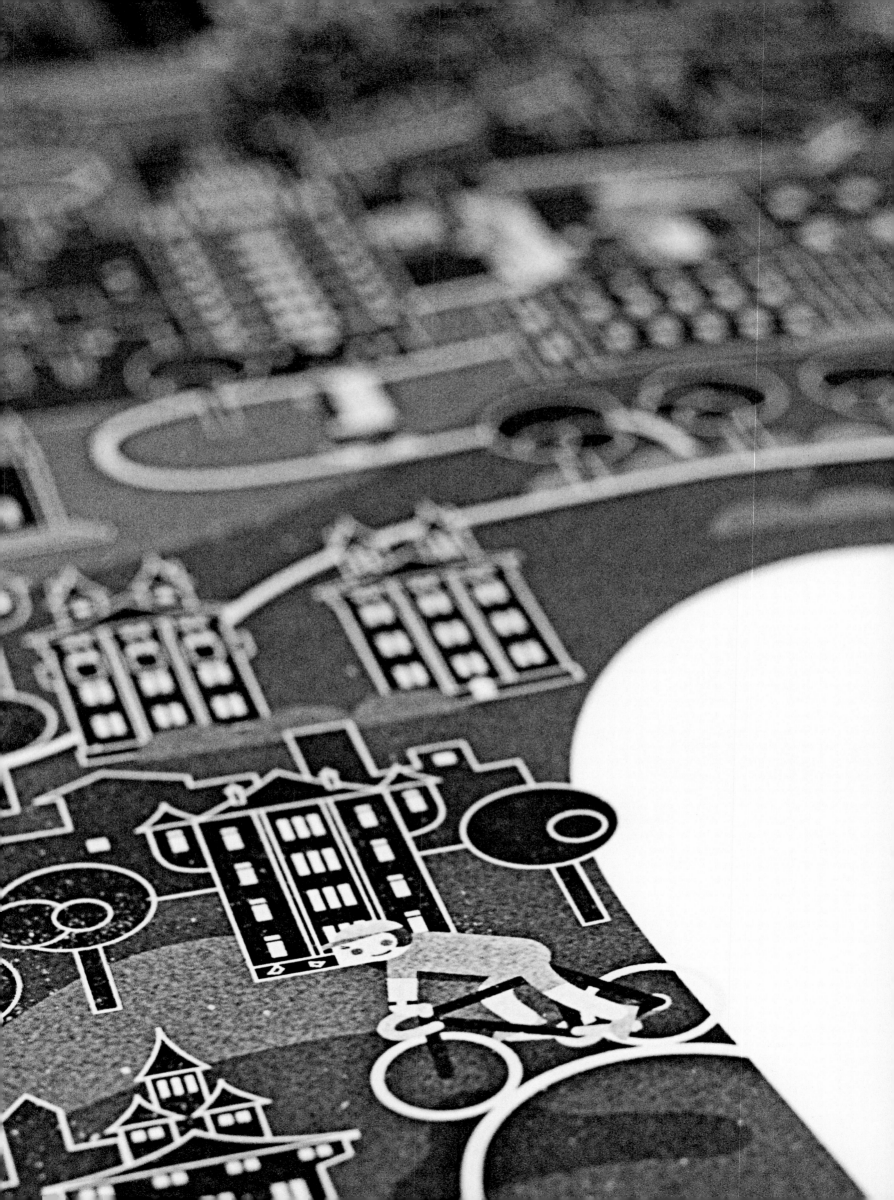

ILOVEDUST

MOSCOW, NEW YORK, LONDON

➥ LEFT PAGE: **MOSCOW / RUSSIA**, RIGHT PAGE: **NEW YORK / USA**, **LONDON / UK**,
2011, PERSONAL PROJECT

LONDON
CAPITAL OF THE WORLD

SAM'S

SELFRIDGES & CO

THE WOLSELEY

THE DORCHESTER

BRUTON STREET & BOND STREET

THE BARBICAN CENTRE

LUXEMBOURG

OTTAWA

THE HAGUE

GENEVA

NEW FUTURE GRAPHIC
LONDON, CAPITAL OF THE WORLD /
MONOCLE MAPS

♦ The maps created by *New Future Graphic* for various publications present important landmarks and venues from a variety of cities. Each location is seen from a ground level perspective, which highlights a panoramic view of what the city has to offer.

➥ LEFT PAGE: LONDON / UK, 2010, FOR DIE WELTWOCHE MAGAZINE ||| RIGHT PAGE: LUXEMBOURG, OTTAWA / CANADA, THE HAGUE / NETHERLANDS, GENEVA / SWITZERLAND, 2010, FOR MONOCLE MAGAZINE

HERB LESTER ASSOCIATES
CITY MAPS

♦ The city maps by *Herb Lester Associates* are written and illustrated by locals for visitors and longtime residents alike. The engaging designs and illustrations reflect the unusual content, which combines humor and curiosity, with a strong sense for visual aesthetics.

➥ **PARIS / FRANCE, AUSTIN / USA, BARCELONA / SPAIN, CHICAGO / USA,** 2012, ILLUSTRATION: CURTIS JINKINS, MIKE MCQUADE, JAVIER GARCIA, KELLI ANDERSON; PHOTOGRAPHY: STEPHANIE LYNN

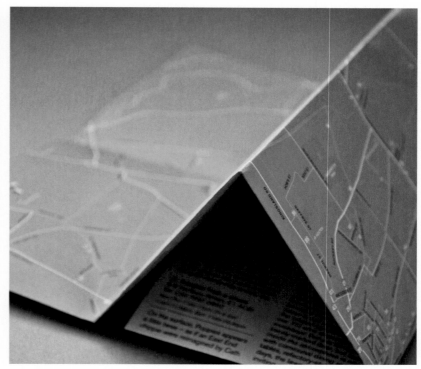

BRENT COUCHMAN

AN EAST LONDON COMPANION /
A GLASGOW COMPANION

♦ An extensive and quirky list of 50 things to do and see in the city of Glasgow, this unusual map includes an unchanged 1960s pub and the city's architectural salvage yard. Designed and illustrated by *Brent Couchman*, it was commissioned for a series of city guides by HERB LESTER ASSOCIATES for travelers who prefer to explore the eccentric side of a city.

➥ LONDON / UK, GLASGOW / SCOTLAND, 2011,
FOR HERB LESTER ASSOCIATES

181

FERNANDO VOLKEN TOGNI

24 HOURS IN
LONDON, HANOI, CAIRO

♦ Combining bold color palettes and vector shapes with layers of detailed information, *Fernando Volken Togni's* 24 Hours series distills the unique characteristics of international cities. Presented in a loosely gridded format, iconic elements are visually connected to one another to create a complete portrait of the city.

➥ **LONDON / UK, HANOI / VIETNAM, CAIRO / EGYPT**, 2012, FIRST PUBLISHED BY QATAR AIRWAYS'S ORYX MAGAZINE

A GUIDE TO THE USUAL & UNUSUAL BY *Herb Lester Associates*

BRENT COUCHMAN
A GLASGOW COMPANION

➡ **GLASGOW / SCOTLAND**, 2011, FOR HERB LESTER
ASSOCIATES

WEEKEND WINE TASTINGS

EVERY SATURDAY FROM 1-3PM, COME TRY SOME OF THE WINES WE FEEL ARE SPECIAL ENOUGH TO SHOWCASE — EXCLAIMING, "YOU REALLY SHOULD TRY THIS!" EACH TASTING CONSISTS OF TEN OR SO ESTATE BOTTLED WINES POURED BY THE 3CUPS CREW AND CURATED BY JAY MURRIE, OUR WINE BUYER AND RESIDENT VINO EXPERT WITH A PASSION FOR WINE AND FOOD BACKED BY OVER TEN YEARS IN THE FIELD.

FREE! 1-3 AM PM

SATURDAYS

1 DATE S M T W T F S

919.968.8993

WWW.3CUPS.NET

3 CUPS

ALWAYS UNIQUE, ALWAYS ENGAGING, AND MOST OF ALL, ALWAYS GREAT TASTING

ALWAYS FOUND AT 3CUPS

VISIT OUR WEBSITE FOR UPCOMING TASTINGS

STORE HOURS: M → SAT 8AM → 7PM

SUNDAY CLOSED

227 SOUTH ELLIOTT RD
CHAPEL HILL, NC 27514

NEXT TO THE WHOLE FOODS SHOPPING CENTER

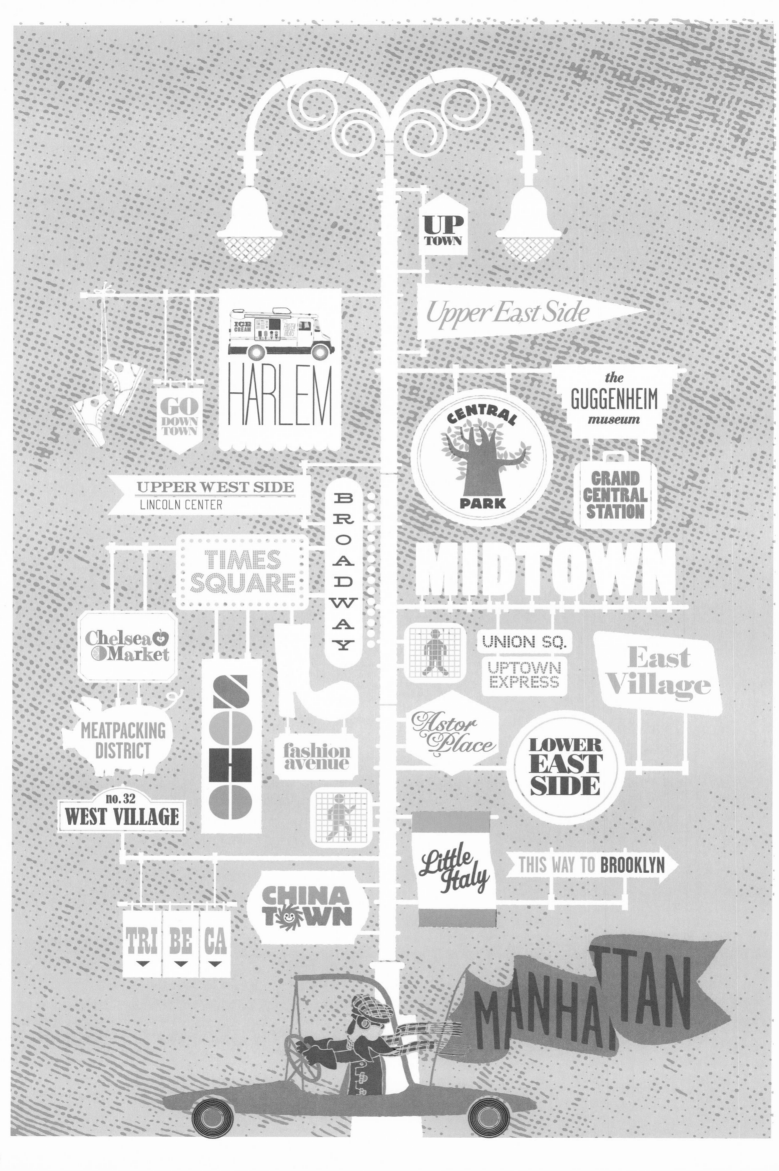

JIM DATZ

CITY POSTERS

◆ For his series of screen prints celebrating iconic city neighborhoods, *Jim Datz* arranged landmarks into a loosely mapped grid of typography and illustration. Drawn in a vintage-inspired style, the posters recall the previous eras that helped make these neighborhoods what they are today.

➡ LEFT PAGE: **MANHATTAN, NEW YORK / USA**, 2008, PERSONAL PROJECT, COLLABORATION WITH THREE POTATO FOUR ||| RIGHT PAGE: **SAN FRANCISCO / USA**, 2012, PERSONAL PROJECT

EDWARD JUAN
TORONTO

♦ The illustrated maps by *Edward Juan* focus on biking and walking trails in North American cities. By drawing them in conjunction with urban landmarks, he emphasizes the alternative possibilities for transportation and outdoor recreation in each city.

➥ **TORONTO / CANADA**, 2011, PERSONAL PROJECT

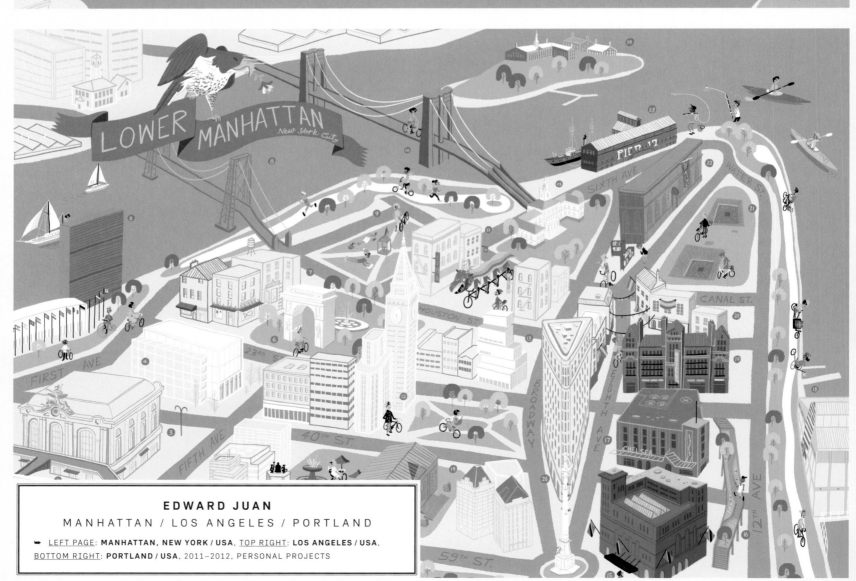

EDWARD JUAN

MANHATTAN / LOS ANGELES / PORTLAND

→ LEFT PAGE: **MANHATTAN, NEW YORK / USA**, TOP RIGHT: **LOS ANGELES / USA**,
BOTTOM RIGHT: **PORTLAND / USA**, 2011–2012, PERSONAL PROJECTS

JIMMY GLEESON
WE ♥ MELBOURNE

♦ The cityscape for We Heart Melbourne is based on a sprawling map of the north and south sides of Melbourne's famous Yarra River. Illustrated for a collection of souvenir home wares for Melbourne's iconic URBAN ATTITUDE stores, this series of simplified geometric shapes features all of Melbourne's main landmarks along with a few hidden treasures.

➥ MELBOURNE / AUSTRALIA, 2012, FOR URBAN ATTITUDE (MELBOURNE), PUBL. IN TIMEOUT MAGAZINE, PHOTOGRAPHY: DAVID GREEN

MIKE LEMANSKI

LONDON

➤ **LONDON / UK**, 2011, FOR NEW LEAVES STUDIO

INVISIBLE CREATURE, INC.

2011 SOUTH LAKE UNION BLOCK PARTY

◆ As an advertisement for a neighborhood block party, *Invisible Creature, Inc.* created a poster that functions as a guide to the amenities and things to do in the neighborhood. The colorful, bold shapes of the illustration create a complex and vibrant environment that reflects the energy of the area.

➥ **SEATTLE / USA**, 2011, FOR VULCAN, PUBL. IN SEATTLE METROPOLITAN MAGAZINE

VESA SAMMALISTO
HARTWALL LAPIN KULTA

♦ Created for World Design Capital Helsinki, this map features the main events and
venues sponsored by the Finnish brewery Harwall Lapin Kulta.

➥ HELSINKI / FINLAND, 2012, FOR HARTWALL, ART DIRECTOR: KIMMO KORHONEN,
USED FOR PRINT ADVERTISEMENTS / PACKAGE ILLUSTRATIONS DURING WORLD
DESIGN CAPITAL HELSINKI YEAR 2012

VESA SAMMALISTO
MALLORCA / NORTHERN ITALY

➡ LEFT PAGE: **MALLORCA / SPAIN**, 2011, RIGHT PAGE: **NORTHERN ITALY**, 2011,
BOTH FOR DIE WELTWOCHE STIL, DESIGNER: GIAN GISIGER (BUREAU MIRKO
BORSCHE)

carniato

EUROPE

ANTOINE CORBINEAU
PRODOTTI TRADIZIONALI ITALIANI /
OPS2 ALMANACH

➤ LEFT PAGE: **ITALY**, 2012, FOR CARNIATO EUROPE, PUBL. AS POSTER FOR CAR-
NIATO EUROPE CLIENTS, ADD.: PLACE ROUGE ‖‖ RIGHT PAGE: **FRANCE**, 2011, FOR
OPS2.COM, GREETINGS POSTER

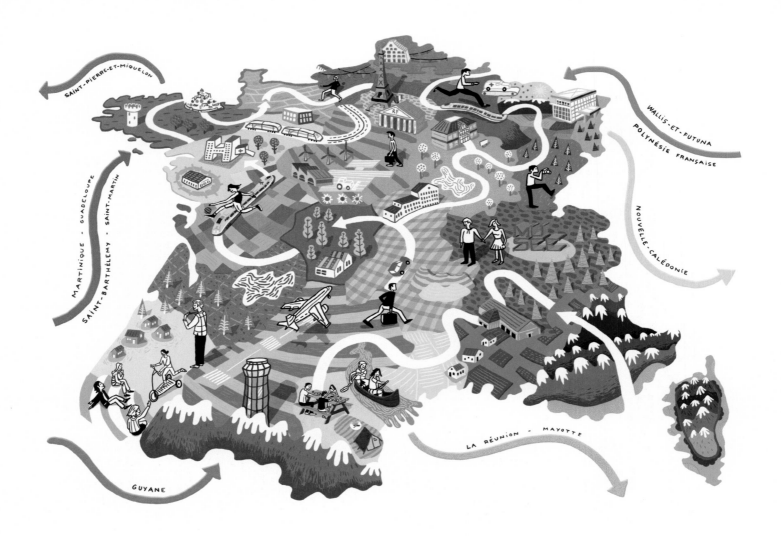

Illustration: Antoine Corbineau

ANTOINE CORBINEAU

DECENTRALIZED FRANCE / BTHERE MAGAZINE MAPS / STREET NAMES SHAPE THE CITY

♦ *Antoine Corbineau's* colorful maps are fanciful interpretations of the cities and neighborhoods he illustrates. For the inflight magazine of BRUSSELS AIRLINES, he completed a series of neighborhood maps from various European cities. His map of Italian wine regions was reproduced on posters for clients of an Italian wine and food distributor.

➥ TOP LEFT: **FRANCE**, 2012, FOR EURO RSCG PARIS, PUBL. IN CNFPT MAGAZINE ⅠⅠⅠ BOTTOM LEFT: **BUDAPEST / HUNGARY**, 2012, FOR INK-GLOBAL.COM, PUBL. IN BTHERE MAGAZINE / BRUSSELS MAGAZINE ⅠⅠⅠ RIGHT PAGE: **ANTWERP / BELGIUM**, 2012, FOR INK-GLOBAL.COM, PUBL. IN BTHERE MAGAZINE / BRUSSELS AIRLINES

MASAKO KUBO

CRUISE THE SEVEN SEAS

♦ The world map by *Masako Kubo* introduces exotic cruises around the world by illustrating the nature and landmarks associated with each tour.

➥ **WORLD**, 2012, FOR NOBLE CALEDONIA, PUBL. IN THE DAILY TELEGRAPH, ART DIRECTOR: SALLY FARR

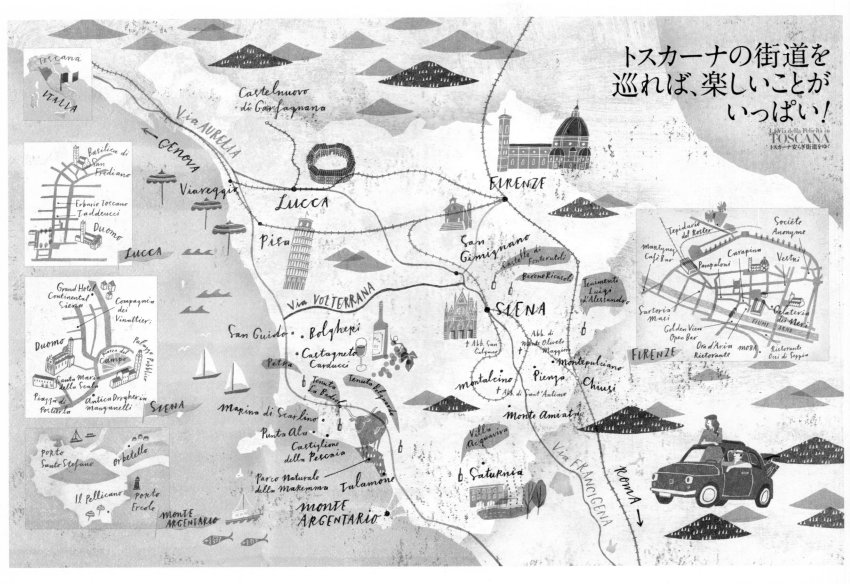

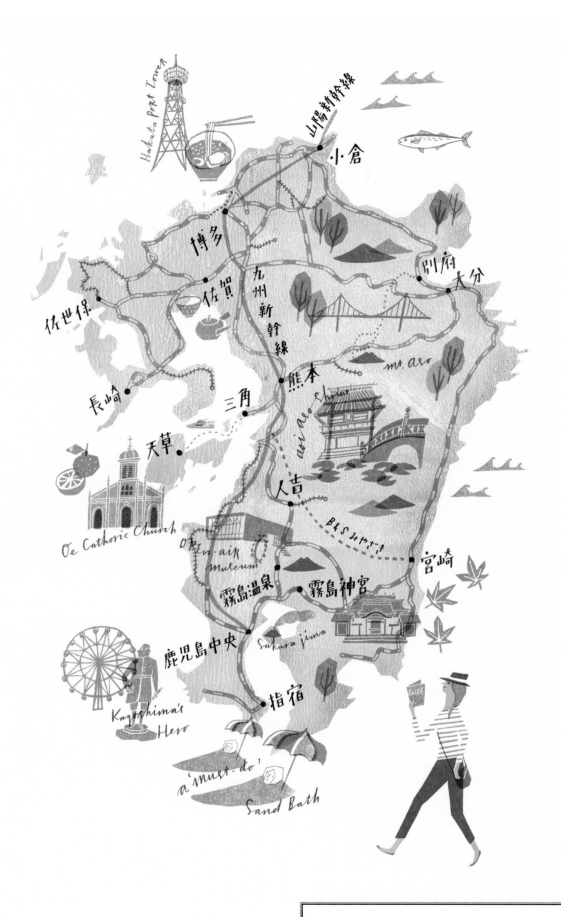

MASAKO KUBO

TOSCANA / SAMANI AND ERIMO GREEN MAP /
KYUSHU TRAIN ALL STARS

◆ Using a friendly, sketchbook-like style, the illustrations of *Masako Kubo* introduce travelers to various international destinations. Her map of Kyushu, Japan, helps promote train travel in the region by suggesting a variety of train-accessible places and activities in the area. An illustration of Tuscany highlights the region's major cities and attractions including local railways, architecture, wineries, hot springs resorts, and seaside towns, while a map of Samani and Erimo, Hokkaido, focuses on the abundant nature surrounding Mt. Apoi.

➥ TOP LEFT: **TUSCANY / ITALY**, 2011, BOTTOM LEFT: **SAMANI AND ERIMO, HOKKAIDO / JAPAN**, 2011, FOR KIRAKUSHA, SOTOKOTO, ART DIRECTION: MICHIO SUZUKI (ADCAMP), DESIGN: ATSUSHI MUTA (ADCAMP) ||| RIGHT PAGE: **KYUSHU / JAPAN**, 2011, FOR BUNGEISHUNJU, CREA TRAVELLER

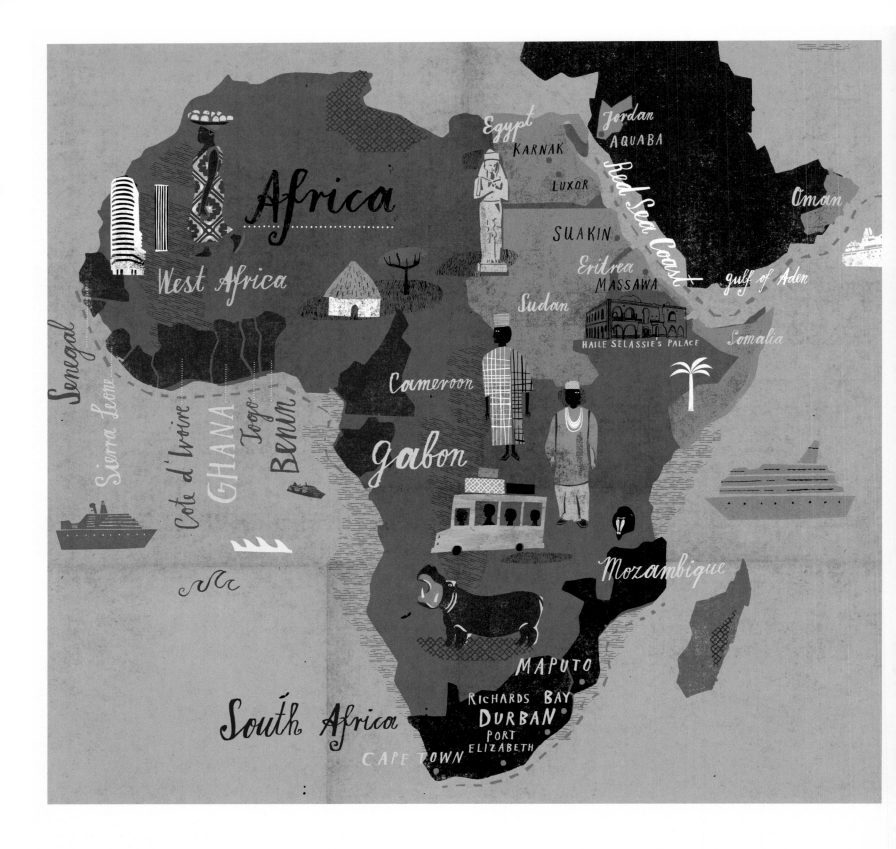

MARTIN HAAKE

CRUISING AROUND AFRICA / WINE IN
SUEDTIROL / SERVICEPLAN IN MUNICH

♦ Color and hand lettering give personality to the countries, regions, and cities in
Martin Haake's maps. His illustration of Munich provides an overview of the city's
most interesting places and things to do, while his map of the world shows international places of happiness.

➥ LEFT PAGE: **AFRICA**, 2011, FOR THOMAS COOK ‖‖ TOP RIGHT: **SUEDTIROL**, 2012,
FOR ZEIT VERLAG, PUBL. IN SUEDTIROL MAGAZINE BOTTOM RIGHT: **MUNICH /
GERMANY**, 2012, FOR SERVICEPLAN, ART DIRECTOR: BEATE GRONEMANN

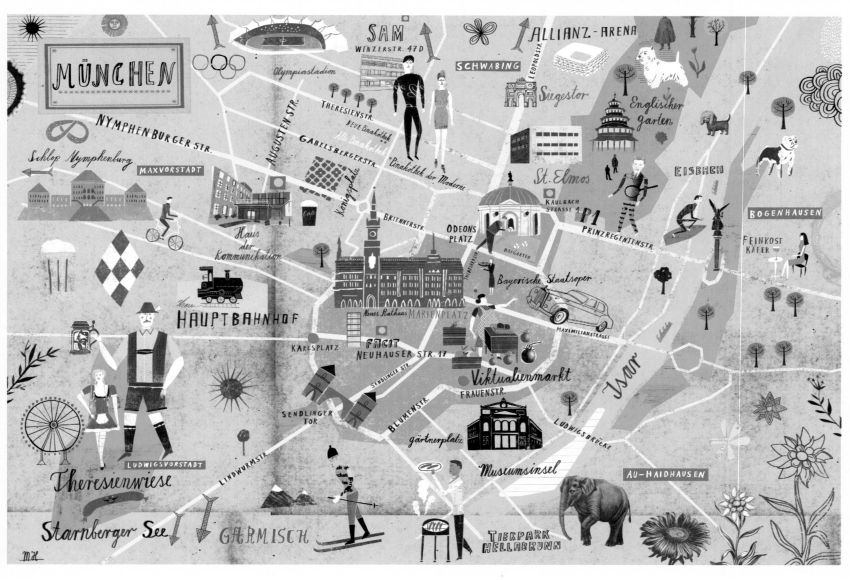

MARTIN HAAKE
HAPPY PLANET

☞ WORLD, 2012, FOR ENKELFAEHIG MAGAZINE, ART DIRECTOR: FRANK VON GRAFENSTEIN

LOTTA NIEMINEN
ANNUAL REPORT

➡ **WORLD**, 2012, FOR SUEZ ENVIRONNEMENT ANNUAL REPORT

ruotsi
38,8

suomi
35,9

34
viro

latvia 33.3

liettua
31.9

tanska
39

alankomaat
37,4

puola
30,6

saksa
35,8

tsekki
33,7

slovakia
32,2

belgia
31,4

luxemburg
30,3

unkari
28,4

itävalta
34,6

romania
30,6

irlanti
34,6

englanti
37

ranska
35

slovenia
33,4

bulgaria
29,5

italia
29,4

kreikka
31,5

portugali
36,1

espanja
32,5

malta
28,1

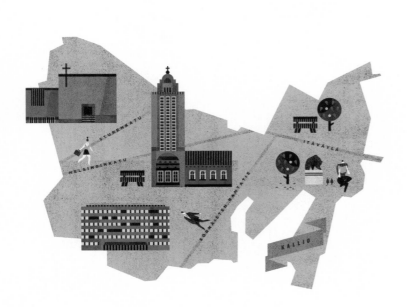

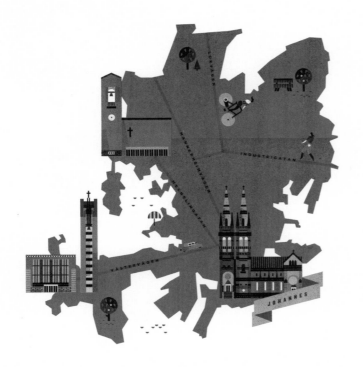

LOTTA NIEMINEN
WORKING / HELSINKI MAPS

♦ *Lotta Nieminen's* slightly abstracted geographical forms use color to emphasize national and neighborhood borders. For an editorial in the customer magazine of the **SOCIAL INSURANCE INSTITUTION OF FINLAND**, she created a map that illustrates the average number of years worked in the EU countries. Her 21-map series of the **PARISH UNION OF HELSKINKI** illustrated the organization's welcome brochures.

➥ <u>LEFT PAGE</u>: **EUROPE**, 2010, FOR KELA, SOSIAALIVAKUUTUS MAGAZINE III
<u>RIGHT PAGE</u>: **HELSINKI / FINLAND**, 2011, FOR PARISH UNION OF HELSINKI

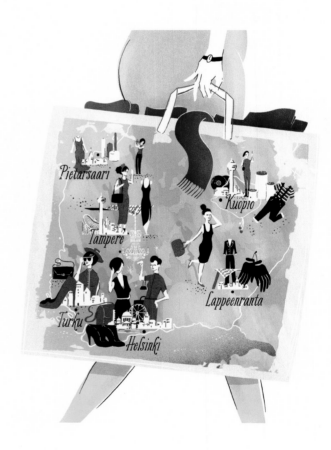

VESA SAMMALISTO

THAMES DIAMOND JUBILEE PAGEANT /
HYVINKÄÄ / GLORIA / MANHATTAN

♦ Known for his dynamic and detailed maps that highlight attractions, landmarks, transportation, commerce, culture, and design, *Vesa Sammalisto* has illustrated places all around the world for magazines, ad campaigns, and cultural events.

➥ TOP: **RIVER THAMES, LONDON / UK**, 2012, FOR HEATHROW TRAVELLER |||
BOTTOM LEFT: **HYVINKÄÄ / FINLAND**, 2011, FOR CITY OF HYVINKÄÄ, CREATIVE
DIRECTOR: TIMO BERRY (BOTH), DESIGNER: IIRA OIVO (BOTH) ||| BOTTOM RIGHT:
SOUTHERN FINLAND, 2011, FOR GLORIA / SANOMA MAGAZINES, ART DIRECTOR:
TIMO TERVOJA, PUBL. IN GLORIA / SANOMA MAGAZINES ||| RIGHT PAGE: **MANHAT-
TAN, NEW YORK / USA**, 2012, FOR WALKER TOWER (NY), CREATIVE DIRECTOR:
RICHARD PANDISCIO & DESIGNER: MIKE GREEN FROM PANDISCIO CO., PUBL. IN
WALKER TOWER — ENGINEERS REPORT BOOKLET

ARCTIC OCEAN

EUROPE

ASIA

AFRICA

PACIFIC OCEAN

INDIAN OCEAN

AUSTRALASIA

OWEN GATLEY

THE MAP OF DISCOVERY

♦ The Map of Discovery was printed as a children's poster that depicts the place of origin of different inventions from around the world.

➥ **WORLD**, 2012, FOR THE TIMES NEWSPAPER (UK)

ANDREW JOYCE
JAPAN
www.doodlesandstuff.com
PAGE 30 / 31

ANDY COUNCIL
UNITED KINGDOM
www.andycouncil.co.uk
PAGE 124 / 125

ANNA FISKE
NORWAY
www.annafiske.com
PAGE 122 / 123

ANNA HÄRLIN
GERMANY
www.annahaerlin.de
PAGE 14, 135

ANTOINE CORBINEAU
FRANCE
www.antoinecorbineau.com
PAGE 200–205

BAKEA
SPAIN
www.bakea.tumblr.com
PAGE 137

BORGARMYND
ICELAND
www.borgarmynd.com
PAGE 26–29

BRENT COUCHMAN
USA
www.brentcouchman.com
PAGE 138, 181, 183

CARLOS ROMO MELGAR
SPAIN
www.c31913.com
PAGE 104

CAROLINE SELMES
FRANCE
www.carolineselmes.com
PAGE 118 / 119

CHRIS DENT
UNITED KINGDOM
www.chrisdent.co.uk
PAGE 140

CINTA ARRIBAS
SPAIN
www.cintarribas.es
PAGE 86

DAVID RYAN ROBINSON
UNITED KINGDOM
www.davidryanrobinson.com
PAGE 32 / 33

DEANNA HALSALL
UNITED KINGDOM
www.deannahalsall.co.uk
PAGE 15–17

DEEAIT X CREATES
AUSTRIA
www.deeait.com
PAGE 172 / 173

DENSITY DESIGN
ITALY
www.densitydesign.org
PAGE 96 / 97

DOROTHY
UNITED KINGDOM
www.wearedorothy.com
PAGE 10 / 11

EBOY
GERMANY
www.eboy.com
PAGE 148 / 149

EDWARD JUAN
CANADA
www.hjolisland.com
PAGE 188–191

ESTHER AARTS
NETHERLANDS
www.estheraarts.nl
PAGE 8 / 9

FAMILLE SUMMERBELLE
UNITED KINGDOM
www.famillesummerbelle.com
PAGE 48–51

FERNANDO VOLKEN TOGNI
UNITED KINGDOM
www.fernandovt.com
PAGE 182

FRANK HÖHNE
GERMANY
www.frankhoehne.de
PAGE 132 / 133

FREECELL
USA
www.frcll.com
PAGE 141

GEN DESIGN STUDIO
PORTUGAL
www.gen.pt
PAGE 98 / 99

GOLDEN SECTION GRAPHICS
GERMANY
www.golden-section-graphics.com
PAGE 92–95

HARRIET LYALL
UNITED KINGDOM
www.harrietlyall.com
PAGE 115

HELLO YELLOW STUDIO
NETHERLANDS
www.helloyellowstudio.com
PAGE 60 / 61, 142, 166 / 167

HERB LESTER ASSOCIATES
UNITED KINGDOM
www.herblester.com
PAGE 180

HEY STUDIO
SPAIN
www.heystudio.es
PAGE 158 / 159

HUMAN EMPIRE
GERMANY
www.humanempire.com
PAGE 154 / 155

ILOVEDUST
UNITED KINGDOM
www.ilovedust.com
PAGE 136, 176 / 177

INVISIBLE CREATURE, INC.
USA
www.invisiblecreature.com
PAGE 194 / 195

JAMES GULLIVER HANCOCK
USA
www.jamesgulliverhancock.com
PAGE 36–39, 113

JAN FELIKS KALLWEJT
POLAND
www.kallwejt.com
PAGE 105

JENNI SPARKS
UNITED KINGDOM
www.jennisparks.com
PAGE 34 / 35

JIM DATZ
USA
www.neitherfishnorfowl.com
PAGE 186 / 187

JIMMY GLEESON
AUSTRALIA
www.jimmygleeson.com
PAGE 192

JOÃO LAURO FONTE
UNITED KINGDOM
www.laurofonte.com
PAGE 56 / 57

JODY BARTON
UNITED KINGDOM
www.jodybarton.co.uk
PAGE 58

JON FRICKEY
GERMANY
www.jonfrickey.com
PAGE 12 / 13

JUDITH SCHALANSKY
GERMANY
www.atlas-der-abgelegenen-inseln.de
PAGE 88 / 91

KATE HYDE
UNITED KINGDOM
www.kate-hyde.co.uk
PAGE 114

KATHERINE BAXTER
UNITED KINGDOM
www.katherinebaxter.com
PAGE 19, 22 / 23

KEITH ROBINSON
UNITED KINGDOM
www.keith-robinson.com
PAGE 24 / 25

KHUAN + KTRON
BELGIUM
www.khuan-ktron.com
PAGE 160–165

LA TIGRE
ITALY
www.latigre.net
PAGE 171

LAMOSCA
SPAIN
www.lamosca.com
PAGE 102 / 103

LORENZO PETRANTONI
ITALY
www.lorenzopetrantoni.com
PAGE 54 / 55

LOTTA NIEMINEN
USA
www.lottanieminen.com
PAGE 170, 214–217

LOULOU & TUMMIE
NETHERLANDS
www.louflouandtummie.com
PAGE 139, 168 / 169

MARILENA PERILLI
USA
www.artrepnyc.com
PAGE 44

MARLENA ZUBER
CANADA
www.maps.marlenazuber.com
PAGE 110–112

MARTA PUCHALA
UNITED KINGDOM
www.cargocollective.com/martapuchala
PAGE 46

MARTIN HAAKE
GERMANY
www.martinhaake.de
PAGE 210–213

MASAKO KUBO
JAPAN
www.masakokubo.co.uk
PAGE 206–209

MATT LAWSON
USA
www.mattlawsondesign.com
PAGE 184 / 185

MATTHEW RANGEL
USA
www.rangelstudio.com
PAGE 68–73

MED NESS
SINGAPORE
www.be.net/ahmericarnation
PAGE 145

MIKE LEMANSKI
UNITED KINGDOM
www.mikelemanski.co.uk
PAGE 4 / 5, 193

NATIONAL GEOGRAPHIC
USA
www.nationalgeographic.com
PAGE 74–76

NEW FUTURE GRAPHIC
UNITED KINGDOM
www.newfuturegraphic.co.uk
PAGE 178 / 179

NILS-PETTER EKWALL
SWEDEN
www.nilspetter.se
PAGE 150–152, 156 / 157

NINA WILSMANN
AUSTRIA
www.vianina.com
PAGE 106 / 107

OLIVER JEFFERS
USA
www.oliverjeffers.com
PAGE 128–131

OWEN GATLEY
UNITED KINGDOM
www.owengatley.co.uk
PAGE 143, 220 / 221

PETER GRUNDY
UNITED KINGDOM
www.grundini.com
PAGE 144

PETER OUMANSKI
USA
www.peteroumanski.com
PAGE 120 / 121

RAYMOND BIESINGER
CANADA
www.fifteen.ca
PAGE 87

ROD HUNT
UNITED KINGDOM
www.rodhunt.com
PAGE 153

RUDE
UNITED KINGDOM
www.thisisrude.com
PAGE 134

RUSSELL BELL
UNITED KINGDOM
www.russell-bell.com
PAGE 6 / 7

SAHAR GHANBARI
UNITED KINGDOM
www.meandsahar.com
PAGE 47

SARAH KING
CANADA
www.sarahaking.com
PAGE 62 / 63

SERGE SEIDLITZ
UNITED KINGDOM
www.sergeseidlitz.com
PAGE 59

SOIL DESIGN
SOUTH AFRICA
www.soildesign.co.za
PAGE 77, 108 / 109

STEPHANIE VON REISWITZ
UNITED KINGDOM
www.stephvonreiswitz.com
PAGE 126 / 127

STEPHEN WALTER
UNITED KINGDOM
www.stephenwalter.co.uk
PAGE 64–67

SUSAN HUNT YULE
USA
www.susanhuntyule.com
PAGE 18, 20 / 21

TAKAYO AKIYAMA
UNITED KINGDOM
www.takayon.com
PAGE 2, 78

TEAMLAB
JAPAN
www.team-lab.net
PAGE 146 / 147

THE FUTURE MAPPING COMPANY
UNITED KINGDOM
www.futuremaps.co.uk
PAGE 82–85

THIBAUD HEREM
UNITED KINGDOM
www.thibaudherem.com
PAGE 45

VESA SAMMALISTO
GERMANY
www.vesa-s.com
PAGE 174 / 175, 196–199, 218 / 219

VIC LEE
UNITED KINGDOM
www.viclee.co.uk
PAGE 40–43, 52 / 53

VIGILISM
USA
www.vigilism.com
PAGE 100 / 101

YOUNG & RUBICAM ITALY
ITALY
www.yritalia.it
PAGE 80 / 81

YUKO KONDO
UNITED KINGDOM
www.yukokondo.com
PAGE 3, 79

ZOE MORE O'FERRALL
UNITED KINGDOM
www.zoemof.com
PAGE 116 / 117

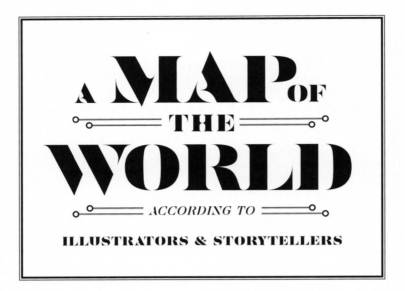

This book was conceived, edited, and designed by Gestalten.

EDITED BY Antonis Antoniou, Robert Klanten, Sven Ehmann, and Hendrik Hellige

PREFACE BY Antonis Antoniou
PROJECT DESCRIPTIONS BY Rebecca Silus

COVER BY Hendrik Hellige
COVER IMAGE BY Vesa Sammalisto
LAYOUT BY Hendrik Hellige and Anne-Marie Gundelwein
TYPEFACES: Quister by Nadia Knechtle, Zimmer by Julian Hansen
FOUNDRY: www.gestaltenfonts.com

PROJECT MANAGEMENT BY Lucie Ulrich
PRODUCTION MANAGEMENT BY Vinzenz Geppert
PROOFREADING BY Bettina Klein
PRINTED BY Nino Druck GmbH, Neustadt/Weinstraße

Made in Germany

PUBLISHED BY Gestalten, Berlin 2013
ISBN 978-3-89955-469-4

5th printing, 2014

© Die Gestalten Verlag GmbH & Co. KG, Berlin 2013

Respect copyrights, encourage creativity!

For more information, please visit
➥ WWW.GESTALTEN.COM.

BIBLIOGRAPHIC INFORMATION PUBLISHED BY THE DEUTSCHE NATIONALBIBLIOTHEK. THE DEUTSCHE NATIONALBIBLIOTHEK LISTS THIS PUBLICATION IN THE DEUTSCHE NATIONALBIBLIOGRAFIE; DETAILED BIBLIOGRAPHIC DATA ARE AVAILABLE ONLINE AT
➥ DNB.D-NB.DE.

THIS BOOK WAS PRINTED ON PAPER CERTIFIED BY THE FSC®.

GESTALTEN IS A CLIMATE-NEUTRAL COMPANY. WE COLLABORATE WITH THE NON-PROFIT CARBON OFFSET PROVIDER MYCLIMATE (➥ WWW.MYCLIMATE.ORG) TO NEUTRALIZE THE COMPANY'S CARBON FOOTPRINT PRODUCED THROUGH OUR WORLDWIDE BUSINESS ACTIVITIES BY INVESTING IN PROJECTS THAT REDUCE CO_2 EMISSIONS (➥ WWW.GESTALTEN.COM/MYCLIMATE).